Bringing Buddhism to the West

A Life of Sangharakshita

Also by Subhuti

Buddhism for Today
The Buddhist Vision
Sangharakshita: A New Voice in the Buddhist Tradition

Dharmachari Subhuti (Alex Kennedy)

Bringing Buddhism to the West

•

A Life of Sangharakshita

•

Windhorse Publications

Published by Windhorse Publications
Unit 1-316 The Custard Factory
Gibb Street
Birmingham
B9 4AA

Cover design Dhammarati

Printed by Biddles Ltd, Walnut Tree House,
Woodbridge Park, Guildford, Surrey, GU1 1DA

The cover shows Sangharakshita near Vajraloka, North Wales, 1980
and at the Kamheri caves, India, farewell tour, 1967
Courtesy of the Clear Vision Trust

British Library Cataloguing in Publication Data
A catalogue record for this book is available from the British Library

ISBN 0 904766 69 1

PUBLISHER'S NOTE: Since this work is intended for a general readership, Pali and Sanskrit words have been transliterated without the diacritical marks that would have been appropriate in a work of a more scholarly nature.

CONTENTS

About the Author

Dharmacari Subhuti was born Alex Kennedy, in Chatham, England, in 1947. Since joining the Western Buddhist Order in 1973 he has been energetically concerned with its development and with that of the Friends of the Western Buddhist Order, the wider movement for which the Order provides a nucleus.

His fields of activity have been remarkably diverse. Among other things he established the London Buddhist Centre and the Guhyaloka Retreat Centre in Spain. He has written two books as well as the present volume, and an outline of the life of Sangharakshita, to be published in 1995. For eight years he served as Sangharakshita's personal secretary. As one of those responsible for the ordination of the Western Buddhist Order's new members, he developed and for some years directed the 'training process' for men preparing to join the Order.

He currently spends much of each year engaged in writing at Guhyaloka, but makes regular visits to England, India, and the USA, where he is much in demand as a speaker and retreat leader.

PREFACE

IN THOSE REMOTE and hazy days of the late sixties, I was a young philosophy undergraduate with long hair and flowery clothes. Cut loose from the reassuring anchorage of the conventional past, I drifted confused into a storm-tossed and formless future. I wanted truth, direction, meaning, and I sought it in drugs, in anarchy, in the vague mysticism of the hippie era. One day, wandering with my angst upon London's Hampstead Heath, I saw a figure gliding towards me. Enveloped in an ankle-length brown cloak, held closed before him, with long, dark hair and bushy mutton-chop side whiskers, his was a striking enough appearance, even in those days when the unconventional was the norm. More striking still was that this was a man in his forties, not some youthful New Age exhibitionist. But what caught my attention most of all was not his garb, it was his manner. He was walking fast, but steadily, evenly, without haste. His face was calm, absorbed, as he gazed a few paces before him, and he seemed contained, compact, sufficient unto himself. There was an extraordinary air of intentness about him, serious and at the same time relaxed, as if he knew exactly where he was and where he was going. Here was a mature man, with the kind of maturity one expects to find in adults when one is young but before long finds they almost always lack. All this I stored away in an instant, as the figure passed out of my view.

A little later I saw that figure again, this time in Hyde Park, during a free concert by the Rolling Stones, which I attended in the aftermath of my first LSD trip. Did I really see that same brown-cloaked form, delicately picking his way through the human flotsam sprawled on the grass? Under the circumstances I cannot be sure, but I can see that image so clearly now: a lone figure, self-contained and graceful, neither part of the scene around him, nor self-consciously apart from it, as the Stones belted out 'Sympathy for the Devil' and the crowd danced, clanking Coke tins together, more or less on the beat.

It was only some time after I met Sangharakshita face to face that I realised it was him I had sighted on those two occasions. Nonetheless, fleeting and distant as they were, they made a deep impression on me. What struck me in him were the very things that I lacked at that time: purposefulness, confidence, mindfulness, individuality. Yet sometimes it seems to me that some deeper attraction was at work: as if I had been inevitably moving towards Sangharakshita for many years, perhaps throughout my life. Slowly I had moved into his orbit, catching many distant echoes of his name, until at last I met him.

My earliest direct encounter with Sangharakshita was at the first, tiny FWBO centre, in a rather dank basement in central London. I stumbled down the narrow stairs and found myself in a small room filled with about a dozen people, packed awkwardly silent around the walls. At the end sat Sangharakshita, seemingly quite at his ease in the somewhat inhibited atmosphere of Englishmen in a public place. There he was with that long hair, those side whiskers, his fingers full of rings, and bright orange robes that he wore more like a shaman's vestment than the habit of a Buddhist monk. He gave me what can only be described as a cheeky grin, gap toothed and familiar, as if he had my measure at a glance. I was captivated in an instant by that unconventionality and directness. There was something untamed about him, as if he was quite simply unaffected by normal social expectations. Raw power ran through him that flashed in his penetrating gaze, while he sat, still and composed. Young would-be rebel that I was, this wild quality was deeply appealing to me—at the same time, it seemed threatening and dangerous, for I knew it passed completely beyond my fragile self-identity.

I glimpsed two more things about Sangharakshita that night. He had a keenly penetrating mind and a deep understanding both of Western culture in its many aspects and of the entire Buddhist tradition. And he was exceptionally kindly and concerned with others. In particular, of course, I felt his immediate interest and concern for me. Both these characteristics emerged as he answered questions after meditation, fielding them with great elegance and clarity and good humour, always searching for what the questioner was really asking and needed to hear. As I left, I knew, though I would not admit it to myself, that I had met my spiritual teacher.

Over the years that followed, I have been privileged to live and work quite closely with Sangharakshita and have come to know him much more deeply. What I saw in those early encounters was but an aspect of him, glimpsed from my own perspective. Now, perhaps, the wild shaman—though still a part of him—is less immediately visible, and his public appearance is more urbane, witty, and charming. What he is like on closer acquaintance is much harder to say. Perhaps it is always hard to put into words what another person is like, but Sangharakshita is a complex and highly gifted man who has led a very full and productive life. It would be hard to capture him in a few phrases. Above all it would be hard to disentangle him from his own creations, for so much of his own spirit has passed into what he has achieved: his writings, his new Buddhist movement, and the men and women who as his disciples have been inspired by him to achieve far more than they ever dreamed they could.

Any exploration of Sangharakshita, the man, must approach from many angles, and in my own writings I seem to have been giving glimpses of Sangharakshita from several points of view. This then is really another in the series. Twelve years ago I published *Buddhism for Today*, an exploration of the principles and practices of the Friends of the Western Buddhist Order, the movement Sangharakshita created—it is a 'Portrait of a New Buddhist Movement', as the subtitle has it. My *Buddhist Vision* presents Sangharakshita's basic Buddhist teachings in a comprehensive pattern, using the Tibetan Wheel of Life as a framework. The recently published *Sangharakshita: A New Voice in the Buddhist Tradition* sets out his leading ideas in the context of his life. Now, in this book, I have given an outline of the principal events in that life, so the reader can see clearly where he has come from and what he has achieved. It is not a biography, rather it is a chronicle. I have attempted no critical appraisal and I have not searched widely for other views of the man and the events of his life.

A full, critical biography will one day be needed and I would like to write it, but this does not seem the moment to do so. A biography is retrospective, summing up the past, recreating it whilst reducing it to some order and giving it some finality. But Sangharakshita is so obviously still working. Although he is now seventy, he still has plenty of creative energy and may well produce more than one entirely new masterpiece of one kind or another in the time left to him. All the threads of his life have not yet been gathered in and the time for biographies has not yet come. Furthermore, Sangharakshita has told me that there are certain elements in his story that he wants to be the first to write about, and I have respected his wishes. I have therefore simply chronicled events, without pushing too far beneath their surface.

In the meantime, until that biography is written, this chronicle will give his friends and disciples an overview of his life. Buddhists of other traditions will have an opportunity to understand better the experiences that have shaped a leading modern Buddhist teacher—and perhaps will gain a brief insight into some aspects of recent Buddhist history. The book has, I hope, wider interest still. Sangharakshita's life exemplifies an important strand in modern history: the meeting of Western culture with Eastern spiritual traditions. He has made something rather unusual of that meeting, allowing the essential spirit of the Buddhist tradition to re-express itself in the modern world. His presentation of the Dharma is at once fully traditional and completely fresh, faithful yet revolutionary. But above all his life shows what a single human being can do, given sufficient courage, determination, and inspired vision.

My main sources of information for this book have been Sangharakshita's own published writings, a number of journals to which he has contributed or which contain news of him (*Stepping-Stones*, the *Maha Bodhi*, the *Buddhist*, the *Middle Way*, the *FWBO Newsletter*, and *Golden Drum*), and Suvajra's book about Dhardo Rimpoche, *The Wheel and the Diamond*, besides anecdotes and memories picked up from Sangharakshita over the years and in several interviews I had with him whilst I was writing. Sangharakshita has checked the final draft and has at least agreed that it is broadly factually accurate. It will be noticed that almost all my sources of information lead ultimately back to Sangharakshita himself. This account is therefore my version of aspects of *his* version of his life.

I found that writing this book had a definite spiritual effect upon me. It helped me first to get to know my own teacher far better than I had ever done before. I not only got to know the details of his life better, but found myself appreciating more than ever his achievement. At several points, such as when I wrote of his renunciation and going forth, I found myself very strongly challenged by the strength of his commitment or inspired by the depth of his vision. I hope that at least something of that challenge and inspiration will be shared by some of my readers.

I would like to express my gratitude to all who have contributed to this book, particularly to Jan Parker for her editorial work, which has definitely greatly improved the final product, as well as to Nagabodhi and Shantavira, as ever. I am, of course, especially grateful to Sangharakshita for all his help in preparing this book and for the encouragement and advice he gave me throughout. As the pages that follow will, I hope, show, we have a very great deal more than that for which to thank Urgyen Sangharakshita, whether we are his disciples in the FWBO, Buddhists from other traditions, or simply men and women concerned for the welfare of our world.

Subhuti,
Guhyaloka,
Spain
January 1995

Chapter One

Early Years
1925–1944

So in my youth did I disport
In that lush wonderland of thought
Which blooms within the guardian walls
Of hushed and silent library halls,
And there from shelf to shelf did range
In eager quest of all of strange
And rich and rare and wonderful,
And terrible and beautiful,
That man, in any age or zone,
Had ever wrought, or felt, or known.

Sangharakshita (1949)

The man we now know as Sangharakshita was born in London in 1925. By that time Buddhism had already established a very precarious toe-hold in England. Scholars had translated much of the Pali Canon of the 'Southern' School into English, along with several sutras of the Mahayana tradition. Sir Edwin Arnold had published his epic on the life of the Buddha, *The Light of Asia*, which was one of the most popular long poems of the Victorian era. And a Londoner, Allan Bennett, had in 1901 been ordained in Burma as a *bhikkhu* or monk in the Theravadin monastic sangha. As Bhikkhu Ananda Metteyya he returned briefly to London in 1908, leading the first Buddhist mission to England under the auspices of the newly formed Buddhist Society of Great Britain and Ireland. This first Society did not last long, but in 1924 Christmas Humphreys, a young English lawyer from a distinguished legal family, founded a Buddhist Lodge of the Theosophical Society in London. Two years later, the Lodge became independent of the Theosophical movement, and was re-established as the Buddhist Society, as which it survives to this day.

It is a curious fact that Ananda Metteyya, the first Buddhist missionary to Britain, should have died only a few hundred yards from the nursing home where Sangharakshita was born just two years later, on 26 August 1925. Sangharakshita was not, of course, the name his parents gave him at birth, which was Dennis Philip Edward Lingwood. The Lingwoods were of East Anglian stock, his grandfather having moved to London to work at the War Office, where among other duties he had written out officers' commissions for signature by Queen Victoria. His father had spent much of his childhood in a small Norfolk village and remained a countryman at heart throughout his life. His mother brought a touch of the exotic to the family, for her grandfather had arrived mysteriously from Hungary when a youth. Dennis's paternal grandmother and many of his numerous uncles and aunts all lived in London and formed a cheerful and loving background to his early years. His grandmother, a woman of great kindness and strength of character, was particularly important to him, and it was through her that he had his first taste of Buddhism—in this life, at least. Her second husband had been in Peking at the time of the Boxer rebellion and, being a confirmed collector of curios, had procured several items from the Imperial Summer Palace after its sack, among which were a scroll of the Buddha surrounded by his disciples, a small statuette of the Bodhisattva of Compassion, and a Tibetan ritual bell. These exercised a great enchantment on the young Dennis, even when he was still a baby and his father had to lift him up to gaze at the fascinating objects.

Mementoes from the Imperial past apart, there was nothing unusual about Sangharakshita's family, unless uprightness and common sense be unusual. His father, Philip Edward Lingwood, was a man of strong feeling, even hot temper at times, who spoke his mind and stuck by his principles. At the same time, according to his son, he was of a generous and forgiving nature, with an exceptional unselfishness that led him to 'cheerfully put the pleasure and happiness of others before his own'. Despite frequently being unemployed, particularly during the Depression of the 1930s, he made sure that his children never lacked for anything—both he and his wife often going without rather than deprive Dennis and his sister, Joan. He had left school early and was apprenticed to a jeweller, but his training was interrupted by the onset of the First World War. He had joined the Army soon after the war began, even though he was under age, and had been wounded in action, losing much of the use of one arm. On discharge from hospital, he had received training in French polishing at a workshop for wounded ex-soldiers and worked at this trade for a succession of firms. He later turned to the restoration of antique furniture, starting his own small business—he did some restoration work in the royal palaces and met Queen Mary on several occasions. He was a friendly and cheerful man who liked to talk and enjoyed the company of his family and companions, making friends easily and having a wide circle of acquaintances from all walks of life. He was a very indulgent parent who never chastised his children—arguing against those in the family who considered him too soft that 'you are only young once'. He and the young Dennis were on very good terms, and the positive and upright character of his father has had a strong influence upon Sangharakshita.

Mrs Lingwood, who was born Catherine Florence Margaret Ketskemety, was of a quieter disposition, gentle and patient, although she too was sociable and liked to chat with her sisters and friends. She was a rather more shadowy figure in Dennis's life, being often very busy, whilst his father was frequently at home when unemployed. Nonetheless she was healthy and positive, if perhaps a bit prudish, and was a careful and kindly mother, always putting her children's interests before her own. Neither of his parents was well educated, although his father read and took some interest in cultural matters. No more were they particularly religious: both had been brought up in the Church of England but neither the churches nor the chapels of Tooting offered much in the way of living faith. From the dry formalism of the established and non-conformist churches they had turned to dabble in spiritualism and the like.

CONFINED TO BED

Mr and Mrs Lingwood must have been bemused as they slowly became aware that their son was exceptionally intelligent, independent, and self-willed. He himself reports that from a very early age he realised that his mind worked much quicker than those around him. However, it was not until he was eight that his life really began to diverge from what might have been expected of a normal boy of his age and background. After he had been in hospital with scarlet fever, it was discovered that he had an abnormally high pulse rate. His doctor diagnosed him as suffering from a valvular disease of the heart and insisted that if he was not confined instantly to bed and forbidden all sudden movement or excitement he would soon be dead. And so it was that for the next two years he lay in his bedroom, seeing no one but his parents and the doctor or nurse, and allowed nothing that would agitate him or lead him to exert himself. His unfortunate parents had the very difficult work of keeping a lively and intelligent boy completely quiet, always with the fear that excitation might kill him.

Their solution was to keep him supplied with books. He had learnt to read early, probably from the *Daily Herald*, the newspaper his father brought home each evening, and had read the first chapters of Genesis from the family Bible at the age of five or six. Now, lying in his bed with nothing else to do, he began to read with a voraciousness which left his parents the hard task of keeping pace with his appetite. In this way he established a habit that has remained with him throughout his life, in many ways making him the man he is—for it has been through reading that he has acquired his very considerable breadth and depth of knowledge. He says that he never learnt anything interesting or useful during his time at school, much interrupted by his illness and the war. He is a self-educated man and the foundations of that self-education were laid during his two years in bed.

His father brought him boys' papers, which fed his boyish taste for adventure and which he imitated in a short story of his own, his first literary effort. He began reading the classics of English literature, notably at this stage *Jane Eyre*, which made a powerful impression upon him. However, it was the sixty-one parts of Harmsworth's famous *Children's Encyclopaedia*, given him by a sympathetic neighbour, which had the most significant impact upon him. For it was through those pages, every one of which he read, several of them many times, that he entered the world of history, literature, and art. He was not only a boy of exceptional intelligence, he also had a lively and natural response to beauty, and was particularly attracted to the plates, many in colour, of the great paintings and sculptures of the world—though it was the work of Michelangelo and Botticelli that particularly appealed to him. Indeed, even at this early age, it is possible to discern a mind that knew its own preferences and which followed its own instinctive attraction to the highest achievements of human culture. He seems to have lived, whilst lying in his bed, in a very vivid and rich imaginative world, filled with the wondrous treasures and glorious people of whom he read.

He himself considers that it may have been the strength of his feelings which led to his illness, if illness he did have. Of a naturally intense nature, his strong emotional responses would set his heart racing, whether from excitement, frustration, or fear—as when he was taken to the doctor. It may be that this was what gave rise to the symptoms diagnosed as a valvular heart disease. After two years or more of him lying isolated in his room, his parents sought a second medical opinion, and took him to an innovative heart specialist who at once declared that the young invalid must be made to return to a normal life. His father then took the difficult and courageous decision to follow this advice. So wasted were the boy's limbs that it was several months before he could walk properly—and even then he was constantly cautioned against hasty or violent motion. However, he never suffered any further problems with his heart, and later medical investigation has discovered no trace of illness or malformation.

Opening the Doors of Art and Literature

Those years in bed then were important ones for Sangharakshita, teaching him a care and economy in movement which is evident today in what Buddhists would call his 'mindfulness' and laying the foundations of his prodigious self-education. From that period on, he was always reading, opening wider and ever wider his literary horizons. At this time too, he began to buy books, haunting the second-hand shops wherever he happened to be, spending whatever money he had on a collection that by the time he was eighteen contained a thousand volumes, some of them quite valuable. Although no books remain from these early collectings, he still loves books, still delights in browsing through bookshops, and has a large collection, filling three rooms, which is the basis of the Western Buddhist Order's library. Throughout the rest of this story, we must imagine him surrounded by books, always reading, consuming often some five or six books each week. But he did not read merely for entertainment or distraction; whatever he read he absorbed with critical attention, copying out passages that particularly struck him and writing comments on each work in several thick ledgers that served as his journal. Many years later he is still able to remember the smallest details of much of what he has read.

However, through those colour plates in the *Children's Encyclopaedia*, it was art that first gripped him and, in his tenth year, as soon as his confinement was ended, he began to draw and paint. So much talent and enthusiasm did he show that his parents and teachers all assumed he would become an artist. At the school to which he now returned one teacher in particular gave him great encouragement and advice in his art as well as in literature, lending him books, encouraging him to write essays, and even to give talks to the rest of the class. In fact, rather dramatically, it was literature that suddenly asserted itself over art when he read Milton's *Paradise Lost*, at the age of twelve, giving rise to what he describes as 'the greatest poetic experience of my life'. The world of poetry opened up to him and he revelled in the great English poets: Keats, Elizabeth Barrett Browning, and Housman, but above all Milton and Rossetti. He not only read but he wrote: an epic inspired by Milton (abandoned after nine hundred lines), many shorter poems, a verse drama, a history of the reign of Queen Elizabeth I (also unfinished), a short story, and a life of Gautama the Buddha.

Why he wrote on the theme of the Buddha is not clear, although Gautama's life, among others, had impressed him when he read of it in the *Children's Encyclopaedia*. At this period, he said his prayers each evening to Jesus Christ, Muhammad, and the Buddha, hedging his bets on who the saviour really was. He had however bought from a curio shop in Brighton—for he now had a small collection of curios of his own—an incense burner in the shape of the Buddha, and in this he reverently burned joss-sticks. But Christianity still claimed him. For four years he attended regularly and conscientiously two or three or more meetings each week of the Boys' Brigade, a quasi-military troop attached to local churches, in this case the Baptist Church nearby. Dennis went chiefly for companionship for, though he had returned to school after his illness, he was so bright that he had quickly found himself in a class with boys two years older than him with whom he had little in common—indeed, he says he was disgusted by the 'meaningless obscenity of their conversation'. The Boys' Brigade offered an altogether more wholesome group to which he could belong, and he responded well to the ideals of clean living, service, and responsibility that the Brigade upheld and which its members did seem to exemplify. He also developed 'one of those dumb, adolescent attachments' to one of the senior members of the Brigade in which it was enough silently to be with the object of his affections—who probably remained in ignorance of the feelings he aroused.

Along with drilling and singing and so forth, the members of the Boys' Brigade were encouraged to attend the Church, and Dennis found himself drawn into Bible study and services. Although he joined in with the activities wholeheartedly, he was never much influenced by the religious views of the Baptists, which appealed almost entirely to the heart and not to the head—and anyway he had already begun to think for himself about religious matters.

Leaving Christianity Behind

Into this stable and happy world of family, school, and Boys' Brigade irrupted the Second World War. It was foreseen that London would be a target for air raids, so children and schools were evacuated to safer parts of the country. Young Dennis went with Clement, his best friend from school, to Barnstaple in Devon, where they were lodged with a local family. Much of his time was spent in the public library and second-hand bookshops. By this time, at the age of fourteen, he was reading the classical authors and was working his way through the collected works of Dr Johnson, a lifelong favourite. He now discovered Schopenhauer, whom he 'recognised at once as a kindred spirit'. His landlady, however, took a violent dislike to Dennis's bookish habits and mature manner, making life very unpleasant for him. So bad did relations become that his mother arranged for him to move to Torquay, where she was staying with her step-brother-in-law and his wife, and he started yet another school. But his education was still his own and now took a new and important turn. It suddenly occurred to him that he need not confine himself to the literature of Europe and opened himself up to the classics of all mankind. Another important turning point came when he discovered, in the Torquay Public Library, Mme Blavatsky's *Isis Unveiled*, the founding work of the Theosophical movement, and this had a very powerful effect on him indeed. He realised, as he says, that he was not a Christian and 'that I never had been and never would be—and that the whole structure of Christian doctrine was from beginning to end thoroughly repugnant to me. This realization gave me a sense of relief, of liberation as from some oppressive burden, which was so great that I wanted to dance and sing for joy. What I was, what I believed, I knew not, but what I was not and what I did not believe, that I knew with utter certainty, and this knowledge, merely negative though it was as yet, gave me a foretaste of that freedom which comes when all obstacles are removed, all barriers broken down, all limitations transcended.'*

---

* *Learning to Walk*, p.91

INNER AND OUTER TURMOIL

It was to be a further year before he did discover what he was. Meanwhile, he left school and took a job in the offices of a coal merchant in the centre of Torquay. As war service claimed more and more of the staff, he found himself virtually running the business—and making sure that he had time to pursue his studies. But, after an absence from home of more than a year, he began to feel homesick and decided to return to Tooting. The London he came back to was battered and strained after the terrible months of the Blitz, throughout which his father had worked as a stretcher-bearer. Although the worst of the bombing was over, he still experienced something of the horror of being caught in an air raid—and, like most Londoners, got used to it. What was not so easy to get used to were the stresses and strains beginning to show in his parents' marriage. There had been quarrels and arguments from time to time, but never with the bitterness that was sometimes present now.

Dennis's inner world too was in turmoil. Momentous changes were taking place within him as conflicting impulses struggled for dominance: religion and philosophy, art and literature, music too—now experienced with a new and passionate intensity—all blended with his awakening senses to feed the raging inner fire. He has said that if he had not come across Buddhism—come across that sublime ideal of Enlightenment in which all the powerful forces of his psyche could be harmonised and find their fulfilment—he thinks he would have become insane. He has referred to those two-and-a-half years after his return from Torquay as among the most important of his present existence, since they settled decisively the direction his life would take.

Shortly after his return, he took a job with London County Council in the vast office blocks of County Hall, across the river from the Houses of Parliament. He was assigned to the Public Health Department as personal assistant to the chief of a branch concerned with allocating nursing staff within a health service ravaged by air-raid casualties. Here he met and fell in love with a clerical assistant in the same branch whom he found one day at her desk reading a work of philosophy. He never declared his feelings to her face to face, although during one holiday in Norfolk with some relations he sent her 'the first and last love letters' he ever wrote—they were 'long, literary, and idealistic' and he never discovered what she made of them. Nonetheless they did spend quite a bit of time together, both in the office and after work. However, she was eventually called up to join the ATS, a military corps for women, and Dennis found himself experiencing the bitter pains of disappointed love—assuaged only by a visit to a bookshop.

His parents were becoming increasingly estranged from each other and this added to the strain and tension he was experiencing. His father had always been a 'ladies' man', very much enjoying the company of women, who in their turn responded to him, and this had often made his mother jealous—though whether with any real foundation he still does not know. Furthermore, their tastes in entertainment were quite different: his mother enjoying romantic films or a meal out at a restaurant in town, whilst his father preferred simpler pleasures, such as an evening chatting with his friends. During the years of the war, his father may have somewhat neglected her, being absorbed in his work as a stretcher-bearer and with the many friends he made in the course of his duties. In 1943, his mother finally decided to leave her husband and to marry a man she had met through her work—a man who clearly gave her the attention she felt she had been lacking. At her instigation, Dennis did what he could to see his father through the pain of separation. As if to complete a severing with the past, the family home was destroyed a few months later by a direct hit from a V1 bomb—just an hour before he himself was due to arrive there and whilst the rest of the family were out.

To match these inner and outer storms, his heroes of this period were 'stricken, tormented, demoniacal figures—Strindberg, Nietzsche, Beethoven'. He read Kant and Hegel and continued his exploration of religion, reading in Gnosticism, Rosicrucianism, and Neoplatonism. He certainly found that he had now travelled very far indeed from his old Boys' Brigade friends and could not revive the connections. He continued to pour out poetry, composing on the bus to and from work, and wrote a novel, now unfortunately lost, rather in the style of D.H. Lawrence.

Music had become for him an obsession—leading to more tension in the home over what programmes were to be listened to on the family radio. Tchaikovsky and Beethoven were the favourites in more intense moods, but he enjoyed Mozart and Haydn and always Bach, whose *Toccata and Fugue in D Minor* had an impact on him that was the musical equivalent of his earlier experience of Milton's *Paradise Lost*. Intoxicated with the sounds, he would be drawn into a concentration so intense that he would sometimes practically lose consciousness of his body. At other times, quite unconnected with music, he would be precipitated spontaneously into mystical experiences. These were of two varieties, one of which had begun to occur to him even before he was evacuated—this was a consciousness of the 'complete absurdity of the mind being tied down to a single physical body'. The other, more striking, experience was of the insubstantial, dream-like nature of the world. For a while he also had a number of 'psychic' experiences, all whilst he was at his work in County Hall, in which events that had not yet taken place would be played out before his eyes—none of them of any great significance. For him, these precognitions substantiated Kant's thesis that time was in consciousness, not consciousness within time.

REDISCOVERING BUDDHISM

An even more momentous experience came in his seventeenth year, when he chanced upon the famous bookshop of John Watkins, off London's Charing Cross Road, during one of his book-hunting expeditions. At that time, Watkins was the principal, if not the only, specialist source of books on the occult and on Eastern religion. Here Dennis purchased two very important Mahayana Buddhist texts, the *Diamond Sutra* and the *Sutra of Wei Lang* (also known as the *Platform Sutra* or the *Sutra of Hui Neng*). Reading these convinced him he was a Buddhist:

'If, when I read *Isis Unveiled*, I knew that I was not a Christian, when I read the *Diamond Sutra* I knew that I was a Buddhist. Though this book epitomizes a teaching of such rarefied sublimity that even Arahants, saints who have attained individual nirvana, are said to become confused and afraid when they hear it for the first time, I at once joyfully embraced it with an unqualified acceptance and assent. To me the *Diamond Sutra* was not new. I had known it and believed it and realized it ages before and the reading of the *Sutra* as it were awoke me to the existence of something I had forgotten. Once I realized that I was a Buddhist it seemed that I had always been one, that it was the most natural thing in the world to be, and that I had never been anything else.'* The *Sutra of Wei Lang* had a similar effect, throwing him into an ecstasy every time he read it.

In Watkins he also discovered a translation of the *Tao Teh King*. Although a classic of Taoism, this edition was published by the Buddhist Society and revealed the existence of Buddhists in London. Dennis began to subscribe to *Buddhism in England* (now the *Middle Way*), a journal published by the Society, and after a time contributed two articles of his own: one on 'The Unity of Buddhism' and the other on the doctrine of the

---

* *Learning to Walk*, p.118

ti-lakkhana—both themes remaining central concerns throughout the rest of his life. The former was published in the journal but the latter was too long and could not be included, although it was very much commended by the editor.

At the end of 1943, having passed his medical examination, much to his surprise in view of his history of illness, he received his military call-up and was posted to a Royal Signals Corps training camp near Leatherhead, in Surrey. To begin with he was numbed by the mindless routine of Army life, but the Royal Signals is a notoriously relaxed body and, once Signalman Lingwood had shown a remarkable aptitude for transmitting in Morse code at high speed, he settled into the undemanding duties imposed upon him. He struck up a friendship with another London lad and was able to return frequently to London to see his parents, now living separately, and to pursue his interest in Buddhism. When he visited the Buddhist Society for the first time, the secretary of the Society and editor of *Buddhism in England*, Clare Cameron, was startled to find that the author of those two assured articles was just a young man of eighteen. He met the Founder-President of the Society, Christmas Humphreys, and at the Wesak celebration of 1944, the anniversary of the Buddha's Enlightenment and Buddhism's major festival, he recited the Refuges and Precepts after U Thittila, a Burmese bhikkhu who had been resident in England for some years, earning great respect for his work as a stretcher-bearer during the Blitz. This recitation of the formula of commitment to the Buddha, Dharma, and Sangha, together with the taking up of the five basic ethical principles, marked Dennis's formal conversion to Buddhism.

Chapter Two

Wandering Days
1944–1950

The dim sun sinks to rest
In a west of watery gold.
The young stars climb the sky
And there like flowers unfold,
In the forest vast of night,
Petals of purest light.
So may my heart unfold,
When the suns of the world have set,
In the forest vast of the Void,
Wisdom with Mercy met
In that tranquil, silent hour,
Like a flower and the scent of a flower.

Sangharakshita (1948)

Spiritual Life in the Army

Rumours of his unit's impending posting were rife at the camp, but of all the possible places to which he might have been sent Dennis was overjoyed to find that it was for India that he was bound. His nineteenth birthday found him on a troop ship in the Atlantic, three days out from Glasgow. In Delhi, where he was initially based, intercepting unidentified transmissions, he explored the magnificent remains of Mogul India and the exotic Hindu present, wandering restless, fascinated and 'somehow frustrated', through the colour, heat, and chaos. He practised meditation, using exercises from a classic by the great Hindu non-dualist philosopher, Shankara, which led to an experience of 'a great peaceful joy' that permeated his whole being. But of Buddhism there was little to be found in North India, and so, after only two months in Delhi, he asked for a transfer to Colombo in Sri Lanka, the home of the Pali Canon and the self-proclaimed cradle of Theravadin orthodoxy.

However, what Buddhism he did encounter in Sri Lanka did not impress him. As he was to find so many times in the future, Sinhalese Buddhism was dry, formalistic, avaricious, and narrow, at least as far as its official manifestations were concerned. Curiously, at this stage he found the spiritual companionship and guidance that he so much longed for within a Hindu group—although he never wavered in his devotion to Buddhism. He had discovered in a Colombo bookshop literature on the lives and teachings of the Bengali Vedantic mystic, Sri Ramakrishna, and his well-known disciple, Swami Vivekananda, who had begun to spread the message of the Advaita (Non-Dual) Vedanta in the West. What caught Dennis's attention was their demonstration that it was really possible to live the spiritual life even today, and he drew encouragement from this to practise himself—rather than merely to study—the teaching to which he was already committed. He discovered that there was an ashram of the Ramakrishna Mission on the outskirts of Colombo and there he became friends with the two resident swamis from whom he imbibed a strong enthusiasm for the spiritual life, so lacking in Sri Lankan Buddhism. Over the next two or more years the Ramakrishna Mission ashrams and swamis, established all over the Indian subcontinent, were to play a major part in his life.

For the seven months he was in Colombo, with very light army duties, much of his free time was spent at the ashram. Here, besides learning about Hinduism in general and the Advaita Vedanta in particular, he was introduced to Indian culture: its music and literature, even its food. The swamis took him to meet his first authentic Hindu holy man, the Yoga Swami, reputedly 160 years old or more. All these experiences, together with his reading, induced in him very strong feelings to renounce the world and dedicate himself wholeheartedly to the spiritual life. A visiting swami from North India, Swami Pavitrananda, a leading member of the Mission and a man of great spiritual energy, impressed upon him the happiness of the monk's life in comparison with that of the worldling and kindled yet further his desire for renunciation. He wrote to his parents, announcing his desire to become a monk—neither seemed surprised or raised any objections, although his mother hoped that he would still see her occasionally.

Pavitrananda advised him to visit the Ramakrishna Mission's headquarters in Bengal and so Dennis applied for another transfer, this time to Calcutta. As well as making contact again with the Mission and its swamis, he met up with an uncle and his family, going with his aunt and cousin to Darjeeling for a holiday. His experience here further intensified his feeling for renunciation. As he watched the shallow and futile posturings of the Europeans' social life, he felt again the unreality and dreamlike nature of the world and was disgusted by the meaninglessness of the lives of those around him. Back in Calcutta, he witnessed Hinduism both in its colourful ceremonies and its terrible caste prejudice—as a *mlechchha*, a foreigner who is lower than the lowest and whose very presence pollutes sacred places, he was forbidden entrance to the Dakshineshwar Temple, where Ramakrishna had once lived—even though Ramakrishna himself had completely rejected caste. He also had an experience of the violence that was breaking out all over India at this time—and indeed had a lucky escape in an encounter with an angry mob during an anti-British riot.

In November of 1945 his unit was ordered to Singapore to monitor, on behalf of the Dutch authorities, transmissions from Indonesian anti-colonial fighters. Dennis and some other members of the unit did not approve of this activity and simply failed to record any signals they did pick up. However, as the war with Japan was now over, duties were light and Dennis was able to pursue his own interests unhindered. He found the local Ramakrishna Mission, the Sinhalese Buddhist Vihara, and the Theosophical Society and immersed himself in their activities, even finding himself called upon to give talks—and thereby discovering a talent which was to be constantly in demand throughout his life. He met a number of monks, both Chinese and Sinhalese, among the latter the well-known Bhikkhu Soma, who encouraged him in the practice of meditation using the technique known as 'Mindfulness of Breathing'. He began to meditate according to this method, sitting on his charpoy under his mosquito net after lights-out, and had immediate success. His mind became light and concentrated, then filled with a keen sense of peace and purity, and finally pervaded by a bliss so intense that he had to break off the practice. He had clearly experienced *dhyana*, that concentrated and elevated state that is the first goal of meditation practice and the basis for *vipassana*, or insight into the true nature of things, that is the ultimate aim of Buddhist meditation. For the time being he realised that he did not have the right conditions for practice, but he resolved to return to it later. This resolution he kept as soon as he found himself in a suitable setting.

At the Ramakrishna ashram he met a young Bengali who was on a medical mission to Malaya on behalf of the Indian National Congress.

Rabindra Kumar Banerjee was a brahmin by birth who had strongly repudiated his caste. This was a radical step indeed, for caste is deeply woven into the fabric of Indian society, even today. Indeed, it is its chief determinant, dictating precisely how people behave towards each other: whom one can marry, with whom one can eat—even whom one can touch. The brahmins consider themselves to be at the very top of the complicated caste structure of graded inequality and they still dominate much of Indian cultural and political life, so Rabindra was giving up a great deal in refusing to consider himself a brahmin. At that time he was deeply involved in nationalist politics. A few months later, perhaps under Dennis's influence, he underwent a major change of heart, becoming convinced that politics did not provide answers and that it was to religion he should devote himself. Although he could be intensely sensitive, volatile, even violent-tempered, he was also warm-hearted, passionate, and overwhelmingly idealistic, and there was an immediate attraction between him and Dennis. They quickly formed a strong friendship and decided to meet up in Calcutta. For the next two-and-a-half years they were to be almost inseparable.

ORGANISED RELIGION

The war was now long over and news came that the unit was to be demobilised back in England. Hearing that it might be difficult to leave England again once he returned, Dennis determined to remain in the East. He applied for leave, went to Calcutta—and never went back to the unit, technically deserting the Army. He and Banerjee met up again in Calcutta and plunged into the work of the Ramakrishna Mission's Institute of Culture. When that proved unsatisfactory because of the Secretary's willingness to use violence to gain possession of Institute property, they moved on to the Maha Bodhi Society of India's headquarters and tried to help there. The Buddhist organisation was no better than the Hindu and Dennis and his friend added disgust with organised religion to their disillusion with the world.

During an 'All-India Religious Conference' in Ahmedabad which he attended as Buddhist representative on behalf of the Maha Bodhi Society, he heard of a renowned Hindu woman mystic, Anandamayi, who travelled in a very unpredictable fashion around North India. He and Banerjee spent the next few weeks at her ashram, watching this woman of undoubted mystical gifts as she carried on her strange spiritual flirtation with her disciples. Although inspired by the atmosphere of serenity which she radiated, they were not impressed by the banal utterances which passed for her wisdom—from a Buddhist point of view, higher states of consciousness may be experienced without the transforming Insight which is the true goal of spiritual life. Worse still, caste distinctions were rigidly observed at the ashram, apparently with Anandamayi's sanction. The two friends could not reconcile her tolerance of this evil with genuine spirituality. Nonetheless, the short period they spent at Anandamayi's ashram was very important. It was here that Dennis finally threw off the last vestiges of Europe and clad himself in Indian style. He had already renounced his given name and called himself 'Dharmapriya', 'Lover of the Dharma'. Banerjee requested a name from Anandamayi and was thenceforth to be called 'Satyapriya' or 'Lover of Truth'. With Anandamayi's blessing, they began to practise the Mindfulness of Breathing meditation twice each day, at her suggestion keeping diaries of their experiences.

GOING FORTH

They had originally been introduced to Anandamayi by an elderly brahmin scholar who had attended the Conference of Religions in Ahmedabad as a representative of Buddhism. He was however very much a Hindu who, like most Hindus, as Dharmapriya was to find over and over again, considered Buddhism to be simply part of Hinduism. However, Panditji claimed to be working for the revival of Buddhism in India and wanted Dharmapriya and Satyapriya to co-operate with him to that end. And so, after leaving Anandamayi, they travelled with him to Kasauli in the Punjab hills. It soon became clear that Panditji was a complete rogue and was simply using them as bait to extract money from well-meaning patrons. Once again, religious organisations were exposed for what they were—self-interest disguised behind a high-sounding name. The two friends decided that the time had come to renounce the world completely. They would 'go forth' as wandering ascetics, without possessions and without civil identity, in the great Indian tradition of which the Buddha himself had been a part. Save for a set of clothes, which they dyed ochre in time-honoured fashion, and a few books, they gave away all they owned and burnt all their identification papers. On 18 August 1947, they set off for Sri Lanka, by train through the length of India, to seek ordination as *shramaneras*, novice monks in the Buddhist Order. This day of Going Forth was one of the most important turning points of Sangharakshita/Dharmapriya's life.

The Immigration Officer at Colombo brought them face to face with the conflict between the worldly and the spiritual: he would not let them land in Sri Lanka since they had no papers and refused to identify their nationalities. Returned to India, the two wanderers now decided that they would walk from the southernmost tip of India to the Himalayas, thereby testing their renunciation. However it only took them a few days to realise that, though in this fashion they would make the most direct contact possible with the people and sights of India, they would not be able to meditate very effectively, meditation being largely incompatible with much external activity. After seeing some of the famous temples of South India and gaining a sadhu's-eye-view of Hindu custom and practice, they took up residence in a deserted ashram of the Ramakrishna Mission in the small town of Muvattupuzha. Here they intended to meditate and study together and do what they could to improve the condition of the ashram.

ENCOUNTERS WITH SOUTH INDIAN SAINTS

In the fifteen months they resided at the ashram, they became a part of the life of the town. They gathered around them a circle of friends and supporters who subscribed to the upkeep of the ashram and participated in its activities. They gave lectures and attended meetings. They followed for much of the time a vigorous routine of meditation and study. For Dharmapriya this period of immersion in a predominantly Hindu world heightened his longing for Buddhism. Friendly as people around him were, the all-pervasive observance of caste, of which he had some striking experiences, repelled him. At the same time, he was deepening his study of Buddhism and reflecting upon the meaning of its principal teachings, such as Conditioned Co-production, the Four Noble Truths, and the Three Characteristics of Existence. The regular meditation sessions and periods of silence and fasting in which he engaged with Satyapriya allowed him to penetrate far more deeply than he had ever done before into these fundamental insights of the Buddha. More than ever before he felt himself to be a Buddhist.

Satyapriya, however much he might have rejected his brahmin background, was still not ready to admit that Buddhism did entail a rejection of Hinduism. On this and a number of other issues, he and Dharmapriya began to clash. A clash with Satyapriya was however not merely a difference of opinion and would easily lead to violent rows. In fact, Satyapriya became increasingly difficult to live with, being morbidly over-sensitive, prone to impulsive fanaticism, and liable to outbursts of anger and even violence. All of this Dharmapriya bore with patience—a patience which perhaps infuriated Satyapriya even more. The strain between them became more and more pronounced.

At this point they discovered at the ashram some literature on the life of a Hindu saint and this greatly moved them both. To their delight, they realised that the holy man was still alive and living in South India. They decided to visit him to ask his advice on their spiritual efforts, hoping perhaps that he might help to ease the tension between them. In marked contrast to Anandamayi, they found Swami Ramdas completely opposed to the caste system, the observance of which he would not allow at his ashram. He was a man of 'childlike simplicity and radiant good humour' who taught by means of a kind of 'transcendental comedy'. Nonetheless, he was full of wisdom and common sense, urging on the two friends the importance of good fellowship between them, insisting that health was essential to effective spiritual practice and condemning *pranayama*, a hatha-yoga technique of breath-control, as without spiritual value—the forcible practice of *pranayama* may have contributed to Satyapriya's mental instability. (Dharmapriya himself had tried *pranayama* when he was in Sri Lanka and had abandoned it since it had had a 'terribly disintegrating effect upon my whole being'.) Swami Ramdas also endorsed their decision to renounce the world and urged them to persist until Enlightenment was attained. Later he gave them a mantra—not, as they had expected, the Hindu 'Ram mantra' that he normally gave his disciples, but *om mani padme hum*, the mantra of Avalokiteshvara, the Buddhist Bodhisattva of Compassion.

After a few quiet and joyful weeks at Ramdas's ashram, the swami sent them off, for it was his custom not to let any of his disciples stay long. He told them to visit the two other great South Indian gurus: Sri Aurobindo and Ramana Maharshi. At the Maharshi's ashram once more they found caste being observed—although they also witnessed the living waves of silence which seemed to emanate from the guru. They received his blessing to take up abode in a cave on the side of Arunachala, the famous sacred mountain near his ashram, and there they gave themselves once more to meditation, study, and reflection. In this cave, Dharmapriya experienced a powerful vision of Amitabha, the Buddha of Infinite Light, which made a deep impression upon him, confirming for him that his period of apprenticeship was over and that he should now seek ordination into the Buddhist sangha. The two journeyed on, now completely abandoning the use of money, and, finding they would not be able to meet Sri Aurobindo, went with a friend from the ashram to Bangalore.

Here, after some alarming encounters with spiritualism, Dharmapriya and Satyapriya met, in the depths of the jungle, another woman mystic, Mother Lakshmi, who lived in a tiny cell under the ground, observing a twelve-year vow of silence. Even more impressive, they met Yalahankar Swami, a one-eyed guru reputed to be 600 years old. This extraordinary man taught by most unconventional means. His sole concern was to lead his disciples to a state of unconditioned spiritual freedom by the overcoming of the only real obstacle to its attainment: egotism. To that end, he would either treat his disciples with extreme disdain or act with the most exaggerated reverence towards them, depending whether their egotism took the form of pride or humility. The swami sent the friends off to the Divyagiri Hills for an experience of intensive meditation in the jungle solitude. Here Satyapriya became again more and more violent, one day coming near to drowning Dharmapriya in a fit of rage.

The Quest for Ordination

Patching things up, they then made their way towards the north of India where they had decided to take ordination. They had determined that they would seek the lower, shramanera, ordination on the full moon of the month of Vaishakha, or Wesak, the anniversary of the Buddha's Enlightenment. Furthermore they had set their hearts on being ordained at Sarnath, the place where the Buddha had first 'turned the wheel of the Dharma' by teaching the five ascetics and bringing them to share his own realisation. Arriving in the great Hindu city of Benares, they saw some of the sights and then set out on foot to walk the ten miles to Sarnath. The monks of the Mahabodhi Society temple there, who they had imagined would welcome them into the order, were far from pleased to see them, and in fact seemed suspicious and hostile, regarding them as a pair of vagabonds seeking a meal ticket. They appeared scandalised that the two friends had been journeying without money as the Buddha had done, and sent them on their way with scant courtesy. This bitter disappointment was too much for Satyapriya who almost decided that he had done with Buddhism and would seek entry into a Hindu order. But Dharmapriya did not waver, determined that he would never abandon Buddhism no matter what Buddhists did.

Fortunately, one of the monks at Sarnath had relented sufficiently to suggest that they consult an Indian scholar-monk, presently teaching at

Benares Hindu University. The Venerable Jagdish Kashyap advised them to go to Kushinagara, where the Buddha had died, to seek ordination from U Chandramani, a Burmese monk who had devoted his life to the restoration of that much-neglected site. Dharmapriya and Satyapriya set off once more, determined against all advice to walk the hundred miles from Benares to Kushinagara in what was the hottest season of the year. Sangharakshita has described this pilgrimage as walking 'through a curtain of fire', so intense was the heat. Even greater was their desire to enter the Buddha's order and they were overjoyed when the kindly old monk finally agreed to ordain them—after a searching interrogation during which he made certain that they were completely clear that he could accept no subsequent responsibility for them. And so, on the morning of Wesak, 12 May 1949, Satyapriya became Buddharakshita and Dharmapriya Sangharakshita.

The two new shramaneras then set out for Nepal where U Chandramani asked them to teach the Dharma to some of his disciples. They set off on foot in their new patched robes of traditional colour and cut, carrying their lacquered iron bowls. These last they had determined to fill by begging in the manner of the Buddha and his immediate disciples. Perhaps for the first time since the final disappearance of the Dharma from India in the Middle Ages, monks of the Buddhist sangha in India went from house to house in the prescribed fashion, receiving at each a few handfuls of cooked food in their bowl. Begging in this way, they walked into Nepal and for a few weeks stayed among the Newars, the indigenous people of Nepal who remained Buddhist despite the persecutions of the Hindu government. Here they learnt the customs and practices of a Buddhist monk in relation to lay-people and continued with their meditation and study—and Sangharakshita with the literary work which he had been engaged in throughout his time in India: letters, poems, articles, essays, and copies of passages from his reading.

On their return to India they sought a place to observe the 'rains residence', the three or four month period during which Buddhist monks traditionally remain in retreat. Finding nothing in North India they determined to go to Sri Lanka, but the physical strains of the last months had told on Sangharakshita and his health began to break down. Once more, the Venerable Jagdish Kashyap came to their rescue, offering to put one of them up at his residence, to support him, and to teach him. After much debate it was decided that Sangharakshita would stay with 'Kashyapji' and that Buddharakshita would go on to Sri Lanka, thus ending their two-and-a-half year partnership. Sangharakshita saw

Buddharakshita go with mixed feelings of sadness and relief, for his 'warm-hearted but irascible friend' had become more and more difficult to live with—although Sangharakshita recognised that without him he might never have 'gone forth' in so decisive and effective a manner.

WITH KASHYAPJI

The Venerable Jagdish Kashyap was an Indian from Bihar, born of respectable peasant stock. He was of a strongly religious temperament and became a *sannyasin** within the Arya Samaj, a Hindu sect which placed great emphasis on the Vedas. The young renunciant eagerly learnt Vedic Sanskrit so that he could read these revered texts—but when he came to study them for himself he found that they contained neither philosophy nor wisdom, being merely a collection of hymns, magical incantations, and rituals. In fact, he later used to argue that the best way to wean Hindus from Hinduism was to get them to study the Vedas. Completely disillusioned with Hinduism he began to study other religions and in that way came across Buddhism, to which he was instantly attracted. He went to Sri Lanka and became a bhikkhu in the Theravada Order, studying at the Vidyalankara Pirivena, a college for bhikkhus, and becoming a Tipitakacharya—a master of the entire Pali Canon. Although he had the highest reverence for the Buddha and his Dharma, he had a low opinion of Sri Lankan bhikkhus in general. He found them rigid, formalistic, and ignorant of the treasures contained in the Pali Canon, which their own ancestors had preserved. He inherited none of the hostility which many Theravadin bhikkhus had for Buddhists of other schools and, although his own field of study and practice was the Buddhism of the Pali texts, he himself was prepared to reverence the Mahayana Bodhisattvas and to acknowledge the entire Buddhist tradition. Since 1937, Kashyapji had been teaching at the Hindu University, although under severe restrictions due to the prejudices of the brahmin authorities.

Kashyapji was a man of both exceptional intelligence and great kindness of heart who clearly came to have the highest regard for his gifted pupil. Indeed, although Sangharakshita regarded Kashyapji as his first Buddhist teacher, Kashyapji himself spoke of Sangharakshita simply as

---

* One who renounces the world within the Hindu tradition

his friend. He was altogether a remarkable man, very humble and unassuming, who lived a very simple life. Whilst he was capable of working day and night when it was required of him, when he had no work he could spend long periods of time asleep. Sangharakshita tells that he would sometimes go into his teacher's room to ask some knotty question concerning his studies and find Kashyapji asleep on his bed. Opening one eye, he would immediately answer the question, completely accurately, knowing precisely the text to which the question referred, and then return to his slumbers.

The next seven months with Kashyapji at Benares Hindu University were among the most tranquil and contented of Sangharakshita's life. Though nominally Professor of Pali and Buddhist Philosophy at the University, Kashyapji had virtually no students or duties to perform, his presence being merely tolerated by the brahmin authorities to placate a wealthy patron. Sangharakshita and he were therefore almost completely undisturbed at their vihara where Sangharakshita applied himself to the study of Pali, Abhidhamma, and Logic under the tutelage of the brilliant and kindly scholar, who proved to be an excellent teacher. Not only did he study those subjects but he read even more voraciously and widely than usual and wrote more poetry. Indeed a struggle developed within him between the 'monk' and the 'poet'—which at one stage resulted in the burning of all his poetry. Fortunately that was not the end of the matter and the monk and the poet continued to coexist within him.

Kashyapji found his position at the University more and more untenable and resolved to take a few weeks' break in order to reconsider his future. He and Sangharakshita accordingly set out on a tour of holy places in Bihar, including the site of the great Nalanda University. As he had previously observed in a number of places in India, Sangharakshita noted that many ordinary Indians responded strongly to Buddhism—perhaps the Dharma could be revived in the land of its origin? Probably the most significant incident of this tour was Sangharakshita's reading of Thomas Merton's *Seeds of Contemplation*, given to him by a Catholic priest. The Trappist monk had, surprisingly, much to say that was relevant to Sangharakshita's own spiritual quest. What struck him in particular was Merton's recommendation for overcoming egoism. He suggested surrender to one's spiritual superior, entirely giving up all will of one's own to him. Sangharakshita decided to apply this in his relations with Kashyapji—a very mild and undemanding man who invariably sought Sangharakshita's wishes before deciding on anything.

An opportunity to put this teaching into practice soon came when the two found themselves in March 1950 at Kalimpong, in the Himalayan foothills. Here Kashyapji finally came to the momentous decision to give up his post at the Benares Hindu University. He needed time to reflect on his future and would therefore leave the hills for the jungles of Bihar where he would spend some time meditating in solitude until he became clear about what he would do next. He told Sangharakshita to stay in Kalimpong and 'work for the good of Buddhism'—and that is what he did.

Chapter Three

DWELLER IN THE SNOW MOUNTAINS
1950–1956

The ashes of all my heartaches,
The dust of a hundred dreams,
Are swept away in an instant
When forth one white peak gleams.
After long storm and struggle,
My heart with quietness fills
At the curve of this jade-green river,
The sweep of these dark blue hills.

Sangharakshita (1950)

FOR THE FIRST TIME in his life, at the age of twenty-four, Sangharakshita was on his own, with only his teacher's injunction to 'work for the good of Buddhism' to guide him. Kashyapji had also told him that 'the Newars will look after you'—the Newars of Kalimpong being of the same people as those among whom he had stayed in Nepal itself, the previous year. Many Newars had settled in Kalimpong, which, situated as it was in India on the borders of Nepal, Sikkim, Tibet, and Bhutan, was a melting-pot of peoples and religions. In fact, in that small market town were to be found representatives of the many races of Nepal—Tamangs, Sherpas, Limbus, Rais, and others—as well as Sikkimese, Bhutanese, men and women from all over Tibet, Indians from Bengal and elsewhere, Chinese, Burmese, Thais, and of course English and other Westerners who had taken refuge from the heat of the Indian plains in this Himalayan haven. As varied as their races were their religions, and Buddhism and Christianity, both in their many traditions and sects respectively, jostled with

Hinduism and Islam and with animist beliefs—even Taoism had its representatives.

For such a small and apparently insignificant township, Kalimpong had unusually broad connections. It was the major staging-post on the only caravan route from India through to Lhasa, the capital of Tibet, and in its heyday had been a centre of considerable wealth. Although caravans still passed through, carrying wool, musk, and yaks' tails for the Indian market, the flow had slowed since the Chinese take-over of Tibet—and was to stop altogether in 1959 with the closing of the border after the abortive uprising of the Tibetan people and the flight of the Dalai Lama. However, from that point on, many important Tibetan lamas found their way into India through Kalimpong, together with many other refugees, both monk and lay. The closeness to the Tibetan border and the Tibetan presence in the town attracted ethnologists and Tibetologists from Europe and America, as well as less scholarly devotees of things Tibetan. Bhutanese and Sikkimese aristocrats, rich and cultured Bengalis sheltering from the sweltering summers of Calcutta, even the pretender to the Burmese throne, all added to the richness which made this Asian microcosm a fascinating and educative backdrop for a very significant period of Sangharakshita's life, for he was to make Kalimpong his base and centre of operations for the next fourteen years.

Kalimpong provided not only a fascinating human setting, it was also a place of astonishing natural beauty. Situated at 4,000 feet in the foothills of the eastern Himalayas, its air is dazzlingly clear and colours shine out with startling brilliance. The town is strung out along a ridge so that on all sides views open up to the mountains of Nepal, Tibet, and Sikkim. Most impressive of all, far to the north, when the clouds clear, there hovers the vast rock mass from which rise the snow peaks of Mount Kanchenjunga, the third highest mountain in the world. Appearing and disappearing at different times of the day and in different seasons, the magical mountain seems to bless and protect the town with its awesome and mysterious presence. But nature is not only sublime here, she is also beautiful. The lush and verdant vegetation flowers with bright and delicate blooms, bringing life and colour to the majesty of perspective. Throughout his stay, Sangharakshita drew unfailing inspiration from the sublimity and beauty of his surroundings, and he considers this to be one of the most important aspects of his time in Kalimpong.

Although Kashyapji had confidently asserted that the Newars would look after him, Sangharakshita found that this was not quite straightforwardly the case. He lodged at the Dharmodaya Vihara, a temple established by the Buddhist Newars as a centre of Theravadin Buddhism, not the degenerate Vajrayana which was their ancestral tradition. Initially he was fed by some prominent Newari merchants, but he soon found that this was not without its problems, and instead went once more on a daily alms-round in the bazaar. In this way he made a deep impression on many people, Buddhist and non-Buddhist, most of whom had never seen a Buddhist monk following this ancient custom, once practised by the Buddha himself. However, when the rains came—a continuous torrent lasting for two or three months—it was no longer possible to continue his alms-gathering. Fortunately, one of his Newari friends collected some money for his support from among the local Buddhists—thus ending his ascetic refusal to handle money. By now he had been in Kalimpong for nearly four months and had begun to gather a circle of acquaintances beyond the rather limited Newari Buddhists, so he never had to go hungry.

THE YOUNG MEN'S BUDDHIST ASSOCIATION

Gradually, Sangharakshita began to 'work for the good of Buddhism'. He was invited to give a lecture or two here and there and conducted the weekly puja or devotional ceremony at the vihara. However, it soon became clear that the Buddhist scene in Kalimpong was far from harmonious: there were rivalries between Buddhists of different racial groups and there were rivalries within those groups. What Buddhist organisations there were in Kalimpong were spiritually moribund and locked in feuds. And so with a small band of his new friends, from a number of different racial backgrounds, including two very eccentric and mutually incompatible Western ex-officers of the British Army, he started a completely new Buddhist organisation. In May 1950, just two months after his arrival in the town, he inaugurated the Young Men's Buddhist Association. Since there were no other Buddhist youth organisations in the town, he thus avoided appearing to set up in competition with existing groups—at the same time appealing to the young men who were less caught up in traditional rivalries than their elders.

The primary objects of the Association, adopted at the inaugural meeting, were 'to unite the young men of Kalimpong and to propagate the teachings of Buddhism by means of social, educational, and religious activities'. Every week there were lectures and debates at the Dharmodaya Vihara, not only on Buddhist themes but on general cultural matters, and educational films were shown twice weekly at the Town Hall.

After a few months, a hut in the vihara grounds was opened as a recreational centre with table-tennis and other games. Youths from all the many backgrounds of Kalimpong, Buddhist and non-Buddhist, came flocking to these activities.

Sangharakshita soon noticed that the principal concern of many of the young men attending the Association's events was their school examinations. Their parents had often made great financial sacrifices to enable them to gain an education and they were expected to repay the investment by getting good, preferably government, jobs. To do that they had to pass exams. But their teachers did little effective teaching at school so that pupils would be compelled to employ them for extra tuition outside school hours—at a considerable price. The boys were thus under great pressure. Sangharakshita's answer to this problem was to begin tutorial classes at the vihara, under the auspices of the Young Men's Buddhist Association. He and his two Western helpers would tutor the boys nightly in the months before exams, Sangharakshita taking them for English and Logic. Besides being of great benefit to the young men themselves, the teaching of English Literature in particular led him to an important realisation, the resolution of his own conflict between poetry and spiritual life. He came to see that when he talked deeply about the inner meaning of a poem he was not merely talking literature—he was talking Dharma, the deep truth of Buddhism. From then on he felt no conflict between the 'poet' and the 'monk'.

Through his tutorial work and his participation in recreational activities—table-tennis was his favourite game—he began to get to know several of the young members of the Association quite well. But he wanted his work to have a wider context than the young men of one small Himalayan township, so in June 1950 he founded and edited a monthly magazine, *Stepping-Stones*. This 'journal of Himalayan Buddhism', in the twenty numbers issued before it ceased publication through lack of funds, achieved a modest fame in English-speaking Buddhist circles, making many connections all over the world for its editor. There were 250 subscribers and, in all, 1,000 copies were produced each month. Many were sent out complimentarily—Sangharakshita continued to send out copies of back-numbers long after the journal ceased publication—and in this way the work of Sangharakshita and the YMBA became quite widely known. Although it was simply and cheaply produced, it contained articles, poems, and stories by now well-known Buddhist writers and scholars of Buddhism and Himalayan culture such as Lama Govinda, Mme Alexandra David-Neel, Marco Pallis, George Roerich,

Edward Conze, Prince Peter of Greece and Denmark, René Nebesky de Wojkowitz, and Herbert Guenther. In his editorials Sangharakshita struck an 'unambiguously spiritual note'. (Many of these editorials, together with articles written for this and other journals at the time, have been published as *Crossing the Stream.*) Not only did this publication give Sangharakshita an outlet for his creative energies, it also forced him to become an organiser, for the principal work of producing this publication and administering the YMBA fell to him.

Fairly quickly, the YMBA established itself as an important feature not only of Kalimpong life but of the Darjeeling District, indeed it began to have an influence much further afield. A YMBA was started in Ajmer in Rajasthan, which soon affiliated to the Kalimpong-based Association. More affiliates were formed in Darjeeling and Gangtok, the capital of Sikkim, after visits by Sangharakshita—although these only seemed to flourish whilst he was present in person. The objects of the Association were widened: 'To unite the young men of India into a brotherhood of love and service that will work for the propagation of the Teachings of the Buddha by means of social, cultural, and religious activities'. A sister organisation, the Visakha Fellowship, was proposed for the young women of India by a student in South India. *Stepping-Stones* acquired a section in Nepali 'with the object of disseminating the Message of the Buddha amongst a larger number of people', Nepali being the *lingua franca* of the Darjeeling district as well as of the Kingdom of Nepal.

Towards the end of his first year in Kalimpong, Sangharakshita returned briefly to the hot and crowded Indian plains, principally to attend the nineteenth anniversary celebrations of the opening of the Mulagandhakuti Vihara at Sarnath, constructed by the great Anagarika Dharmapala. He took advantage of this gathering of bhikkhus from all over India to fulfil a heartfelt ambition: he received his 'higher' ordination as a bhikkhu, U Kawinda Sayadaw, a distinguished Burmese elder, acting as his *upadhyaya* or preceptor. Unusually for ordinations in the Theravada tradition, there were monks from several different nationalities making up the 'chapter' necessary for full acceptance into the bhikkhu sangha: Burmese, Nepalese, Sinhalese (including Sangharatana, the secretary of the Maha Bodhi Society's Sarnath branch, and Saddhatissa, later a noted scholar who became the head of the Maha Bodhi Vihara in London), and Kashyapji from India. Just outside the *sima,* or ordination 'boundary', sat Kusho Bakula Rimpoche, the head lama of Ladakh who, having been ordained a monk in the Tibetan tradition, was not eligible to join the chapter for the ceremony. Nonetheless, his presence seemed to emphasise that Sangharakshita was not merely entering one particular sect of Buddhism but a community which united monks of all schools. Indeed, the fact that surrounding the *sima* there were many white-robed lay-followers made it clear that what was really happening was that he was being welcomed into the Buddhist community as a whole, not just into its monastic wing. Although the ceremony was conducted in almost unintelligible Pali and no explanation was given, the occasion was a very happy one, during which he had an 'extraordinary sense of peace, satisfaction, fulfilment, acceptance, and belonging'.

From Sarnath, he went on to Lucknow for a few days, where he lectured to local Buddhist groups and at the University. Here he met the great Indian scholar of Buddhism, Dr Surendranath Dasgupta, as well as the Austrian scholar, Dr H.V. Guenther, who became a regular contributor to *Stepping-Stones*. Returning to Kalimpong after this important and fruitful tour, Sangharakshita found that his work for the good of Buddhism had received a considerable check—and, as he was so often to find, that check came from other Buddhists. The librarian at the Dharmodaya Vihara, a former bhikkhu who had been compromised with one of his female devotees and forced to marry, had not been happy with Sangharakshita's work since it began. The YMBA had brought Buddhist activity back to the vihara, thereby restricting the librarian's ability to hire out its rooms to his own advantage. For some time he had been feeding stories about wild parties and destruction of property back to the vihara's authorities in Nepal. A monk had been sent to restore order and for a few weeks past, though he could find no disorder to vanquish, he had been an unpleasant presence about the vihara. When Sangharakshita returned from his ordination at Sarnath, he found that in his absence this monk had simply shut down YMBA activities and expelled him from the room he had been occupying. He now insisted that Sangharakshita would have to pay in order to stay there at all. Gradually the new incumbent made his life at the vihara more and more untenable—besides heaping him with constant abuse and threats, he cut off his water and electricity. Why the vihara authorities had taken such exception to Sangharakshita never became clear, the tangled roots of the problem being buried deep in the petty jealousies and conflicts of small town life. One thing was clear, however, they preferred the vihara to return to its former moribund state rather than see it flourishing as it had done for the last few months.

Sangharakshita found himself completely alone in all this difficulty. His closest supporters were unwilling to help him because they did not want to upset members of their own community—and chose therefore to remain neutral. But help did come, and from an unexpected quarter. An elderly Burmese man swept up to the doors of the vihara in a taxi and invited Sangharakshita to come and stay with him. Prince K.M. Latthakin was the nephew of the last king of Burma and his wife was the king's second daughter. If Burma had not become a republic Prince Latthakin would probably have been king, and he was therefore known locally as 'Burma Raja'. Despite his illustrious ancestry, he now lived in Kalimpong, on a small pension from the Indian Government. He and his wife were devout Buddhists and, hearing of Sangharakshita's predicament, offered him the use of their guest bungalow, situated a few yards from their own. The little bungalow was beautifully sited and very peaceful. Here he could settle again into the routine of meditation, study, and writing which has always been the steady base-note of his life. Here too he could receive the friends he had begun to make among the people of Kalimpong, and particularly among his students in the YMBA.

The bungalow was, however, far too small to offer premises for the social, cultural, and religious activities of the YMBA. Some rooms were therefore rented in 'Banshi's Godown', a run-down, deserted warehouse in a rather insalubrious area nearer the centre of town. Quickly, the members reappeared and the activities of the Association recommenced with renewed vigour. Without the free accommodation provided by the Dharmodaya Vihara, membership subscriptions were inadequate to cover the expenses of the YMBA. Sangharakshita had therefore to learn a new skill: fund-raising—calling on various likely sympathisers throughout Kalimpong and asking them to contribute to the funds of the Association.

THE RELICS OF SHARIPUTRA AND MAUDGALYAYANA

Together with the recreational facilities, social events, debates, and films and lectures on cultural matters, the Association was of course engaging in religious activities. Sangharakshita and others gave talks on the Dharma, conducted regular puja ceremonies, and celebrated the major Buddhist festivals. As time went on, Sangharakshita began to galvanise the many different kinds of Buddhist in Kalimpong to celebrate together. His first success in this field came in 1951, when he arranged for the reception of the relics of the Buddha's two foremost disciples, Shariputra and Maudgalyayana. The relics had been taken from their stupa at Sanchi by a British archaeologist in the nineteenth century and deposited in London's Victoria and Albert Museum. They were now to be returned to

India for re-enshrinement. They were first being taken on a triumphal tour of Buddhist Asia, everywhere inspiring great devotion and renewed enthusiasm for the Dharma. Hearing that the relics were to be taken to Gangtok, the capital of Sikkim, Sangharakshita asked that they should also be brought to Kalimpong.

Arrangements for the visit of the relics entailed much organisation and committee work. It particularly required the surmounting of hostilities and suspicions, some of which derived from contemporary local rivalries and some from ancient and traditional differences. Sangharakshita himself encountered the latter when he visited the largest Tibetan monastery in the area to enlist the support of the monks. The red-robed Tibetan monks have, until recently, usually only read about their yellow-robed counterparts in scriptures and commentaries—and therefore view them all as narrow-minded followers of the Hinayana—the 'Lesser Way'. The abbot of the monastery greeted Sangharakshita with reserve—which quickly melted when he discovered that this particular yellow-robed monk followed the Bodhisattva Ideal. Contemporary rivalries were not so easily dissolved, but gradually Sangharakshita did bring sufficient harmony amongst the Buddhists of Kalimpong for them to worship together the sacred relics of the two friends who had been the Buddha's leading disciples.

Before the relics came to Kalimpong they were to be received in Gangtok, and Sangharakshita, together with Kashyapji and Sangharatana, was asked to accompany them there. Besides taking part in ceremonies and receptions, Sangharakshita found himself administering innumerable blessings by lowering the reliquary on to the heads of each of the thousands of devotees who came to reverence the relics. But he noticed that, strong as was the faith of the Sikkimese people, their actual knowledge of the Dharma was very weak. Clearly much needed to be done to revive and strengthen Buddhism in this 'Buddhist' land. He gave a number of lectures before the royal household, which constituted a modest beginning in the education of the Sikkimese in the Dharma. These were very well received and this visit was to prove the beginning of a long association with the small mountain kingdom.

From Sikkim the relics were to be taken into Tibet and Sangharakshita was to have accompanied them. He had been looking forward to this visit with great eagerness but it was not to be. Sikkim was an Indian protectorate and its foreign policy was the responsibility of the Indian Government. China had recently annexed Tibet and a visit from a British monk might be seen as a provocation—and the Indian Government with its strongly pro-Chinese policy above all did not want to provoke its ally. Orders had come from Prime Minister Pandit Nehru himself not to allow Sangharakshita to enter Tibet. Sadly he watched the caravan cross the border with the relics and his friends. He was never to enter Tibet, though living on its border and within its cultural influence for fourteen years.

His time in Sikkim had another significance, for this was the first extended period he had spent with his teacher, Kashyapji, since he had been left by him in Kalimpong. Slowly he started to unburden himself of the difficulties he had had to face at the Dharmodaya Vihara. To his surprise he found Kashyapji entirely unsympathetic and unwilling even to discuss the matter, simply being admonished by him to forgive what had happened. Sangharakshita had assumed that breaches of the harmony of the sangha or spiritual community as gross as those to which he had been subjected would be serious matters on which his teacher would wish to advise him and which he would be eager to resolve. But Kashyapji had, it seemed, no expectation of harmony. Sangharakshita gathered from stray remarks he made that he too had suffered at the hands of other monks and had ceased to expect anything from them. For Kashyapji there was no spiritual community. This terrible realisation made Sangharakshita feel even more on his own than ever.

The visit of the relics to Kalimpong in March 1951 was very successful and stirred up new enthusiasm amongst the local Buddhists, as well as bringing them together in a way that had never happened before. Sangharakshita then accompanied the relics to Darjeeling where the same feelings of intense devotion were stimulated in the hearts of the local Buddhists. Against this background of renewed fervour, he was able to pursue the plans for a Darjeeling branch of the YMBA—plans which were, unfortunately, never to materialise, although Sangharakshita's own lectures and frequent visits were very much appreciated.

The success of the sacred relics' Kalimpong visit offered a unique opportunity. Inspired and united by the devotion called forth by the relics, the Buddhists of Kalimpong would be unusually receptive to renewed Buddhist activities. It was therefore imperative to establish the YMBA on a much firmer footing. The expenses of Banshi's Godown were too great and Sangharakshita himself, living at Burma Raja's guest cottage some two miles out of town, was too far from the Association's headquarters and from where most of its members lived. And so, in June 1951, a dilapidated, but beautifully sited, bungalow was rented where both the headquarters and Sangharakshita himself could be housed under one roof. Named 'The Hermitage' by the owners in honour of its new occupant, it was situated a little way out of town on a ledge cut from the hill-side. Although much more cramped than the warehouse premises, the attractive setting of the new headquarters and the greater accessibility of the President made the activities of the YMBA more successful than ever, several members spending much of their out-of-school time at The Hermitage, playing table-tennis, reading in the library, and talking with Sangharakshita.

A VISIT FROM LAMA GOVINDA

Although he and the headquarters were now in one and the same place, Sangharakshita withdrew somewhat from the organisation of the YMBA's local affairs. He set up an 'Activities Committee', made up of members of the Association, so that he could concentrate on editing and publishing *Stepping-Stones* and establishing YMBA branches elsewhere. The journal had proved remarkably successful, attracting a notably brilliant band of regular contributors. One of these, in particular, had made a strong impression on Sangharakshita, both through the articles he had contributed to *Stepping-Stones* and through personal correspondence; so much so that, even before he had met him, Sangharakshita felt that he and Lama Govinda, the German artist, scholar, and teacher, were 'kindred spirits'.

One striking respect in which they shared a common outlook was in their attitude to Buddhism as a whole. Sangharakshita had been very disappointed to find that many of the modern Theravadin practitioners he encountered had a very narrow perspective, which excluded all other traditions. By contrast, he had, from his earliest acquaintance with the Dharma, felt himself to be heir to the entire tradition and had seen Buddhism as one whole—the subject of his first article, published in *Buddhism in England* in 1944, had been 'The Unity of Buddhism'. Govinda, too, argued in an article for *Stepping-Stones*, 'Buddhism as Living Experience', that the only criterion for determining what is the Dharma is 'whatever leads towards the realisation of Enlightenment' and that, with this criterion in mind, one should be open to the whole Buddhist tradition, not just one part of it. The two thus shared a common view of the unity of Buddhism, based upon an uncompromising vision of spiritual growth towards Enlightenment. Not surprisingly, they were very eager to meet. The chance came in September 1951, when Lama Govinda and his wife, Li Gotami, came to spend a few days with Sangharakshita at The Hermitage.

Lama Govinda had commenced his spiritual quest in Theravadin Sri Lanka but, on encountering the rich and deeply significant iconography of Tibetan Buddhism, had become a follower of the Mahayana. Later he married and, with his Indian Parsee wife, herself a gifted artist, had travelled into Tibet, notably visiting the ruins of Tsaparang, an ancient capital of Buddhist Western Tibet (the story of his travels is told in his *The Way of the White Clouds*.* Govinda had become the disciple of the great Tomo Geshe Rimpoche and was now a devoted practitioner of Tantric Buddhism. He was a man of very wide learning and deep understanding and contributed a number of highly acclaimed articles to *Stepping-Stones*.

When the two men met, they found they had a very great deal in common. They were kindred spirits indeed—as, to a lesser extent, was Li Gotami, Govinda's wife. During the days of this first meeting, they discussed many things, ranging 'over the whole field of Buddhist thought and practice'. They found themselves in agreement on whatever they talked about and Sangharakshita realised that he had more in common with Lama Govinda than with any other Buddhist he had so far met. Not only did they share the same outlook on Buddhism but they were both artists—Sangharakshita was a poet and Govinda a painter as well as a poet. Both considered their art to be an integral part of their spiritual path and they explored together in discussion the inner connection between art and spiritual life.

So successful was the meeting that Lama Govinda and Li Gotami invited Sangharakshita to spend a further week with them at Ghoom, a small town situated a few miles from Darjeeling. Here they visited the monastery temple—the oldest in the district. It was in this temple that Govinda had met his teacher, Tomo Geshe Rimpoche, and Sangharakshita too had been deeply impressed by its atmosphere when he visited six years before, during a brief stay at Darjeeling with an aunt. As he watched Lama Govinda and Li Gotami pass round the temple, pausing before the statuettes or frescoes of Buddhas and Bodhisattvas and murmuring in front of each figure the mantra appropriate to it, he was deeply affected both by the reverberations set up in him by the mantras and by the evident devotion with which his two friends recited and 'seemed to feel, behind each image, the living spiritual presence of which

---

* Published by Rider, London 1972

the image was the representation or, indeed, even the veritable embodiment'.

This experience naturally led on to discussions about meditation upon the various Buddha and Bodhisattva figures. Although Sangharakshita already knew something of Vajrayana Buddhism from his reading, Govinda made plain to him its general principles and philosophical background so that he saw how it fitted into the Buddhist Path as a whole. Thus, through this meeting with Lama Govinda, he not only met a kindred spirit but gained from him a clearer understanding and experience of a dimension of spiritual practice that was later to become of great importance to him.

LIFE IN KALIMPONG

Shortly after his return from Ghoom, where he left Lama Govinda and Li Gotami, Sangharakshita flew to Nepal, where he stayed for two weeks, once more accompanying the sacred relics on their tour of Kathmandu and Patan. Since his first visit to the kingdom, Nepal had undergone a considerable change. The repressive and caste-based regime of the hereditary Prime Minister had been forced to liberalise and the Prime Minister himself was shortly to be deposed. During his visit, Sangharakshita was able to meet the King and to remonstrate with him for the better treatment of his Buddhist subjects, in particular urging him to give his government's support to a Buddhist school. He also urged him in strong terms not to allow Christian missionaries into the country. In Kalimpong and Darjeeling, Sangharakshita had seen the disastrous effect many missionaries had had on indigenous culture, which they systematically undermined—and his bhikkhu friends had seen the same in Sri Lanka. Since the missionaries were often backed by the considerable resources of the West, they were a very powerful destructive force. Nepal was still relatively free from their depredations and Sangharakshita advised the King to resist their entry.

His return to Kalimpong was met with another crisis: he was running out of money for his work. An appeal in *Stepping-Stones*, despite its wide readership, brought insignificant response and, in February 1952, after twenty issues, Sangharakshita was forced to cease its publication. Indeed, the YMBA itself was threatened by lack of funds. Subscriptions and donations to the Association did not at all cover the rent on those parts of The Hermitage used for its activities. Sangharakshita himself had to subsidise some of the expenses from his own resources—which were very limited indeed. At this period, he had a small monthly allowance, given him by the same wealthy industrialist who had financed Kashyapji's vihara at the Benares Hindu University. Apart from that he had no regular income. All the tuition he gave to YMBA members was free, although he did have two or three paying students, mainly relatively wealthy Tibetans, to whom he taught English. He also received some income from poems published in the *Illustrated Weekly of India* and from articles and book reviews for the *Aryan Path*, a Theosophical journal. Apart from that, he would from time to time receive small donations from well-wishers. In fact, during the whole of his time in India he did not have an adequate regular income—and at times he would be completely without funds. However, he says that he never worried about money and successfully lived from hand to mouth throughout those fourteen years.

The next months were spent mainly in Kalimpong, continuing with literary work, with the affairs of the Association, with lecturing, with tutoring, and with an ever-widening circle of friends and acquaintances. The small but cosmopolitan town offered a rich variety of characters from a wide range of backgrounds. One of his earliest friends here was Marco Pallis, the noted English explorer and author of *Peaks and Lamas*, one of the first modern accounts of encounters with Tibetan Buddhism, the reading of which in 1945 had given Sangharakshita his first real insight into the subject. Although perhaps more of a Universalist than a Buddhist, Marco Pallis was deeply interested in the Dharma and shared Sangharakshita's concern at the decayed state of Buddhism in the area, supporting him in his work and contributing to *Stepping-Stones*. The two became good friends and met quite frequently. However, in 1952 Marco Pallis was expelled from the area by the Indian Government, probably because of his clandestine support for Tibetan opposition to the Chinese. He remained in contact with Sangharakshita and, later, at a time of crisis, proved himself a very good friend, adviser, and support. The young Austrian ethnologist, Dr René Nebesky de Wojkowitz, lodged at The Hermitage for a while and was a lively and agreeable companion. Sangharakshita came to know two other scholars living in the area, although less well: Prince Peter of Greece and Denmark, together with his wife, the Princess Irene, and Dr George Roerich. Beyond the European community in Kalimpong, his acquaintanceships were very wide indeed: he knew the head of the local branch of the Central Intelligence Bureau, a Buddhist of Sikkimese origin who, having been deeply impressed by the sight of Sangharakshita going on his alms-round, took a fatherly interest in him; he knew the daughter-in-law of Rabindranath Tagore, who came up to Kalimpong for the summer months to avoid the heat of the Bengal plains; he knew many people from all the backgrounds of this Himalayan melting-pot. Of course, he especially got to know several of the young members of the YMBA, many of whom spent much of their free time at The Hermitage.

Among others, Sangharakshita came into some contact with the Christians of the town. As Tibetans poured across the border, fleeing the Chinese, missionaries of all denominations began to gather in the hill districts, often rather callously trying to take advantage of the refugees' poverty to make converts. Some were foolish enough to try to convert Sangharakshita, but most saw him as evil incarnate: a Westerner, born a Christian, who had gone over to the demon-worship of Buddhism. Some Christian monks whom he did befriend and with whom he had interesting and open-minded discussions on religion were, after a while, forbidden to visit or converse with him. Although one or two impressed him with their humanity, altogether he got a very unpleasant impression of Christian missionary activity, the missionaries on the whole being narrow-minded and unscrupulous in their pursuit of converts, using bribery and threats to achieve their ends. He himself had occasion to protest to the authorities at some of the manipulations by which they sought to press people into conversion—which added to his reputation for being anti-Christian. He later gained a similar reputation for being anti-Hindu, but in both cases the truth was that he simply spoke out fearlessly against the abuses and evils that some of their practitioners perpetrated. Since he also spoke out against the abuses and evils of Buddhists, often much more publicly and thoroughly, he could scarcely be accused of partiality.

Inner Life

It is evident that the young English monk made a strong impression on the many people he met. In fact, by the age of twenty-seven, with very little outside help and guidance, he had established himself as an important figure in the town. What was it that sustained and inspired him? Perhaps none of his many acquaintances really knew what motivated him. Beneath the surface of his activities and friendships there moved an intense and powerful inner life which is glimpsed in his poetry of this period, which reveals him deeply stirred by the beauty of his Himalayan setting, wrestling with the tension between love as personal attraction and as Universal Compassion, and empowered by the image of the Bodhisattva, who works for the salvation of all beings.

Although he had been inspired by the Bodhisattva Ideal from his earliest contact with Buddhism, his time in India until he arrived in the hills had been mainly concerned with renunciation and the Arhant Ideal of personal liberation. His efforts had been directed towards freeing himself from the ties of the world and penetrating the truth of the Dharma for himself. Now, on his own and working for the good of Buddhism, he felt himself more and more in need of help and guidance from a higher source. As he has often found in his life, Sangharakshita came across the book that he needed at the time when he needed it. On his first arrival in Kalimpong, he had found at the Dharmodaya Vihara a copy of an English translation of the *Shiksha Samuchchaya*, the 'Compendium of Training', by the great seventh-century Indian Buddhist sage and poet, Shantideva, better known for his *Bodhicharyavatara*. The *Shiksha Samuchchaya* is a compilation from the scriptures on the theme of the Bodhisattva and his work: the Bodhisattva who dedicates himself to the attainment of Supreme Enlightenment for the sake of all living beings, even though this involves myriad lifetimes of unflagging spiritual effort. On reading the *Shiksha Samuchchaya*, he realised that here, in this principle of Universal Compassion, the most sublime of ideals, was the source of strength he needed if he was to stay in Kalimpong and 'work for the good of Buddhism', as Kashyapji had enjoined him. He found in the Bodhisattva Ideal a spiritual support which 'provided me with an example, on the grandest possible scale, of what I was myself trying to do within my own infinitely smaller sphere and on an infinitely lower level.'

Whatever else was happening at the vihara, and whenever his outward engagements would permit, Sangharakshita continued with his own meditation, study, and writing. Every year he would faithfully observe the rains retreat, during the later part of his stay in Kalimpong not stirring from the compound of the vihara for three months or so, studying, meditating, and writing more intensively than ever. At that time works on Buddhism in English were still quite few and he was able to keep abreast of them all. What translations of scriptures there were in English he read and reread, notably the *White Lotus Sutra*, *Lankavatara Sutra*, and Perfection of Wisdom sutras, and these were a source of great inspiration and insight to him. Of course, he read as voraciously as ever in the classics of English and world literature.

Sustaining all his activity was his unceasing spiritual practice and reflection upon the Dharma. Every day would start with a period of meditation, still the Mindfulness of Breathing or *anapanasati* which he had first taken up in Singapore and had practised almost every day since his time at Anandamayi's ashram. He says that from his earliest efforts he had no difficulty in becoming concentrated and absorbed, experiencing, from the outset, the very positive effects of integration and calmness which are its fruits. Through this practice, the intensity of his nature was deepened and steadied. Each evening he would meditate again and perform puja, usually reciting the *Ti Ratana Vandana*, the 'Salutation to the Three Jewels'—Pali verses expressive of intense faith in and devotion to the Buddha, Dharma, and Sangha. His shrine-room, during this period, was in an octagonal summerhouse in the grounds of The Hermitage, and here, with great reverence, he placed a small standing statue of the Buddha given him by Lama Govinda, three *thangkas* (Tibetan painted scrolls) depicting the Buddha and his two chief disciples together with the legendary sixteen Arhants, given him by Marco Pallis on his departure from the district, and various other prints. This shrine-room and the devotional objects it contained were clearly the focus for the very strong feelings that Sangharakshita had for the Buddha, his teaching, and his community, and he never neglected to give those feelings expression in both his puja and his poetry.

But study and formal spiritual practice by way of meditation and puja were certainly not the sum of Sangharakshita's inner life. From his earliest contact with Buddhism, when he had read the *Sutra of Wei Lang* and the *Diamond Sutra*, he had constantly reflected upon the Dharma. Naturally, his days in the Army had seriously restricted his study and contemplation, although even the mindless routine of barracks life had certainly not stopped it. During his wandering days in South India he had been free to pursue his urgent desire to understand the Dharma and to penetrate more deeply into it. This required no forced effort on his part. Even though he had at first to make some effort to meditate, he never had to make an effort to reflect upon the Dharma: as soon as he turned his mind to it, he was immediately concentrated. He was, in a sense, interested in nothing else, and simply followed his natural inclination to absorb himself in what most concerned him. This current of reflection and contemplation continued when he settled in Kalimpong—as it continues to this day. All the time he would be trying to gain insight into the Buddha's teachings and, he says, hardly a day went by when he did not give himself to this reflection, whether sparked off by his reading or through some spontaneous inner prompting.

He found no one with a deeper penetration of the Dharma who could help him clarify his understanding yet further. There were few if any at that time with whom he could share his inner life and ideals, and probably no one really knew what the issues and preoccupations were that most concerned him. In Lama Govinda he had found a kindred spirit, but there were, perhaps, no others—even among the Buddhist monks with whom he was acquainted. Some of those who were supposed to be his friends and collaborators were actually obstructive under the guise of giving him help and guidance. These must have been lonely and frustrating times for him, but with his deep faith in the Buddha and his teaching, and the unfailing inspiration and support of the Bodhisattva Ideal, he continued to work for the good of Buddhism without dismay.

THE MAHA BODHI SOCIETY

Sangharakshita's field of work for Buddhism was not long confined to the hill districts. An opening into the wider Buddhist world came through the Maha Bodhi Societyof India. He had already met Devapriya Valisinha, its General Secretary, on a number of occasions, and a sympathy had sprung up between them. Commiserating with him over the demise of *Stepping-Stones*, Valisinha had written, urging him to ally himself with some larger Buddhist organisation, rather than trying to set one up on his own. Over the next years, Sangharakshita did begin to co-operate more and more with the Society, at that time the leading Buddhist organisation in India.

The Maha Bodhi Society had been founded by one of the great figures of modern Buddhism, Anagarika Dharmapala (1864–1933), a Sinhalese who had struggled to awaken Sri Lankan Buddhism from the deep slumber into which it had sunk and who had been the first effective Buddhist missionary to the West, visiting Europe and America several times to propagate the Dharma. However, perhaps his greatest work, and the one which lay closest to his own heart, was his attempt to restore the holiest shrines of Buddhism in India to proper care and respect. Above all, he was horrified at the plight of Bodh-gaya, the place where the Buddha gained Enlightenment, and therefore for all Buddhists the very centre of this Earth. Not only had the site fallen into great disrepair but it was in the hands of Hindu landowners who had no intention of letting Buddhists regain control over their own most hallowed place. Anagarika Dharmapala was a man of strong faith and deep inspiration and he vowed his life to the revival of Bodh-gaya. In 1891 he founded the Maha

Bodhi Society, first based in Bodh-gaya and then moved to Calcutta, and the next year he began publication of the *Maha Bodhi*, an English language periodical that was for many years the leading international journal of Buddhism. The Society and its various branches throughout India were now the principal focus for the revival of Buddhism in India.

After Dharmapala's death, despite the intense fervour of its founder and his ecumenical spirit and international outlook, the Society had settled down into a dull and narrow Theravadin orthodoxy. Worse still, its Governing Body was dominated by Hindus and it was not possible to propagate any aspect of the Dharma that was inimical to Hinduism. Despite the heroic and dedicated efforts of Devapriya Valisinha, who was a personal disciple of Dharmapala and utterly devoted to completing his vision, the Society had ceased to be a truly effective vehicle for the revival of Buddhism, partly because of the crippling domination of the Hindu board members and partly because of the lack of real spiritual commitment on the part of the mainly Sinhalese *bhikshus* who ran its activities. Sangharakshita had already had his own experiences of that spiritual degeneracy when he worked at the Society's headquarters back in 1947, as well as when he sought ordination from the monks of the Maha Bodhi Society's vihara in Sarnath.

Nonetheless, he saw Valisinha's point that he should ally himself to some larger organisation and he was happy to do what he could to help the Society. In 1952, Valisinha suggested that Sangharakshita come down to Calcutta to write a 'biographical sketch' of their founder for the Diamond Jubilee Souvenir of the Society, working from some of Dharmapala's own diaries, from Valisinha's recollections, and from an unpublished—and unpublishable—biography previously commissioned by the Society. In doing this work, in the autumn of 1952, Sangharakshita was able to help Valisinha and to get to know him better but, more importantly, he was able to 'discover' Dharmapala. He discovered him not only as an activist and missionary but as an idealist and man of vision with a strong inclination to meditation. It was clear that in Dharmapala Sangharakshita had found another kindred spirit: a precursor and source of inspiration for the work which was to occupy his own life.

The finished article, some 30,000 words long, was a great success when it appeared in November 1952 in the long-delayed Diamond Jubilee Souvenir, receiving wide acclamation. But Sangharakshita's work on the biography had an important effect on its author: it awakened in him a deep respect for this great modern Buddhist hero and an appreciation of his founding vision for the Maha Bodhi Society, as well as a sympathy for the hard-working and dedicated Devapriya Valisinha—although the disciple was clearly not up to the task left to him by his master. Sangharakshita wished to do what he could to help Valisinha to bring the Society back to something like Dharmapala's original vision and was happy to ally himself with it to some extent. In 1953, the Young Men's Buddhist Association was therefore transformed into the Kalimpong branch of the Maha Bodhi Society of India. Thereafter, the branch received a small monthly grant towards basic expenses—though not for Sangharakshita's personal support. However, Sangharakshita, who by now had developed a vivid awareness of the limitations and failings of many 'religious' organisations, was very careful to retain complete independence from the parent body.

From that time on, he continued to work with the Maha Bodhi Society: continued, that is, to try to breathe back into it something of the spirit of Dharmapala. In 1954 he was appointed to the Editorial Board of the *Maha Bodhi* and for the next ten years was the effective editor—and remained on the Editorial Board until 1968. Three or four times each year he would come down from the Darjeeling hills to Calcutta and see to the publication of the next edition. For most issues he would write an editorial, report news of happenings in the Buddhist world, and often contribute an article or two. For a while he contributed a column called 'In the Light of the Dhamma'. Adopting a traditional literary device, he wrote this column under the *nom de plume* of Himavantavasi, 'Dweller in the Snow Mountains', appearing as an innocent backwoods Buddhist, offering trenchant and often ironic comment on current goings-on in the Buddhist world. The observations of this literary persona were especially popular with many bhikkhus, who appreciated Himavantavasi for openly saying much that they could only whisper among themselves.

While he was in Calcutta, he would usually give a few lectures at the Society and other locations. He became very popular with certain audiences in Calcutta, particularly with elderly, educated Bengalis, often of a theosophical bent and therefore quite receptive to the Dharma. Another aspect of his work for the Society was that it gave him the opportunity to meet many bhikkhus from a great variety of traditions and nationalities, and he gained thereby a wide understanding of the state of the modern monastic sangha throughout the world.

Though Sangharakshita began a long connection with the Society by writing Dharmapala's biography, at no time was he under any illusions about its decadence. He refused to become a member, especially because its President was a Hindu—indeed he was a brahmin who had led opposition to the Hindu Code Bill, whereby the great Dr Ambedkar had tried to reform Hindu society, which would have had the effect of ending the brahmins' social and political domination. Indeed, this domination was even replicated in the Maha Bodhi Society itself, since caste Hindus controlled its Governing Body—most of them having little sympathy with Buddhism as a genuine, independent spiritual tradition. On several occasions, Sangharakshita found that he was not able to publish what he wanted to in the *Maha Bodhi* because it offended the religious, social, or political sensibilities of the Hindus on the Governing Body. He therefore made sure that he was never too closely identified with the Society, refusing to accept any money from it for his personal support, since this might limit his freedom of action for the good of Buddhism.

ENCOUNTERS IN BOMBAY

In November 1952, once the biographical sketch of Dharmapala had been successfully completed, and the Diamond Jubilee edition seen through the press (a task which Sangharakshita took on to help Valisinha), he went to Sanchi for the re-enshrinement of the relics of Shariputra and Maudgalyayana. At the International Buddhist Conference held in honour of the event, Sangharakshita was able to make a public plea before Dr Radakrishnan, the Vice-President of the Republic of India, for the anniversary of the Buddha's Enlightenment to be made a public holiday in India, the land where he had lived and taught. Somewhat grudgingly, Dr Radakrishnan agreed to take up the matter.

Lama Govinda and Li Gotami were also present for the celebrations and he was able to spend more happy and fruitful hours with them, particularly exploring the archaeological remains of Sanchi. Towards the end of the event, he was introduced to Raj Kapoor, one of the greatest stars of the Indian film business, known as the 'Clark Gable of India', who also ran his own production company, RK Films. Kapoor had sought him out because he had an idea for a film about a monk at the caves of Ajanta during the time when Buddhist monasteries had flourished there. He needed an adviser to help him both develop his idea and to make sure it was historically accurate, and Valisinha had recommended Sangharakshita. The star therefore invited Sangharakshita to come to Bombay at the expense of his film company to discuss the story with him and work with one of his script writers, Arjundev Rashk. Feeling that he should exert what influence he could to make sure that Buddhism was not too drastically misrepresented, Sangharakshita agreed—and the next day found himself on a train to Bombay, courtesy of RK Films.

For the next three weeks, Sangharakshita spent quite a bit of time with the mercurial film star, as Kapoor developed and discarded approach after approach for *Ajanta*, his projected film. Rashk, the scriptwriter, had been delegated to look after him while he was in Bombay and the two men formed a friendship which outlasted his brief incursion into the Indian film world. He also took advantage of his presence in Bombay to fulfil another purpose: he went to visit Dr Ambedkar, leader of the Untouchable communities of India, at his house in Dadar.

Dr Ambedkar was such a prominent figure in Indian politics that Sangharakshita could hardly fail to have been aware of him. Even though he had taken little interest in current affairs in his wandering days, he had followed the controversy surrounding the Hindu Code Bill, which had led to Dr Ambedkar's resignation from the Government as independent India's first Law Minister. When he read Dr Ambedkar's article, 'Buddha and the Future of His Religion', in the April–May 1950 issue of the *Maha Bodhi*, Sangharakshita realised how genuine and deep was the Untouchable leader's interest in Buddhism and decided to contact him. He wrote, in June of that year, expressing appreciation of his article and telling him of the formation of the YMBA. Ambedkar replied, congratulating Sangharakshita on the founding of the Association and concluded, with characteristic bluntness, 'Great responsibility lies on the shoulders of the Bhikkhus if this attempt at the revival of Buddhism is to be a success. They must be more active than they have been. They must come out of their shell and be in the first rank of the fighting forces. I am glad you have started the YMBA in Kalimpong. You should be more active than that!'

Dr Ambedkar's interest in Buddhism was genuine and deep indeed. All his life he had worked for the social, economic, and political development of the 'Untouchables' of India, placing himself at the head of a movement embracing millions of people. The movement had its roots in the terrible oppression of the Hindu caste system of what Dr Ambedkar called 'graded inequality', which condemned millions to an inhuman slavery, sanctioned and enforced by religious belief. It was held that the mere touch of an 'Untouchable' would pollute a caste Hindu, who would then have to purify himself with various ceremonies and ritual ablutions. Untouchables were not supposed to receive education, were consigned to 'unclean occupations', and barred from participation in most Hindu religious practice. Under the influence of Western liberal ideas, some

Untouchables did begin to rise out of the subjugation of caste. The greatest and most influential of these was Dr Bhimrao Ambedkar, a towering figure by the standards of any time or place. As a young man, his exceptional intelligence had been recognised and, aided by a liberal-minded native prince, he had studied in the United States, England, and Germany. He refused to take personal advantage of the qualifications he acquired and dedicated his life to the uplift of his people. He had worked within politics, becoming Law Minister for the newly independent India and being responsible for the drafting of its constitution. He had founded a political party, engaged in labour organisation, started educational projects, and agitated in every way he could for the eradication of caste. To the Untouchables of India, particularly those of Maharashtra where he came from, he was a true hero, almost a god. Eventually he concluded that the Hindus would not change and that caste was an ineradicable part of Hinduism. He would leave Hinduism and enter a new religion, bringing his followers with him. As he investigated the available options, his choice fell more and more on Buddhism.

When the two men met at Ambedkar's house in Bombay, Dr Ambedkar immediately and bluntly made plain his disapproval of the Maha Bodhi Society's domination by Hindus. Sangharakshita was able to reassure him that he shared that disapproval and for that reason would not ally himself with the Society by being in its pay or even by becoming a member.

The Unity of Buddhism

After leaving Bombay, Sangharakshita visited Lama Govinda and Li Gotami at their residence in Deolali. He then returned to Kalimpong to reimmerse himself in the activities of the Maha Bodhi Society branch. From time to time, over the next years, he would make forays out from his base in the hills to the plains of India, visiting Calcutta for *Maha Bodhi Journal* work and the usual lectures and teaching activities. On his way down to Calcutta, on two occasions, he gave well-attended lectures on Buddhism and Art at Visvabharati University, Shantiniketan, the famous cultural institute founded by the poet Rabindranath Tagore. He would also frequently make visits to Darjeeling, trying to stimulate the rather tenuous Buddhist revival there. In February 1954, he made a tour of Buddhist centres in Assam, where there were some of the only Buddhists in India who could trace their tradition back to the time of the Buddha. Here too he did what he could to stimulate the revival of Buddhism.

1954 also saw the publication of a collection of his verse, *Messengers from Tibet and Other Poems*, by Hind Kitabs, a Bombay publisher. His poetry had been appearing in various publications since 1950, notably in the *Illustrated Weekly of India*, and he had achieved some modest acclaim as a poet among a circle of educated, English-speaking Indians.

Yet another new field of activity opened up for him in July 1954, when he was invited to Bangalore to give a series of lectures at the Indian Institute of Culture (later known as the Indian Institute of World Culture), an organisation established by Sri B.P. Wadia, a member of a very wealthy Bombay Parsee shipping family, and his French wife, Mme Sophia. The Wadias were Theosophists who believed, along with many others, that Mme Blavatsky's message was essentially Buddhist. The main body of the Theosophical movement had, however, under Mrs Annie Besant, increasingly interpreted Blavatsky in Hindu and Christian terms. The Wadias were therefore members of a breakaway organisation, the United Lodge of Theosophists, that purported to keep alive the original message of Theosophy. They were keen to maintain their Buddhist links and it was thus that Sangharakshita came to be invited to lecture on Buddhism at the Indian Institute of Culture in Bangalore, an organisation that among other things handled the publishing activities of the United Lodge. Later he often spoke at Theosophy Hall, the Lodge's Indian headquarters in Bombay, and contributed to the *Aryan Path*, a journal sponsored by the Lodge. The talks at Bangalore were very well received and he was invited to write them up for publication by the Institute.

Sangharakshita began his writing at The Hermitage in October 1954 but he was not to have a clear run at what was to prove a monumental work. He was forced to leave the bungalow he had come to love so well and move to another, called Craigside. But even here he was not to be at peace and had to move again just a few months later, still immersed in his *magnum opus*, to another bungalow, Everton Villa. As if these interruptions were not enough, he also found himself assisting a friend in writing an article on Tibetan Buddhism, besides continuing to oversee and participate in the activities of the Maha Bodhi Society Kalimpong branch. The work, *A Survey of Buddhism*, completed in March 1956, grew in the writing and comprised, when published, some 200,000 words. It is a brilliant and lucid account of the major Buddhist teachings, striking at once for its intellectual clarity and its inspiration and devotional fervour. Having established the basic and universal teachings of Buddhism in their context, Sangharakshita shows that all the different schools and traditions of Buddhism are aspects of a single whole, each drawing out different dimensions of the original insight of the Buddha. Recent scholarship has thrown some of his historical account into doubt and his own perspective on Buddhism has deepened, modifying some of the views he then expressed. Nonetheless, the work is of enduring value. The book achieved immediate and almost universal acclaim on its publication in 1957. However, in its pages as elsewhere in his writings, Sangharakshita sternly and explicitly attacked certain elements of the modern Theravada School for their narrow-minded sectarianism. Reservations were expressed about this, not only from upholders of the Theravada but from those who considered that Buddhists should not criticise one another. Sangharakshita has never been of this opinion, and has always spoken out against what he considers to be abuses and distortions of the Dharma from whatever source. Although this has made him some enemies, many have appreciated his saying what they dare not say even about their own schools.

The other literary project he became involved in whilst he was writing *A Survey of Buddhism* consisted in rewriting the work of a Tibetan friend. Lobsang Phuntsok Lhalungpa, an official of the Tibetan Government-in-Exile, had been asked to write a chapter on 'Buddhism in Tibet' for an American book, *The Path of the Buddha,* which aspired to present Buddhism from the Buddhist point of view. Lhalungpa relied for his account of Tibetan Buddhism on discussions with Dhardo Rimpoche, an incarnate lama resident in Kalimpong. Lhalungpa's English being, at that time, quite poor, he relied for his writing up of that account on Sangharakshita. He thus became a sort of intermediary between Sangharakshita and Dhardo Rimpoche, the former putting into good clear English what Lhalungpa had written up of what he had understood from the latter. There was much toing and froing in order to clarify exactly what the Rimpoche had said and to make sure that what had been written did accurately represent Tibetan Buddhism. In the course of this demanding work, Sangharakshita gained a thorough grounding in Tibetan Buddhism and an appreciation of the mind of the Rimpoche whom he had yet to meet.

SIKKIM

During this much disrupted period of literary work, Sangharakshita made a visit to Gangtok at the invitation of the Maharajkumar, the Crown Prince, who had made a strong connection with Sangharakshita when he visited the kingdom in 1951 with the sacred relics. The connection had been continued and deepened through the Maha Bodhi Society, of which the Maharajkumar was elected President (a genuine Buddhist one, for a change, partly as a consequence of some skilful manoeuvring by Sangharakshita)—he later became a Patron of the Maha Bodhi Society Kalimpong branch. Over the years, Sangharakshita gained great popularity with the Sikkimese royal family, particularly with the Maharajkumar, and he would visit once or twice each year, sometimes at the invitation of the Maharajkumar and sometimes at that of Sri Apa Pant, the Political Officer of the Indian Government, responsible for liaison between the kingdom and the central government, who invited him to give several series of lectures. Sangharakshita found his visits very interesting, both for the opportunity to assist in the revival of the Dharma in a devout but ignorant land and for the privileged glimpse into a small principality at work. Just as must have been the case in the little principalities of Italy and Germany before their unification into the modern nations, the principal officers of state all knew one another personally and public business would be casually discussed over dinner. Sangharakshita tried to ensure that the Maharaja did act as the 'Dharma Raja' he was supposed to be, protesting vigorously when the Crown Prince's wedding was celebrated with large quantities of beer and meat, specially killed for the occasion. He later even became involved in a project to educate the monks of the royal monastery in the rudiments of Buddhist doctrine—their knowledge of Buddhism being mostly confined to rituals and ceremonies—a project which unfortunately foundered.

Meetings with Dr Mehta and Dr Ambedkar

In November 1955 Sangharakshita returned to Bombay to help complete the screenplay for Raj Kapoor's film. A final script was, however, never arrived at—Raj Kapoor had moved on to other schemes and the film was never made. But there was plenty for Sangharakshita to do in Bombay. He lectured at Theosophy Hall, the headquarters of the Wadia's United Lodge, on the theme 'Inspiration—Whence?'. A Parsee woman came to him after the talk and insisted that, in view of the subject-matter of his talk, he should meet a friend of hers. She introduced him to Dr Dinshaw Mehta, also a Parsee, who was to become one of Sangharakshita's closest friends in India.

Dr Mehta was a noted naturopath who had treated many of the famous men of the Indian National Congress, even Gandhi himself. He had established a religious organisation of his own, the Society of the Servants of God, which centred upon messages Dr Mehta received in trance and transcribed by means of 'automatic writing'. He tried to interest Sangharakshita in these 'guidances' but it was all too apparent that 'God', or whoever it was from whom the messages came, had sometimes been listening to Sangharakshita's own lectures! Eccentric though he was, a very warm friendship developed and it was with Dr Mehta that Sangharakshita usually stayed when in Bombay. Dr Mehta was very supportive of the work amongst the ex-Untouchables that soon became one of Sangharakshita's major activities—Dr Mehta himself always made a point of employing so-called 'low caste' people as his servants—unthinkable to orthodox Hindus. His wide knowledge of pre-independence politics and of the history and culture of Maharashtra was very useful to Sangharakshita as he developed his activities amongst the ex-Untouchables. His rock-like integrity and honest and independent spirit more than made up for the eccentricity of his religious beliefs—about which, Sangharakshita thinks, even Dr Mehta had some doubts.

Whilst he was in Bombay, Sangharakshita also pursued his connections with the ex-Untouchables and lectured at the Japanese temple at Worli and other localities where ex-Untouchables lived, communicating to them the basic principles of the religion which their great leader had now advised them to embrace and to which he himself was very seriously contemplating conversion. Sangharakshita took advantage of his presence in the city to visit Dr Ambedkar a second time, on this occasion at Siddharth College of Arts, founded by Ambedkar himself. Ambedkar explained that he had in fact now decided to convert to Buddhism and enquired how formal conversion took place, asking whether Sangharakshita could conduct the ceremony for him. Replying that although he, or any other duly ordained bhikkhu, was qualified to do so, Sangharakshita recommended that, for greater impact on the Buddhist world, it would be better if a much more senior and well-known monk performed the ceremony. He suggested U Chandramani, the Burmese monk who had conducted his own shramanera ordination, and was the seniormost *bhikshu* in India. Dr Ambedkar then asked for a written account of everything Sangharakshita had told him and asked him to speak to some of his followers on the meaning of conversion. A few days later Sangharakshita addressed a crowd of some 3,000 of Dr Ambedkar's disciples on this theme.

Both his meeting with Dr Mehta and his further connection with Dr Ambedkar were to have important consequences for the remainder of Sangharakshita's stay in India, opening up new fields to him, both inner and outer. After basing himself in Kalimpong for six years, Sangharakshita had developed a wide range of contacts and several different spheres of operation throughout India. The breadth of his activities is astonishing, drawing together such contrasting worlds as that of wealthy Parsee Theosophists and the desperately poor Untouchables. One very important contrast in his life we must remember is that between the peace and beauty of the Darjeeling Hills and the noise and bustle and heat of Calcutta, Bombay, and the Indian plains. Since the journey from Kalimpong to Calcutta alone is an arduous one, given the crowded, dirty, and inefficient state of Indian transport, his tours away from the hills must have been taxing in the extreme. Since childhood, he had been rather frail in appearance—pictures of this time show him gaunt and ascetic—but he was tough enough to take the discomfort of these travels and did so without hesitation or complaint. His work for the good of Buddhism was gathering momentum and he was becoming known as one of the most active and forthright modern exponents of Buddhism.

Chapter Four

The Place Where the Three Ways Flourish
1956–1964

Visitors all day!
Morning mist, afternoon flowers—
And now the full moon.

Sangharakshita (1959)

THE YEARS 1956 AND 1957 were very important for world Buddhism. By agreement of practically all Buddhists, the period between the Vaishakha Purnimas (the full moons of the Indian lunar month May–June) of those years was to be celebrated as the 2,500th anniversary of the Buddha's *parinirvana* or death. The Indian Government too had decided to honour the country's most famous son, declaring the period to be the Buddha Jayanti year. Buddhists all over the world anticipated a great revival of the Dharma, and certainly it transpired to be the year in which the mass conversion of ex-Untouchables began. It was a watershed for Sangharakshita too: the year in which his work for the good of Buddhism began to take decisive form.

Guidance from Another Dimension

Early in 1956, before the Jayanti officially began, Sangharakshita took a step that he had been contemplating for some time and which marked a new departure in his inner life: he received Tantric initiation.

Sangharakshita's path had been, on the whole, a lonely one: for the first year or so of his life as a Buddhist he had had no contact with other Buddhists. He had then met some of the few followers of the Dharma in Britain and, thereafter, encountered many others in India. But none of them was able to offer him any real guidance. He had, for the most part, to find his own way forward, with the words of the Buddha in the scriptures and the writings of great Buddhist sages to guide him, together with his own reflections and insights. In many ways, his greatest spiritual help had come from Hindu gurus, notably Swami Ramdas. From some of these gurus he gained a definite experience of a higher dimension and encouragement to follow the path—encouragement he had scarcely had from any Buddhist so far. Kashyapji, though a brilliant teacher of Pali and Buddhist studies, as well as a good-natured companion and loyal friend, was hardly a man of great spiritual attainment, and Sangharakshita could not truly look upon him as his spiritual mentor.

Sangharakshita himself saw this as a definite problem. Had he found a teacher, he would have unhesitatingly placed himself under his instruction. But so far he hadn't met anyone whose penetration of the Dharma was greater than his own. This left him with one of the most basic problems of spiritual life: how could one get beyond ego by ego's unaided efforts? Unless there was some intervention from outside himself, to which he could submit his ego, all his efforts at transcending ego would be tainted with ego. As we have already seen, some light came from the Trappist monk, Thomas Merton, who wrote of this paradox in his book *Seeds of Contemplation*, which Sangharakshita had read in 1950 while he was travelling with Kashyapji after leaving the Benares Hindu University. Father Merton advocated the complete subjugation of one's egoistic will to one's spiritual superior. Sangharakshita forthwith began to apply this advice, submitting his will to that of Kashyapji—no easy matter when his teacher was a man of such mild manner and so eager to consult Sangharakshita on every matter. Nonetheless, it was in obedience to Kashyapji's injunction to 'stay here and work for the good of Buddhism' that he settled in Kalimpong and remained there for fourteen years.

Once more on his own, however, after Kashyapji had left him in the Himalayan township, the problem remained—perhaps redoubled: now he needed guidance as never before, since he was concerned not only with his own spiritual progress but with guiding others. He drew his inspiration principally from the Buddha and, particularly, from the Bodhisattva Ideal—but in many ways that was not enough: he knew that he needed some more effective link with a higher reality. A clue to the way forward arrived when he learnt something of the philosophical background to Vajrayana meditation from Lama Govinda. But it was through his contact with Dr Mehta that he finally came to see what he must do.

Dr Mehta's own view was that spiritual progress without 'divine' help was impossible. He himself practised a form of automatic writing, which he claimed was God-inspired. Dubious as might be the source of Dr Mehta's guidance, it still had an important spiritual impact on Sangharakshita. Dr Mehta repeatedly pressed him to take advantage of the 'guidances' he received through his automatic writings, stressing again and again that spiritual progress cannot be made by relying on one's own egoistic efforts alone. Contact must be established with some higher dimension from which guidance can be derived. According to Dr Mehta, such guidance could come in a number of different ways and from a number of different levels—the highest being, of course, his own inspired writings. However, this advice was by no means uncongenial to Sangharakshita; he had already had various experiences of guidance, notably the vision of the Buddha Amitabha which had come to him in the cave on Arunachala, near the ashram of Ramana Maharshi, which he had taken as a sign that he should go to Sarnath and seek ordination. He also, from time to time, would receive a kind of guidance in his meditation, hearing a voice, usually uttering a single sentence. Shortly after meeting Dr Mehta in 1955, he spent a few days in intensive retreat at Dr Mehta's house in Poona and had a number of experiences that confirmed that he needed to find, so to speak, an inner guru—since he had been unable to find any completely satisfactory external one. He could not, of course, accept the validity of Dr Mehta's guidance, but he realised that Vajrayana initiation was the way in which he could make that essential connection with a higher reality.

In Tantric initiation, the guru imparts to the disciple, usually by means of a ritual, a connection with an idealised Buddha or Bodhisattva, embodying a particular aspect of the Enlightened consciousness, such as Wisdom or Compassion. Thereafter, the disciple contemplates the visualised form of that Buddha or Bodhisattva in meditation, thus deepening and strengthening his experience of the Enlightened mind itself. Naturally, the ceremony is only really efficacious to the extent that the guru has himself some real contact with the transcendental realities he is trying to convey. If he has such a contact, the ritual becomes a kind of formal introduction, whereby the disciple is brought into contact with that further dimension and henceforth can connect with it himself through the form he visualises in meditation. Sangharakshita saw that here was the means of gaining guidance from a higher reality. Here was the way to get beyond egoistic striving by opening oneself up to that higher transcendental influence.

Sangharakshita was determined that he would only seek initiation from someone he considered to be in definite contact with that higher reality. In February 1956 he received initiation from Chetul Sangye Dorje, a Tibetan lama of whom he had heard much from his Tibetan friends—and who later was to make a deep impression on Thomas Merton, as he attests in his *Asian Journals*. The Chetul ('One Without Concerns') was indeed a strange and unorthodox figure, although very highly thought of by Tibetans, including those of the Buddhist hierarchy. He was not a monk but a wanderer who came and went across the borders of India, Nepal, and Tibet, no one knowing when he would arrive or leave. He followed the Nyingmapa School of Tibetan Buddhism and was said to be very learned in the scriptures. The Regent, who had ruled Tibet during the Dalai Lama's minority, had been deeply impressed by him and had himself taken initiation from him, as had other leading lamas, despite the fact that he was still a relatively young man, at that time about thirty-five years old. His appearance was quite rough and unpleasing, almost brutal, but there was about him that touch of another dimension for which Sangharakshita had been looking, and he felt a strong spiritual attraction to him. The Chetul gave him the initiation of Green Tara, a female Bodhisattva who embodies Compassion, and said that all the great pandits of the past had meditated upon her. For the next seven years Sangharakshita faithfully performed the Green Tara practice every day. Through this meditation, and others he was initiated into later, he felt his whole spiritual life to be guided from a higher dimension. He had found at last the inner guidance which he had so long desired, beyond the level of his own ego.

Sangharakshita never got to know the Chetul very well—he was too elusive a character for that. But the day after the initiation he came to Everton Villa, where Sangharakshita was then staying, and explained through an interpreter the significance of the initiation. He also delivered a startling prediction—'at a time when this seemed impossible'—that Sangharakshita would have a vihara of his own, and even bestowed a name upon it: Triyana Vardhana Vihara, 'The Place where the Three Yanas Flourish'. The Chetul also gave him several other definite instructions arising out of his experience in meditation. On this occasion he composed, 'in a mood of high spiritual exaltation', the Tibetan original of the following stanzas:

In the sky devoid of limits, the teaching of the Buddha is
The sun, spreading the thousand rays of spiritual discipline;
Continually shining in the radiance of the impartial disciples,

May this realm of the Triyana be fair!
In accordance with this request, made in the Fire-Monkey Year
On the ninth day of the first month by the Maha Sthavira Sangharakshita,
This was written by the Shakya-upasaka, the Vidyadhara Sangye Dorje:
May there be happiness and blessings!

THE BUDDHA JAYANTI

Sangharakshita naturally seized on the Buddha Jayanti year as another opportunity to unify and galvanise the Buddhists of Kalimpong. He formed a committee to co-ordinate festivities, consisting of local Buddhist dignitaries, with himself as General Secretary—and inevitably the one who did all the work. Again he overcame the various diplomatic complications involved in such an enterprise, particularly having to handle the very prickly Bhutanese aristocrat, Rani Chuni Dorji, who was President of the committee. In May 1956, at the start of the Jayanti year, the town's celebrations were held. Once more they were a great success, being by all accounts 'the biggest and most colourful the town had ever witnessed'.

In November that year, Sangharakshita toured the Buddhist holy places of India as guest of the Indian Government—one of fifty-seven 'Eminent Buddhists from the Border Areas' being entertained in honour of the Buddha Jayanti. The tour took in Bodh-gaya, Rajgir, Nalanda, Sarnath, Kushinagara, Lumbini, and Sanchi with detours to various prestige 'development' projects which the Government felt it important that the 'Eminent Buddhists' should see, such as dams and cement factories. The tour ended in New Delhi with the massive Jayanti celebrations, sponsored by the Government. The party was introduced to the President and Vice-President, as well as the Prime Minister, Pandit Nehru, with whom Sangharakshita had some private talk. They also had the opportunity to meet the Dalai and Panchen Lamas who were in India for the Jayanti. This was Sangharakshita's first encounter with the spiritual—and at that time, at least nominally, temporal—head of the Tibetan people.

DR AMBEDKAR AND THE CONVERSION OF THE EX-UNTOUCHABLES

Perhaps even more significant than his meetings with these various dignitaries was Sangharakshita's third meeting with Dr Ambedkar, which took place in Delhi—Sangharakshita having brought the Eminent Buddhists from the Border Areas to congratulate Ambedkar on his conversion to Buddhism, which had taken place just a few weeks earlier. At their previous meeting, Sangharakshita had advised Dr Ambedkar to ask U Chandramani to conduct his conversion ceremony and this he had done, Ambedkar taking the Refuges and Precepts from the Burmese elder in Nagpur on 14 October 1956, and then in his turn administering them to 380,000 of his followers. Sangharakshita, though invited, was unable to attend since he had a previous engagement in Sikkim. He was thus very pleased to have the opportunity to congratulate him on the great step he had taken.

It was however apparent that Dr Ambedkar was very ill. During the course of the meeting, he became more and more exhausted as he spoke of his hopes and fears—mostly fears—for the new movement of conversion he had inaugurated. Although the great man spoke so softly that only Sangharakshita could hear him and although he was clearly on the verge of collapse, he refused to let the delegation go—or rather refused to let Sangharakshita go, because it was to him exclusively that he had been talking. 'I had the distinct impression that he somehow knew we would not be meeting again and that he wanted to transfer to my shoulders some of the weight that he was no longer able to bear himself. There was so much still to be done, the sad, tired voice was saying ... so much to be done....'

Although Sangharakshita and Dr Ambedkar only met three times, their conjunction was clearly significant for them both. Some of the latter's closest lieutenants have reported that the great leader had a high regard for the English monk, saying that there were only two bhikkhus his followers should trust: Sangharakshita and an Indian of unwavering hostility to caste. For Sangharakshita himself the meeting with Dr Ambedkar opened up a sphere of activity which had never previously concerned him and which was to become a very significant part of his life. Till then his interests had been almost entirely religious, philosophical, and artistic. He had never given much consideration to the social dimension of Buddhism nor had it occurred to him that the Buddha's teaching could become a means to social, even political, emancipation for the oppressed masses. But once he had met Dr Ambedkar and seen the potential in the conversion movement, he threw himself wholeheartedly into this work, conducting conversions himself and educating the new Buddhists in the religion of which they were now members.

After the Jayanti celebrations in Delhi, Sangharakshita briefly visited Bombay and then set out for Kalimpong. He had however decided that he would stop off at Nagpur, the location of the conversion of

Dr Ambedkar and so many of his followers. Since he had been unable to be present at the great occasion, he wanted to congratulate the new Buddhists and give them what help and encouragement he could. He arrived at Nagpur by train from Bombay on 5 December. Just an hour-and-a-half after his arrival came the news that Dr Ambedkar had died the previous night. His followers were overwhelmed with grief: seven weeks after the mass conversion their great leader was dead. Not only were they grieving deeply for the loss of their beloved 'Babasaheb' but they were overwhelmed with hopelessness and despair. It was their faith in Ambedkar that had carried them forward against the odds of their poverty, centuries' old oppression, and the hostility of caste Hindus. What could they do without him? It was particularly through their faith in him that they had left behind their Hindu gods and become Buddhists. The local leaders beseeched Sangharakshita to rally the stricken masses by speaking to them, so he asked them to arrange a condolence meeting. That evening, standing on the seat of a rickshaw as an improvised platform, Sangharakshita spoke to a crowd of 100,000 or so. In the darkness he had seen the vast mass of people assembling in complete silence, a near impossibility for an Indian crowd, highlighting their desolation. Others had tried to speak but, one by one, had sat down again, choked with tears. Sangharakshita exhorted the vast crowd of weeping men and women to remember that Dr Ambedkar lived on in their hearts and in his great work to bring about the revival of Buddhism in India. He urged them to pay their homage to him by carrying on that work. This simple message had its effect and the great crowd began to recognise hope where previously there had been only despair.

Over the next four days Sangharakshita gave more than forty talks, all pointing out Dr Ambedkar's greatness and calling on his followers to take up his work. He conducted conversion ceremonies for another 30,000 or so and taught the significance of the Refuges and Precepts, the recitation of which constituted conversion, and of the twenty-two vows formulated and taken by Dr Ambedkar himself which were the ex-Untouchables' declaration of freedom from caste and of their conversion to Buddhism. Sangharakshita's presence in Nagpur at this time was almost miraculous. The new Buddhists had become Buddhists simply on the strength of their faith in Dr Ambedkar—they knew almost nothing of what it signified. There was a very real danger that, with his death, they would not be able to find a way forward. Sangharakshita was there, at the moment when he was needed, to encourage them to continue on the path their great guide had shown them. The local Buddhist leaders said that Sangharakshita had 'saved Nagpur for Buddhism' and he is still honoured and respected by the Buddhists of Nagpur second only perhaps to Dr Ambedkar himself.

Triyana Vardhana Vihara

After this deeply stirring event which wedded him to Dr Ambedkar's movement for life, Sangharakshita returned to Kalimpong. The extraordinary happenings of this *annus mirabilis*—in his own life as well as in that of world Buddhism—continued. In January 1957 the Dalai Lama visited the Kalimpong branch of the Maha Bodhi Society, and donated an image of the Buddha Amitabha. This year also saw the publication by the Indian Institute of World Culture of *A Survey of Buddhism*, which quickly attracted very favourable reviews. One Sri Lankan journal described it as the chief event of the Buddha Jayanti year—despite its strictures on the modern Theravada. Indeed, many Theravadin bhikkhus were delighted that someone had at last pointed out the narrowness and lack of spiritual vision of many modern presentations of the Dharma.

For Sangharakshita, the Buddha Jayanti year was crowned by the fulfilment of Chetul Sangye Dorje's prediction that he would soon have his own vihara. The owner of Everton Villa wanted to sell the property and was willing to help him to secure another. The opportunity arose to buy another bungalow for a very good price, several wealthy friends—notably Marco Pallis, an English writer who had lived in Kalimpong during the early part of Sangharakshita's stay, and the Maharaja of Sikkim—provided the money, and at last he had his own vihara. The house was situated about two miles outside Kalimpong on a spur looking west towards the Kanchenjunga range. It was a beautiful and peaceful site with some four acres of its own land which Sangharakshita enthusiastically put under cultivation, deriving a good yearly income from the sale of oranges, and keeping the vihara stocked with vegetables—in the face of local scepticism, he proved an excellent horticultural manager.

The new vihara was officially inaugurated in May 1957 with the name that Chetul Sangye Dorje had suggested: the Triyana Vardhana Vihara. The vihara aimed to function in a threefold capacity:

'As a centre for the systematic study of Buddhism in all its aspects, for research, and for the production of Buddhist literature, both original and translated, in English, Nepali, Hindi, Marathi and other languages. As a meditation centre, where both monks and laymen will be provided with all facilities for the practice of dhyana according to the traditional methods, and where arrangements can be made for longer or shorter periods of spiritual retreat. As a centre for the ordination and training of Bhikshus, Shramaneras, and lay Dharmaduta workers, in order to meet the growing need for dedicated workers now being felt both in the hill areas and the plains as a result of the movement of Buddhist revival.'

Sangharakshita felt the importance of that revival very keenly, finding himself at an important juncture in time and space: he was from the West where interest in Buddhism was beginning to blossom, he lived in India where millions were converting to the Dharma, and he lived in a town on the border of Tibet, a land that had preserved the full glory of Indian Buddhism as a living spiritual tradition and from which some of the foremost teachers were now escaping in the face of the terrible depredations of the invading Chinese. All these currents—the awakening of the West to the Dharma, the reawakening of Buddhism in India, and the opening up of the spiritual treasures of Tibet—underlay the new foundation, the Triyana Vardhana Vihara. Its non-sectarian character was unique: Sangharakshita continued to look to the entire Buddhist tradition for inspiration and guidance, as he had done from the outset.

Over the next seven years, from 1957 to 1964, he spent most of his time at the vihara. Whilst in residence, he would always continue with his study, meditation, and literary work, and from time to time spend periods in more intensive retreat. From the beginning of his stay in Kalimpong he had observed 'the rains', the three-month retreat that bhikkhus are supposed to keep during the monsoon season, but now that he had his own vihara he was able to observe it more strictly, not leaving the confines of the compound and spending his time in meditation and study, often keeping silence. At other times he would lead a more active life, attending to the affairs of the Kalimpong Maha Bodhi Society, giving lectures, conducting ceremonies, and meeting a wide range of people from the area—besides overseeing the cultivation of the small estate. He would often visit Gangtok and Darjeeling and other nearby townships for Buddhist activities.

Although he spent much of these next years in this remote and high corner of the world, Sangharakshita built up a circle of acquaintances all over India, and indeed, by correspondence, all over the world. His sphere of operations had now become very wide indeed. From time to time he would make forays down from the hills: to Calcutta for the work of the Maha Bodhi Society and its journal, often visiting and lecturing at other places at the same time, such as the Visvabharati University; to Bombay and Maharashtra where he had many friends and where he worked more and more among the ex-Untouchable Buddhists; and to South India where he had contacts among Theosophists sympathetic to Buddhism. We must therefore now try to picture his remaining years in India by following each of these threads thematically rather than chronologically, imagining them twisted together in the rich and rewarding life of Sangharakshita.

Dhardo Rimpoche

One of the most important strands in that life was his deepening connection with Tibetan Buddhism. Kalimpong being so near to Tibet and providing a home for so many Tibetans, it was not hard for him to immerse himself in the magnificent wealth of Tibetan religious tradition. Above all he found that tradition to be alive, spiritually alive, as witnessed by the fervent devotion of its humblest adherents and the deep learning and wisdom of its leading teachers, many of whom passed through Kalimpong at some point. He had already been fortunate enough to receive initiation from Chetul Sangye Dorje, and in the next few years he gained initiation and teaching from a number of other prominent lamas, most of them *tulkus* (i.e. recognised as incarnations of previous great teachers).

As we have seen, Sangharakshita had had to find his own way upon the spiritual path since he had never found a real spiritual guide. Fortunately, from his earliest contact with the Dharma, he had had an immediate and powerful response to it and an intuitive grasp of its true meaning that required no external explanation. As he himself says, it was as if he was not new to Buddhism but was merely picking up the threads of a dedication to the Three Jewels carried over from some previous existence. In the absence of any fleshly teacher, he took Tantric initiation in order to make contact with the higher spiritual energies embodied in the Buddhas and Bodhisattvas. From then on it was they who were his teachers, and his whole spiritual life was guided from that dimension. Nonetheless, in Kalimpong he did make contact with some remarkable men who were able to grant him initiation, help him to deepen his knowledge of the Dharma, particularly in its Tibetan expression, and, in one case, offer him some guidance in his meditation practice.

His connection with Dhardo Rimpoche, the lama who became his closest friend and teacher, began very slowly. The two men had first come into contact indirectly in 1954 through their mutual friend, Lobsang Phuntsok Lhalungpa, who wrote an article on Tibetan Buddhism with the benefit of Dhardo Rimpoche's learning and Sangharakshita's literary skill. Through this intermediary, who had to go back and forth between the Rimpoche and the English bhikkhu, Sangharakshita began to appreciate the depth of understanding of the Rimpoche whom he had not yet met.

When he did meet Dhardo Rimpoche, later in 1954, he found him a little aloof, but set this down to the fact that he was a member of the Gelugpa School, the 'reformed' tradition to which the Dalai Lama belongs and that lays great stress on monastic discipline. However, though the Rimpoche was a Gelugpa by training and present practice, his origins were not of that school. He was the thirteenth tulku or 'incarnation' of the abbot of Dorje Drak Monastery at Dhartsendo, a trading post on the border with China, and, until his immediate predecessor, all these had been Nyingmapas. The twelfth tulku too had begun his life as a Nyingmapa but had found his way into the Gelugpa tradition. He was a man of very considerable learning and spiritual renown and was invited, whilst on pilgrimage, to visit Drepung Monastery, the largest of the great Gelugpa monastic universities near Lhasa. He decided to stay, and studied in the Gelugpa tradition, rising to become abbot of the entire monastery, a most unusual achievement for a monk from another tradition. He became an important figure in the government of Tibet and was one of the chief advisers, supporters, and friends to that great reformer, the thirteenth Dalai Lama. The early years of the twentieth century were tumultuous times for Tibet, and the twelfth Dhardo Rimpoche found himself playing a leading political and diplomatic role in Tibet's efforts to maintain independence in the face of British and Chinese ambitions.

After the death of the twelfth Dhardo Rimpoche, the thirteenth Dalai Lama was keen to find his successor and sent investigating parties to Dhartsendo. A young boy was found who passed the requisite tests, and he was installed as the abbot of Dorje Drak Monastery and later taken to Lhasa to be trained in the Gelugpa tradition. After excelling in his 'geshe' degree, the culmination of long and very exacting training in Buddhist studies undertaken in the monastic colleges, Dhardo Rimpoche was to have gone to the Tantric college, but his health gave way and he travelled to India for medical treatment. He proved so popular among Tibetans in India that he was asked to return to become abbot of the newly established Ladakhi monastery at Bodh-gaya. One day, looking out of the window of his room in the monastery, he saw a yellow-robed figure on the terrace of the Maha Bodhi Society rest house. In itself, this was nothing unusual—but the monk was European. Rimpoche was astonished and intrigued that a Westerner too was interested in Buddhism. He called his attendant to look and announced 'Now the Dharma has gone even as far as the West.' When he met Sangharakshita in Kalimpong, he realised that he was that same yellow-clad European.

The scorching heat of the Indian plains in the summer is almost fatal to many Tibetans, brought up as they are on the high Himalayan plateau, so every year Dhardo Rimpoche would spend three or four months in Kalimpong. From 1950 onwards, the Chinese started to enforce their claim to Tibet and refugees began to pour over the border into India, most of them completely destitute. Rimpoche was well aware that the Chinese domination of his country meant that he would never be able to return, but worse, that the culture of Tibet, which over a thousand years had grown to be a complete support for the practice of the Dharma, would be destroyed. He felt strongly that he must do something to help the refugees and preserve what he could of Tibetan culture so that, even in exile, Tibetans would devote themselves to the Dharma. His work as abbot of the Bodh-gaya monastery ensured that the opportunity for full-time study and practice was available outside Tibet—but what of the younger generation? How would they acquire the basis of knowledge and devotion which would make them want to join such a monastery? He set up, in Kalimpong, the Indo-Tibetan Buddhist Cultural Institute, which ran a school for refugee children in which lessons in Hindi and English would be combined with traditional Tibetan studies. Because of this latter emphasis the school was not eligible for Indian Government grants, so Rimpoche had to scrape together whatever money he could to maintain the Institute. Later he was forced to give up the abbotship of Bodh-gaya monastery, though he had also become abbot of the famous Yi Ga Choling Monastery at Ghoom, just outside Darjeeling—probably the oldest Buddhist monastery in India and the one that Sangharakshita had visited with Lama Govinda in 1951. However his duties here were light and he devoted himself now almost entirely to work with refugees.

It was this remarkable, selfless man who became Sangharakshita's closest teacher and personal friend whilst he was in Kalimpong. After they had worked together, through Lobsang Lhalungpa, on Lhalungpa's article on Tibetan Buddhism, the two men met and began to work together in other ways. Sangharakshita was associated with Rimpoche in the founding of the Indo-Tibetan Cultural Institute in 1954 and assisted him in whatever way he could, mostly fund-raising, writing letters and reports in English, and helping to deal with officialdom. Dhardo Rimpoche being somewhat reserved, friendship did not really blossom between them until 1956 when they found themselves travelling together among the fifty-seven 'Eminent Buddhists from the Border Areas' visiting the Buddhist sacred sites during the Buddha Jayanti celebrations as guests of the Indian Government. The yellow-robed Theravadins in the party considered themselves the only validly ordained sangha and held themselves separate from the rest, insisting on honorifically sitting at the front of the bus that carried them from place to place. Sangharakshita however, traitor in their eyes to his yellow robe, sat at the back with the red-robed Tibetans, always placing himself next to Rimpoche. Thrown together in this way, they got to know each other well, delighting in each other's company and finding that they were very much of one mind.

Each of them has told many anecdotes to the credit of the other and it is clear that they had the profoundest respect for each other. They worked together not only for the Tibetan refugees but 'for the good of Buddhism' in Kalimpong, often sharing platforms at functions and ceremonies and becoming the acknowledged leaders of the Buddhists in the area. Indeed, when the Chinese invaded a portion of India in 1962 and the border regions were thrown into turmoil at the threat of further invasion, the two of them were specifically asked to stay in Kalimpong by government officials so that Buddhists would not stampede away from the endangered areas.

Through his work on Lhalungpa's article, Sangharakshita had been deeply impressed by Dhardo Rimpoche's mind. But that mind not only contained deep learning and clear understanding but expressed overwhelming compassion. So striking was this quality that Sangharakshita came to consider that Rimpoche was not a mere follower of the Bodhisattva Ideal but that he was himself a Bodhisattva, activated only by Wisdom and Compassion. This connection with a living Bodhisattva was of immense spiritual importance to Sangharakshita, for the ideal of the Bodhisattva had been an inspiration to him from the moment he became a Buddhist. Although he had been ordained into the Theravadin monastic sangha, he had never considered himself limited to its particular teachings but had drawn sustenance especially from the Mahayana vision of the spiritual life as being lived not for one's own sake alone but for that of all beings. It was from this loftiest of all ideals that he had gained the inspiration and support to carry on with his own work when he had first arrived in Kalimpong. After several years as a bhikkhu and as a worker for the good of Buddhism, he felt that he was ready to take on that Bodhisattva Ideal fully and explicitly, especially as he had now met someone whom he 'had come to revere as being himself a living

Bodhisattva'. On 12 October 1962, therefore, he took the Bodhisattva ordination from Rimpoche and the next day received from him a full and detailed explanation of the sixty-four precepts taken at the time of ordination.

Sangharakshita learnt as much as he could of Tibetan Buddhism from Rimpoche. Though a staunch Gelugpa, Dhardo's approach was completely non-sectarian and he insisted that all the schools of Tibetan Buddhism are different manifestations of the same truth. Rimpoche was deeply impressed by Sangharakshita's ability to understand whatever he taught him. At first he had assumed that a Westerner would not have the background and training to become a true bhikkhu, but he soon found that, in Sangharakshita, he had a pupil of very rare quality. He has said of him:

'If you are asking whether Bhikshu Sangharakshita is the reincarnation of a Rimpoche or not that I cannot say straight out. But I am a hundred-percent sure that he is a truly remarkable and outstanding, deep-minded person. I say this because, when we used to talk about the profoundest aspects of Buddhism, Bhikshu Sangharakshita had no difficulty at all in understanding them with ease. That in itself is a proof that he has a natural inborn ability to understand the higher things which ordinary people cannot understand easily.... I did not have any other disciples like Sangharakshita. He was unique in the sense that he used to learn from me and at the same time practise it and then he used to teach it to other people. Only a few people can do this—learn and teach at the same time—because most students do not understand what they have learnt and so can't teach it to others.'

For Rimpoche it was a matter of great joy that he was teaching a Westerner, particularly one of such exceptional spiritual aptitude. He had at one time formed the intention of going to the West himself to teach the Dharma, but as soon as he began to get to know Sangharakshita he realised that a Westerner would be far more effective there and, some years before Sangharakshita himself had ever even considered the possibility, he began to hope that he would return to his homeland. When the opportunity did arise, he gave him all encouragement and blessing to go to England to establish the Dharma there. For this reason, he said, 'I took it as a matter of great joy and responsibility that whenever the opportunity arose I should be of help to Bhikshuji.'

Whilst Sangharakshita gained great inspiration, knowledge, and example from him, Rimpoche also considered that he learnt much from his English disciple. The fact that a foreigner from a country where

Buddhism was hardly known could understand the Dharma so readily and could work so hard to propagate it was, said Rimpoche, an inspiration to him to study and practise more deeply. He also learnt from Sangharakshita that teaching could take place in a context of friendship. Rimpoche had been accustomed, like all Tibetan lamas, to teach in a very formal manner. He would sit on a high throne, put on his pandit's cap, and, after various ritual preliminaries, would deliver a discourse of some hours' length without interruption or questioning. But he and Sangharakshita would simply sit together, conversing in Hindi, discussing questions raised by Sangharakshita or working on the translation of Tibetan texts, exploring the meaning as they went along, all in a very friendly and informal spirit. He found this a very effective way of teaching and gained a reputation thereafter for being very approachable and unceremonious.

Before Sangharakshita left for England in 1964, Rimpoche gave him the initiation of White Tara, a female Bodhisattva especially associated with Wisdom and with long life. He considered this to be particularly important insofar as Sangharakshita would be engaging in extensive teaching and would need as much inspiration and support as possible.

Other Teachers

The warm and deep friendship that developed between Dhardo Rimpoche and Sangharakshita was slow in maturing because of Dhardo's rather reserved character. However, there was one incarnate lama who went out of his way to befriend Sangharakshita from the first time they met in 1954. Khachu Rimpoche was abbot of Pemayangse Gompa near Gangtok, the royal monastery of Sikkim, and he had been recognised as the eighth tulku of Lhatsun Rimpoche who had introduced Buddhism into the kingdom. He was a Nyingmapa and completely devoted to his tradition and to Guru Padmasambhava, its founder. Besides being a man of great learning and a gifted sculptor, he was a very deep meditator and visionary. He would live very much in accordance with his inspirations and intuitions and displayed a remarkable ability to see into the minds of others—Sangharakshita would sometimes translate for him when he talked with Europeans and he observed on one occasion that Khachu Rimpoche was answering the questions—abstruse ones on the nature of nirvana—before he had had time to translate them. However, for all his gifts, he was a very unassuming man, very warm, cheerful, and communicative.

Sangharakshita would visit Khachu when he was in Gangtok and from time to time the Rimpoche would visit him at his vihara, often turning up unannounced. He too gave various instructions arising out of his meditative experience—once insisting that two banners of victory should be raised above the vihara since he had seen them fluttering there in his meditation. Khachu Rimpoche was the leading disciple of one of the greatest figures in modern Tibetan Buddhism: Jamyang Khyentse, himself the tulku of one of the foremost lamas of nineteenth century Tibet. The previous, first, Jamyang Khyentse Rimpoche had been the principal founder of a movement to transcend the sectarian divisions of Buddhism in Tibet by encouraging lamas from different schools to interchange initiations, pooling thereby the initiatory lineages. This 'Ri-me' movement the second Jamyang Khyentse continued. Originally a Shakyapa, he now functioned mainly within the Nyingmapa School, although in accordance with the non-sectarian principles of the Ri-me movement.

Khachu Rimpoche was very keen indeed that Sangharakshita should meet Jamyang Khyentse and take initiation from him, suggesting he should ask for the Manjughosha initiation since Jamyang Khyentse was reputed to be an incarnation of Manjughosha, the Bodhisattva of Wisdom. When they did meet in 1957, the Rimpoche told him he would give him not one but four initiations—Avalokiteshvara, Vajrapani, and Green Tara as well as Manjughosha—and that he should wait until he was summoned to the ceremony. Sangharakshita was in bed at the vihara with a raging fever and very bad toothache when the call came. However, he felt that, in the circumstances, he should still go and, in great pain, made the arduous journey across the mountains by jeep. Sangharakshita remembers particularly that, during the ceremony, as each of the Bodhisattvas was being introduced, Jamyang Khyentse Rimpoche's face would light up, as if in recognition—for him the visionary world was a living and present reality.

The giving of four initiations in one ceremony was most unusual and clearly had a very special significance. Jamyang Khyentse later on commissioned for Sangharakshita a *thangka*, or scroll painting, on which were depicted the four Bodhisattvas and a number of great Buddhist teachers of the past. Sangharakshita himself was shown twice, once teaching the Dharma and again meditating in a cave. Jamyang Khyentse Rimpoche took some pains to explain that, through this initiation, he had transmitted to Sangharakshita the essence of all the teachings of all the gurus in the *thangka*, a fact to which he seemed to attach great importance. Sangharakshita was now, he said, their spiritual heir and successor. By virtue of the Rimpoche's spiritual eminence and the nature of this particular initiation, Jamyang Khyentse is Sangharakshita's most important teacher from the Vajrayana point of view, what the Tibetans would call his 'root guru'. He was able to meet him a number of times before the Rimpoche died two years later in 1959.

Jamyang Khyentse Rimpoche gave Sangharakshita no further initiations, but he was insistent that Khachu should pass on to him the initiation of Padmasambhava, the founder of the Nyingmapa School and, according to tradition, the Indian teacher who had implanted Buddhism in Tibet. Sangharakshita had first encountered the impressive and magical figure of Guru Rimpoche, as he is known by Tibetans, in 1950, in a sculpture three or four times life size in a temple in Darjeeling. He had been deeply moved by this experience, and wrote 'In seeing the figure of Padmasambhava I had become conscious of a spiritual presence that had in fact been with me all the time. Though I had never seen the figure of Padmasambhava before, it was familiar to me in a way that no figure on earth was familiar: familiar and fascinating. It was as familiar as my own self, yet at the same time infinitely mysterious, infinitely wonderful, and infinitely inspiring.'

In 1962, Khachu Rimpoche came to the vihara in Kalimpong and gave Sangharakshita the initiation, thus deepening his connection with Guru Rimpoche and with the Nyingmapa tradition. Khachu at the same time gave him a new name, 'Urgyen'—the Tibetan form of the Sanskrit 'Udiyana', the land in the north-west of India of which Padmasambhava was said to have been king. The day following the initiation, Sangharakshita came across a Tibetan monk in the bazaar, selling a few woodblock prints of texts in Tibetan script. Wanting to help the monk, who was clearly destitute, Sangharakshita gave him what money he had and bought the texts. Khachu Rimpoche was delighted to find that they were Nyingmapa, mostly related to Guru Rimpoche, and took this to be an important confirmation of the success of the initiation. One of the texts was the *Tharpe Delam* or 'Easy Path to Emancipation' which, among other things, gives an account of the 'Four Foundation Yogas' or preliminary trainings. In particular, the 'Going for Refuge and Prostration Practice' was explained—a very vigorous exercise in which one prostrates full length, over and over again, before a visualised tree in which are represented all the highest ideals of Buddhism, with Guru Rimpoche at the centre as their principal embodiment. Getting the necessary permission from Khachu and translating the text in conjunction with Dhardo

Rimpoche, Sangharakshita took up the prostration practice for the remainder of his stay in Kalimpong.

Another important Nyingmapa lama figures among Sangharakshita's teachers: Dilgo Khyentse Rimpoche, also a tulku of the first Jamyang Khyentse. (Some great spiritual masters are said to be able to produce several new tulkus—five 'incarnations' of Jamyang Khyentse were recognised.) Dilgo Khyentse had escaped from Tibet after the Chinese invasion and settled in Kalimpong with his wife and two daughters (in his youth he had been advised by his physicians that he would have a recurring illness unless he married). Since he had managed to bring scarcely anything with him when he left Tibet, he now lived in great poverty in a small bungalow on the outskirts of town. Sangharakshita visited him there several times and was always received in a very friendly and unassuming fashion. Even though he had been a very famous lama in Tibet and had been much sought after for initiations and teachings, he was a quite unspectacular and even ordinary man. Nonetheless, Sangharakshita speaks of him as one of the most impressive men he has ever met—although the impressiveness was of a very subtle kind. In fact it was his lack of pretence and his very gentle, even fatherly manner which made its impression. When Sangharakshita visited him he would usually find him reading, and it was apparent that he was a man of great learning, the author of many commentaries on the scriptures. He gave Sangharakshita several initiations, principally those of Amitabha (with the *po-wa* or Consciousness Transference empowerment), Kurukule, and Jambhala. Sangharakshita has very positive memories of him and recalls him particularly for his sweet, gentle smile.

Dudjom Rimpoche, the last of his Tibetan teachers, was a married Nyingmapa tulku and leading authority on the Nyingmapa tradition. He had a very different style from Dilgo Khyentse, living in the manner of a king, surrounded by formality. He was therefore much less approachable and it was not so easy to get to know him, although Sangharakshita formed a very high regard for him. From him Sangharakshita received a number of initiations.

The last of his teachers vehemently refused to be considered a teacher, yet Sangharakshita learnt a great deal from him, particularly receiving guidance from him in his personal meditation. Yogi C.M. Chen was born in China where he had spent the early years of his life. Starting with an interest in Taoism, he had practised the Dharma under a Chinese teacher and then sought out Tibetan Vajrayana masters. He had studied very widely and deeply and had devoted much of his life to meditation.

Latterly he had settled in Kalimpong, establishing his hermitage not in the solitude of the hills but on the edge of the bazaar. During a period of some twenty-eight years he did not leave his small bungalow and received few visitors. Most of his time was spent in meditation, although he devoted half an hour each day to writing, pouring forth a stream of small pamphlets on esoteric themes in appalling English, the works being a mixture of almost comical literalness and astonishing penetration.

He was a very excitable and emotional man, with an intense inner life, full of visions and strange occult and psychic experiences. But he was also very warm-hearted and Sangharakshita has especially fond memories of him. Sangharakshita met him in the late fifties and went to see him once a week—a great concession from Mr Chen and a measure of the regard he had for the English monk. During their weekly meetings, Mr Chen would discuss various aspects of the Dharma, drawing on his immense knowledge of both Chinese and Tibetan Buddhism. He had studied mainly in the Nyingmapa tradition but he had also practised Ch'an and gave Sangharakshita a very thorough grounding in that school—he had little time for Zen, the Japanese form of Ch'an, and less for modern Western explications of it, some of which drove him to tears when he considered how people were being led astray. One particular series of talks Mr Chen gave privately to Sangharakshita and Khantipalo, an English bhikkhu who stayed for a period at the vihara, was a detailed survey of the entire field of Buddhist meditation. This material was written down by Khantipalo, and has since been published as *Buddhist Meditation: Systematic and Practical*. The work includes rather charming vignettes of Khantipalo, Sangharakshita, and Mr Chen, meeting in that tiny bungalow near the Kalimpong bazaar. Although Mr Chen would not consider himself a teacher and would not take on disciples or give initiations, Sangharakshita gained much from his contact with him and respected him highly, for, despite his eccentricities of manner, he had a very good mind and deep understanding of Buddhist doctrine, being able to unravel and explain matters that others had been unable to clarify.

FRIENDS AND DISCIPLES

In his fourteen years in Kalimpong, Sangharakshita became acquainted with a surprisingly wide range of people. Besides the incarnate lamas who became his teachers, he encountered many others as they passed through Kalimpong, which was for many their first stopping point after leaving Tibet. Sangharakshita made a point of visiting every lama who arrived in the town, to welcome them and offer assistance. In this way he came to meet many of the principal teachers of Tibetan Buddhism, getting to know several of them quite well. One who settled in the town was Tomo Geshe Rimpoche, the incarnation of the wonder-working guru mentioned by Lama Govinda in his *Way of the White Clouds*, and Sangharakshita became very friendly with him. He met the Dalai Lama and the Panchen Lama in connection with the Buddha Jayanti celebrations and later the Dalai Lama visited his vihara in Kalimpong. After 1959, when the Dalai Lama had fled from Tibet, Sangharakshita had several more meetings with him, advising him on various matters, such as on what subject to address the ex-Untouchables of Bombay when he had been asked to speak to them (at his suggestion, the Dalai Lama spoke on the Bodhisattva Ideal). He had many friends among the bhikkhus of all the various traditions working in India: Thais, Burmese, Sinhalese, Nepalese, Vietnamese, and Japanese. He met Pandit Nehru on two occasions—his daughter, Indira Gandhi, and her two sons, Rajiv and Sanjay, hovering in the background. The great man was very eager to show him the giant pandas the Chinese government had given him. Tendzin Norgay, Sir Edmund Hillary's companion in the ascent of Mount Everest, was a devout Buddhist and met Sangharakshita several times in Kalimpong.

Many scholars in Buddhism and Tibetology would come to Kalimpong and Sangharakshita would usually meet them: among them Dr David Snellgrove, Dr René Nebesky de Wojkowitz, John Driver, Dr Lilian Silburn, and Dr Herbert Guenther. Two scholars, Prince Peter of Greece and Dr George Roerich, lived in Kalimpong and Sangharakshita got to know them well, especially as they participated in the activities of the YMBA and contributed to *Stepping-Stones*. Many foreign visitors came to see him at the vihara, including Christmas Humphreys, the English lawyer who founded the Buddhist Society, and Allen Ginsberg, the American 'beat' poet—Sangharakshita has written a very amusing description of their first encounter, originally contributed to a festschrift in honour of Ginsberg's sixtieth birthday and now published in *The Priceless Jewel*.

His closest personal friends in Kalimpong, during the latter half of his stay, were Kazi Lendup Dorje and his wife, the Kazini Elisa-Maria. The Kazi was a leading Buddhist nobleman from Sikkim, a very shrewd and wily politician who later became the first democratically elected Chief Minister of the kingdom, himself organising its full incorporation into the Indian Republic. His wife was of Baltic extraction and had been educated in Edinburgh. She was a woman of even greater shrewdness than her husband and had lived a very colourful life, working as a journalist for a French newspaper and living for a while in Kemal Ataturk's palace in Turkey. She was, in Sangharakshita's words, a 'born behind-the-scenes politician' and from her he began to learn about the wider world of international politics—until the 1956 Suez crisis and the Chinese invasion of India he had had little knowledge of or interest in world events, being completely absorbed in the world of the Dharma. The Kazini was his chief confidante and adviser, being helpful with legal matters since she had studied law at Edinburgh University and had a fine legal mind. There is no doubt that Sangharakshita acquired a great deal of his considerable practical shrewdness from his association with her. She herself converted to Buddhism and took him as her teacher.

A great many others became his disciples whilst he was in India—he has estimated that he initiated into Buddhism and personally instructed more than 200,000 men and women, the vast majority being followers of Dr Ambedkar in Maharashtra. In Kalimpong, many local Buddhists—and indeed others—would participate regularly in the activities of the vihara, particularly in attending Sangharakshita's lectures. Indeed in all the places he spoke, whether to the ex-Untouchables of Western India, the Himalayan peoples of the Darjeeling District, the Buddhists of Assam, the educated élites of Calcutta, or the Theosophists of Bangalore and Bombay, he was an extremely popular speaker. He combined his deep understanding of Buddhism with an ability to convey his material in an engaging and lucid manner that made it relevant and attractive to his audience—he had, as one Indian journalist put it, 'a remarkable gift for clear and attractive exposition'. He spoke not only with the authority of his own comprehension of his subject but with the warmth of his love for it. He could also be very humorous, having a delightful, ironical wit and an eye for the ridiculous in human behaviour.

There were a number of closer, more personal disciples who stayed with him at the vihara or visited him regularly. He ordained several shramaneras, some of whom lived and studied with him. He also taught many people English, finding that teaching the language and its literature was also a medium for communicating the Dharma. He had started teaching in order to help the young members of the YMBA to prepare for their college examinations, but found that, as he became more and more engaged in preaching and writing, he had no time for this and had to confine himself mainly to tutoring one or two students as a way of providing an income, otherwise giving preference to those who might be able to use their English for the service of the Dharma. Several Tibetan monks came to learn from him, particularly after the uprising against the Chinese in 1959, including Rechung Rimpoche, Tomo Geshe Rimpoche, and the abbot of the local Gelugpa monastery.

The vihara had many visitors, some staying for quite long periods. Monks from all over the Buddhist world, and several from the West, would come to study and meditate with him. Some would come from the hot plains of India during the summer months for a rest and to enjoy Sangharakshita's company. One or two of the 'new Buddhists' from the ex-Untouchable communities came to the hills to study with him more intensively than was possible during the hectic tours in western India.

LITERARY WORK

His literary work has always been dear to Sangharakshita and throughout this period his output was prodigious. Besides the articles and editorials he wrote for *Stepping-Stones* and the *Maha Bodhi*, he often contributed to the *Aryan Path*, a journal of the Wadias' Theosophical movement, as well as to the *Middle Way*, the quarterly journal of the London Buddhist Society, and to other Buddhist periodicals world-wide. He continued to write poetry, which was published in various journals. His first book, *Messengers from Tibet and Other Poems*, published in 1954, had achieved a modest success, and he became quite well known and popular among educated, English-speaking Indians through the poems he contributed to the *Illustrated Weekly of India*, which had a circulation of 100,000 or so throughout India. After he had completed and published *A Survey of Buddhism*, he commenced the story of his early life and wandering days in India—these memoirs took many years to bring to completion and have now been published as *Learning to Walk* and *The Thousand-Petalled Lotus*. He was then asked to contribute articles on Buddhist topics to an encyclopaedia in the Oriya language, compiled by the government of the state of Orissa. The articles grew into a full length book, published in England in 1967 as *The Three Jewels*, a penetrating and exhaustive account of the Buddha, Dharma, and Sangha from a lofty perspective. He also completed a survey of the Buddhist scriptures which, for the first time, shows the sacred texts of Buddhism to belong to a single tradition. Although written in 1963, it was not published until 1985, under the title *The Eternal Legacy*.

Besides his own writing, Sangharakshita was concerned to stimulate others in their literary endeavours. A number of works were written whilst people stayed as guests of the vihara, and Sangharakshita did what he could to help and encourage them. The vihara also sponsored translations: some Pali scriptures into Nepali and Tibetan and one of his talks, 'What is Dharma?', into both Hindi and Marathi. Sangharakshita himself worked with Dhardo Rimpoche, Dudjom Rimpoche, and other scholars on the translation into English of Tibetan meditation sadhanas and other texts—notably, at the request of the Dalai Lama, Tsongkhapa's *The Three Chief Paths.* In 1959 Sangharakshita persuaded a leading Bombay publishing house, Chetana, to begin a series of pocket-sized volumes on Buddhist topics intended for 'the intelligent general reader'. Under his editorship 'the Buddhist Library' brought out four works: *A Short History of Buddhism* by Dr Edward Conze, *Long Discourses of the Buddha,* a translation of the first sixteen *suttas* of the Pali *Digha Nikaya* by Mrs A.A.G. Bennett, *The Buddha's Middle Way* by Bhikkhu Khantipalo, and *Crossing the Stream,* a collection of his own editorials and articles. More publications were projected but, since the impetus for the series came very much from him, his departure for England brought the enterprise to a halt.

THE NEW BUDDHISTS OF INDIA

Until his return to England in 1964, Sangharakshita spent some time most years touring among Dr Ambedkar's followers in the states of Maharashtra, Gujerat, and Uttar Pradesh, principally in the cities of Bombay, Nagpur, and Poona. In Poona he found that the Buddhist movement was already vitiated by factionalism and politics, making it difficult for him to carry out his activities without seeming to ally himself with one or another party. To circumvent this problem an organisation of women was founded under his guidance, the Poona District Buddhist Women's Association, which was untainted by the squabbles of the male-dominated groups. It was under these auspices that Sangharakshita usually worked in Poona, and the Association published Marathi translations of several of his talks.

In Nagpur, Sangharakshita had a number of friends and helpers, chief among them A.R. Kulkarni who, though born a brahmin, had completely rejected caste and had embraced Buddhism, albeit of a rather idiosyncratic kind. He was a retired advocate in his sixties, a man of great energy and fire, honest and blunt, even outspoken. Not only did he translate Sangharakshita's lectures into Marathi, he also made organisational arrangements and protected him from his sometimes overzealous disciples. From him Sangharakshita learnt a great deal about Maharashtra and the Maharashtrians.

The preaching tours that Sangharakshita undertook most years, sometimes twice a year, were extraordinarily busy. One such journey lasted for seven-and-a-half months, from October 1960 to April 1961, and may serve as an illustration of the nature of such peregrinations. From Kalimpong Sangharakshita travelled to Bodh-gaya where he was joined by a Thai bhikkhu, Vivekananda, who accompanied him throughout the tour, and an English shramanera, later ordained as Bhikkhu Khantipalo, who came for the first part, both assisting and supporting him in whatever way they could. At Jabalpur they stopped briefly to officiate at a name-giving ceremony and to lecture at the Jain library. Then they went on to Nagpur where they spent two weeks, packed with activity, starting with four meetings and talks on the first day, which was the anniversary of Dr Ambedkar's conversion. Thereafter they visited the various localities in which Buddhists lived, in and around Nagpur.

At the end of October the tour continued to Bombay where Sangharakshita spent one month, again speaking at many places throughout the vast city, mainly to ex-Untouchable audiences, on themes such as 'Buddhism and God', 'Mindfulness', and the Avalokiteshvara mantra. He also spoke to a quite different audience, this time educated English-speaking Indians who were followers of Mme Blavatsky at Theosophy Hall, his topics being 'The Spiritual Path of Buddhism' and 'Literature and Ethics'. Throughout the city he performed various ceremonies, mainly name-givings and conversions, and of course met many hundreds of people who wanted to have personal talks or simply literally to see the bhikkhus.

In November they travelled to Ahmedabad, the capital of Gujerat, and spent a week preaching, meeting people, and carrying out ceremonies in the usual Buddhist localities and under the auspices of the usual local Buddhist organisations that had sprung up under Dr Ambedkar's inspiration. Sangharakshita also spoke at the International Academy of Philosophy on 'Buddhism Today'. He then journeyed to Ajmer in Rajasthan where he gave four lectures in three days, before moving on to spend a month in Delhi, the capital of the Republic, giving many talks both to Dr Ambedkar's followers and at the Sri Lankan Pilgrims' Rest House, presided over by the Sri Lankan High Commissioner. After briefly visiting Lama Govinda, he returned to Ahmedabad for three days to give a series of nine public lectures. He then spent January and February in Poona, during which time he conducted thirteen mass conversion ceremonies, initiating some 25,000 people into Buddhism, and gave the new converts comprehensive instruction in their duties and responsibilities as Buddhists. Sangharakshita also delivered a series of eight lectures for the Poona District Buddhist Women's Association on 'The Position of Women in Buddhism'. He went to various villages and towns around Poona, everywhere giving talks and conducting ceremonies. During a brief visit to Bombay, he gave a talk at Theosophy Hall on the *Diamond Sutra*. On his return to Poona, he conducted a special training course in Buddhism, every evening throughout March, covering all the major teachings of the Dharma, the *Dhammapada*, and basic meditation. The course was probably unique insofar as it gave ordinary lay followers of Dr Ambedkar a thorough introduction to the theory and practice of their new religion.

The last lap of his tour took him to Bangalore in South India for three days, where he lectured at the Maha Bodhi Vihara and reconnected with old friends. Then it was back to Poona where he addressed large crowds at several meetings on the anniversary of the birth of Dr Ambedkar and dedicated the site of a vihara. More large anniversary meetings awaited him at Ahmedabad and Bhusawal. In Ahmedabad, he presided over the inaugural meeting of the Buddhist Society of Gujerat, founded under his guidance by five young Gujeratis he had initiated into Buddhism. He arrived at Nagpur in time for the anniversary celebrations of the Buddha's Enlightenment, during which he attended several functions a day for several days, giving numerous talks. On his way back to Kalimpong, he lectured at the Maha Bodhi Society in Calcutta and was taken deep into the jungle at Ranchi to speak about Buddhism to aboriginal tribespeople who were turning to the Dharma. The tour finished back in Kalimpong on 19 May, Sangharakshita having given over two hundred full length lectures, each of them completely original, and having travelled more or less continuously for seven-and-a-half months, visiting more than half the states of India.

Although more extensive and prolonged than most of his tours, this was representative of the distances travelled and the range and variety of people he contacted during other trips of this kind. Travel was mainly by railway, third class, money always being tight, or else, when distant villages were being visited, by bullock cart. Accommodation would often be very basic and food sometimes quite rough. But Sangharakshita found no difficulty in entering into the simple lives of his ex-Untouchable disciples. With astonishing versatility he could speak to the often illiterate peasants and labourers of Poona or Nagpur or to the intellectuals and educated élite of Theosophy Hall, entrancing them all. One of his greatest gifts is his ability to talk to simple, uneducated people without talking down to them. He finds a way of communicating the profoundest truths of Buddhism in a way they can easily understand without compromising clarity or profundity. Above all, he can rouse and fire their fervent faith in Dr Ambedkar. He has since said that so complete and heartfelt was the faith of many of these ex-Untouchables that it could have carried them all the way to Enlightenment. Unfortunately, that faith was increasingly exploited by people who sought only to use it for personal power. As the years went by, Sangharakshita saw Dr Ambedkar's movement, begun with such fervour and high hope, degenerate into factionalism and power-seeking. Even his tours could not reverse that trend.

THE CALL OF THE WEST

Sangharakshita had, since his arrival in Kalimpong, kept up an extensive correspondence with Buddhists all over the world, including some of his old acquaintances in Britain—particularly Clare Cameron, who had been the Buddhist Society's Secretary when he had first joined. She, however, severed her connection with the Society and his main correspondent thereafter was Jack Austin, a young bank clerk, later the leading exponent of Shin Buddhism in Britain, who kept him informed of goings-on in the small world of English Buddhism. He also read the various English-language Buddhist journals and soon realised that there was a great deal of confusion among Buddhists in the West and even a growing disharmony within the English Buddhist movement. The two leading Buddhist organisations in London were increasingly locked in a bitter feud and no one seemed able to draw the few Buddhists in Britain together. The young movement seemed to be degenerating into squabbling and acrimony before it had really begun. In 1963 the idea arose, among the leaders of all factions, of inviting Sangharakshita, by then the seniormost English bhikkhu, to return for a few months to try to bring harmony to the Buddhists of Britain.

When he left the Army to become a wanderer, Sangharakshita considered that he was breaking completely his ties with England. Indeed from the time of his going forth he had never even corresponded with his parents and he had rather avoided Europeans—most of those he met in Kalimpong being rather neurotic. He had assumed he would never return to his native land and was quite happy to be settled in India, especially in Kalimpong. He found India itself very congenial, feeling that many features of the Buddha's teaching still permeated society despite the pernicious omnipresence of caste. His work was going very well: he had achieved a great deal among the ex-Untouchables; through his work as editor of the *Maha Bodhi* he was able to have an influence on Buddhism world-wide; in Kalimpong he was respected widely and well, being known amongst the Tibetans as Imji Gelong Rimpoche—'Greatly Precious English Monk'. He had awakened Buddhism in the district into new life and had achieved the extraordinary distinction of reviving the death anniversary celebrations of Tsongkhapa, the founder of the Gelug-pa School, and seeing them attended by a large number of Rimpoches from all schools. Tibetans said that only he could have achieved this—they themselves were too much caught up in traditional factions—and he received a personal letter of congratulations from the Dalai Lama. In many ways he had no reason to leave.

However, he had begun to feel that his stay in Kalimpong could not last much longer. The Chinese threat to the border areas made it unlikely that the Indian Government would continue to tolerate the presence of a foreigner—especially as malicious people had spread rumours that he was a communist spy (others claimed that he was an agent of the CIA). He had for some time been expecting that he would be asked to leave, as had other Europeans before him. Not only was his work in Kalimpong threatened, but his work amongst the ex-Untouchables had reached something of an impasse. With the death of Dr Ambedkar and the waning of the initial enthusiasm for Buddhism, the movement of conversion had become bogged down in politics. There were few other openings for him in India. From the outset he had had few illusions about the Maha Bodhi Society and its journal and all his later experience had confirmed that the Society was virtually moribund, despite the valiant efforts of Devapriya Valisinha, its General Secretary. He had on several occasions had his writing censored by the Governing Body—for instance, he was not permitted to publish an editorial critical of the Chinese invasion of Tibet with its inevitable destruction of Buddhist culture. He was the only bhikkhu engaging in effective and sustained Dharma work in India in connection with the Society, even though he was not supported by it.

Finally, he felt a certain disillusion with India itself and the direction its politics had taken since Independence. Sangharakshita had been deeply sympathetic to the Indian independence movement, particularly as it had pursued its goal non-violently. The new India had promised to be based on genuine moral and spiritual ideals and he had felt able to throw in his lot with the emergent nation. But gradually the Indian Government, even under the great Pandit Nehru, showed itself to be essentially self-interested, prepared to set aside moral principles when those interests were threatened. Thus the Government allowed China to invade Tibet virtually without protest, even though India was the legatee of Britain's treaties with Tibet, guaranteeing protection against China—India wanted to maintain Chinese friendship. Then the Indian Government was prepared to condemn the British, French, and Israeli invasion of the Suez Canal Zone whilst it condoned Russian intervention in Hungary—Russia was an important Indian ally. Finally, the Government seized Goa from the Portuguese by force, despite the principle of non-violence which had underlain their own independence struggle. Sangharakshita was affected quite deeply by these demonstrations of lack of genuine moral principle in the Indian Government and he felt disinclined to remain.

New opportunities to 'work for the good of Buddhism' seemed to await him in the West. With the encouragement of Dhardo Rimpoche and other friends, he decided to take up the invitation to make a short visit to England. He would assess the situation there, and then decide on his future. So, in the summer of 1964, having made a final tour among the ex-Untouchables in Maharashtra, he set out by air for London.

Chapter Five

Return to England
1964–1967

I

How bare and dead the branch! But look, again
Burst forth pink buds, as soon as touched by rain.

II

The red leaf falls upon the lake below.
Ah well, perhaps the water's lovelier so!

III

Though vigorously the high wind shakes the bough,
The unripe fruit sticks on to it, somehow.

Sangharakshita (1961)

WHILST SANGHARAKSHITA WAS rather disillusioned with the India he was leaving, he had some expectations of the Britain to which he was returning. By 1964, its great empire had been largely relinquished and the nation was gradually adapting to its new status as a post-colonial power. Earlier that year, a Labour government had been formed with high hopes of forging a classless and prosperous Britain in the 'white heat of technology'. Sangharakshita himself had imbibed a sympathy for the Socialist cause from his father and other family members and had some idealistic hopes of the new government.

He had some hopes, too, for Buddhism in Britain. There clearly was a rising tide of interest, as he already knew from his correspondence and from his reading of the *Middle Way*, the journal of the Buddhist Society, and of the *Sangha*, that of the Hampstead Buddhist Vihara. At the same time, there were very obviously problems—even considerable problems. Although Buddhism had been known in the West for two or three centuries, it was only relatively recently that scholars had come to have some reasonably accurate picture of its doctrines, and it was even more recently that some Britons had actually begun to think of themselves as Buddhists and to try to practise its teachings. They were necessarily on the whole a rather cranky and even neurotic collection of people, frequently seeing in Buddhism some projected fantasy of their own. Some, often from a Theosophical background, were looking for secret teachings and psychic powers. Some saw Buddhism as a form of extreme asceticism and made of it a kind of new protestantism, highly moralistic and repressive of all colour and emotion. Others again were simply attracted by Buddhist philosophy and had an approach that was almost entirely intellectual. Many had seized upon one or other school or teaching and tried to adopt it wholesale, without separating what belonged to the culture within which it had flourished from what was essential to the Buddhist Path. Many again were convinced that their own chosen brand of Buddhism was the only true one. It was amidst this confusion that the Dharma struggled to take root in the West.

The two leading Buddhist organisations in England were the Buddhist Society and the Hampstead Buddhist Vihara administered by the English Sangha Trust. The Buddhist Society, under the able if autocratic leadership of Christmas Humphreys, had developed a style of its own based largely in Mr Humphreys's own Theosophical roots and upper middle class background. Its approach was predominantly theoretical—although not necessarily scholarly—and there was a definite caution about the practice of meditation: Mr Humphreys advised Sangharakshita, soon after his return to England, that English people would not be able to meditate for longer than five minutes at a time. Mr Humphreys also had reservations about the monastic sangha—perhaps with some justification in view of experience in Britain so far.

The Hampstead Buddhist Vihara, on the other hand, definitely aspired to do things in the 'traditional' way—the tradition chosen in this case being a particular, rather narrow, interpretation of Thai Theravada. The Vihara had been established largely with funds donated by Henry Newlin, a wealthy, eccentric businessman with Buddhist sympathies. However, Mr Newlin had intended the Vihara to be non-sectarian, and he was already severely disappointed that so exclusive a line had been taken. The present incumbent was a Canadian who had been ordained a bhikkhu in Thailand and who vigorously advocated a technique of meditation known as vipassana—a technique that in his hands seemed to do quite a bit more harm than good. A feud had developed between

Right Sangharakshita's mother in her Voluntary Aid Detachment uniform, 1918

Above Sangharakshita's father, 1923

Right Three years old, 1928

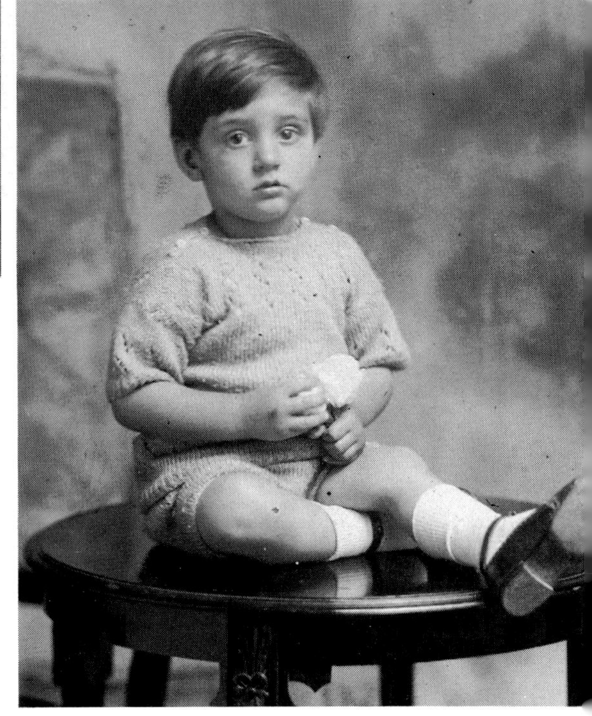

Top left In Singapore, near the harbour, 1946

Top right With Buddharakshita in Kushinagara shortly after their shramanera ordination in May 1949

Right With Sangharatana in Sarnath, 1967 Farewell Tour. The Mulagandhakuti Vihara is in the background

With Thupten Chhokyi, a French nun, and Kachu Rimpoche at Everton Villa, Kalimpong, in the 1950s

Above Jagdish Kashyap in 1967

Right View of the Triyana Vardhana Vihara and cottage (right) in Kalimpong

Top left Dilgo Khyentse Rimpoche, 1950s

Top right Dudjom Rimpoche in the ceremonial dress of a Nyingmapa lama

Left Chetul Sangye Dorje, 1950s

Bottom left Dhardo Rimpoche, 1967

Bottom right Mr Chen at his home in Kalimpong, 1967

U Chandramani speaking at the ceremony when Dr Ambedkar (sitting, right, next to Mrs Ambedkar) and 380,000 of his followers converted to Buddhism in Nagpur on 14 October 1956

Above At Stonehenge, 1965

Middle right At the Hampstead Buddhist Vihara, 1965, after the shramanera ordination of Virya (behind, right) with Virya's parents and friends and (far left) Thich Minh Chau, Sangharakshita's friend and helper

Bottom right With Christmas Humphreys at the Buddhist Society's Summer School, 1964

Above Addressing a street meeting in Ahmedabad, 1967 Farewell Tour

Right With the Dalai Lama in Dharamsala, 1967 Farewell Tour

Left With Li Gotami, Lama Govinda, and (standing) Terry Delamare at Kasar Devi, Govinda's ashram in Almora, Uttar Pradesh, 1967 Farewell Tour

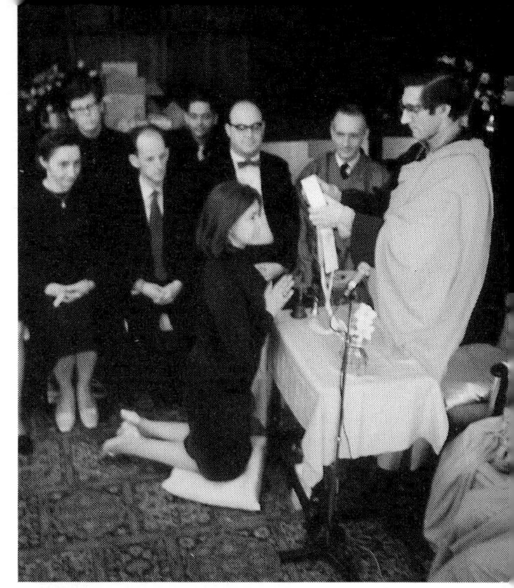

Top right Sara Boin becoming Sujata. Others wait their turn at the first ordinations into the Western Buddhist Order on 7 April 1968 in Kensington, London

Middle right With mutton-chop whiskers in his shaman phase, early 1970s during a TV interview

Bottom right At Broomhouse Farm, Brandon, Suffolk in the early 1970s

Above The Windhorse mural over the courtyard of the London Buddhist Centre in Bethnal Green as building work nears completion in 1978

Top The Order at the 1978 Convention

Bottom Leading study at Padmaloka Retreat Centre in Norfolk, 1979

Top At the 1982 women's ordination retreat in Sussex

Right Sangharakshita in his study at Padmaloka, 1990

Bottom In conversation with the poet and scholar, Kathleen Raine, at Independent Arts in Croydon, 1988

With the San Francisco sangha during the 1993 tour of America

Top left Appliqué banners depicting Dr Ambedkar, the Buddha, and Sangharakshita, made for the 1992 visit to India and used at mass meetings in Poona and Nagpur

Bottom left With Lokamitra (left) leaving the TBMSG's medical centre in Dapodi during his 1992 visit to India

Meditating in the London Buddhist Centre's shrine-room, July 1993

this bhikkhu and Mr Humphreys—and was being carried out with considerable acrimony. Relations between the Vihara and the Society had, as a consequence, deteriorated very badly.

Perhaps the most difficult aspect of Sangharakshita's task was, since British Buddhists were drawn mainly from the middle and upper classes, an overwhelming concern with making Buddhism 'respectable'—that is, acceptable to others of those classes. The classic English obsession with preserving an appearance of conformity with the social pretensions of others was imported even into Buddhism. Buddhists must not be seen to be different. Buddhists must be found a place in the English Establishment. Mr Humphreys himself told Sangharakshita that he should think of himself as 'the Buddhist equivalent of the Vicar of Hampstead'. The atmosphere in the English Buddhist movement generated by this concern was constrained and dull, and the version of Buddhism promulgated was so watered down that it was devoid of almost all vitality. It had been so diluted that it did not at all threaten the ordinary bourgeois lives of its followers. It did not call upon them to make that radical change in one's whole being, inner and outer, which is the essential message of the Dharma.

AT THE HAMPSTEAD BUDDHIST VIHARA

It was thus with mingled hope and apprehension that Sangharakshita arrived in England on 12 August 1964 at the invitation of the English Sangha Trust, and took up residence at the Hampstead Buddhist Vihara a few days before his thirty-ninth birthday. He came with a vivid consciousness of the significance of his mission, realising that it was probably the most important step in British Buddhism since the return of Ananda Metteyya, the first English bhikkhu, at the beginning of the century. By then, Sangharakshita had been ordained for fourteen years, had founded his own vihara, and had gained an international reputation. He was deeply versed in the teachings of the major schools of Buddhism and had received ordination and initiation into all three *yanas*, the major divisions of the Buddhist tradition. He plainly had the experience, understanding, and authority to unite and lead the Buddhists of Britain.

Sangharakshita was determined that British Buddhism should not fall into a narrow sectarianism but should be a Triyana Buddhism. He was particularly aware that many aspects of the social structure of traditional Buddhism would not transplant to the West and that Buddhism in Britain was likely to take a quite different form from Buddhism in the East. Soon after his arrival, he wrote in an editorial for the *Buddhist*, the journal of the Vihara (the editing of which he immediately took on, changing its name from the *Sangha*), 'At this stage in the development of the Buddhist movement in England, it is unlikely that the traditional pattern of sangha–laity relations will be perpetuated in the extreme forms it has taken in some parts of the Buddhist world, and perhaps undesirable if it were possible.'

Sangharakshita plunged swiftly into his work, giving talks at the Vihara and visiting the Buddhist Society and most of the provincial groups and societies. He had come, as he declared, principally to draw together the various schools of Buddhism in Britain, and he set about doing so by visiting them all, establishing his own impartiality and goodwill. Towards the end of his first month, he attended the Buddhist Society's annual Summer School, held at a large conference centre just outside London. The Summer School offered participants a taste of various aspects of Buddhism, mainly through talks, although some meditation was practised. Sangharakshita quickly established himself as a witty and engaging speaker and made a strong impression on many who attended. He found there was an excessively sectarian emphasis on the different schools of Buddhism with their particular teachings and practices, at the expense of an understanding of the unity of the Dharma in a single spiritual vision. He therefore started to stress the basic teachings, common to all, and the primary 'classical' meditation practices, the Mindfulness of Breathing and the *Metta Bhavana* ('development of loving-kindness'). He developed a new way of teaching meditation by guiding groups through each practice stage by stage—an experiment which quickly showed results since the voice of the leader helps to keep practitioners focused. He was teaching just Buddhism, and a Buddhism that was relevant to the times and cultural background of his hearers. It was clear to participants in the Summer School that Buddhism in Britain was beginning to look up with the arrival of this dedicated and brilliant bhikkhu.

After the Summer School, he called a 'Sangha Sabha' or Council of the Sangha, bringing together the few Theravadin bhikkhus in Britain who now formally constituted themselves as a Chapter—the first time this had happened in the West—with U Thittila, the Burmese monk from whom Sangharakshita had first taken the Refuges and Precepts in 1944, as President, and Sangharakshita himself as Secretary. He was also recognised by the Sabha as Incumbent of the Hampstead Vihara and Head of the English Sangha by virtue of his seniority and experience. The Council directed him, together with another bhikkhu, to prepare *samaneras* or novice monks for full ordination. Thus within his second month in England he had established a basis for co-operation and clear organisation among the Theravadin monks in Britain.

Sangharakshita brought all his considerable energy and capacity to bear on his task of drawing together the various Buddhist groups in Britain. His main focus was the Hampstead Buddhist Vihara itself. The Hampstead address was a prestigious one, this area being a pleasant North London enclave of large and well-built Victorian houses, occupied for the most part by members of the professional classes, although it also had a reputation as a meeting point for artists and intellectuals. The Vihara was situated in a three-storey house on a major thoroughfare in the district, an adjacent house also being owned by the English Sangha Trust, the organisation that owned and administered the Vihara, and let out as flats to provide an income.

On Sunday afternoons he would lecture at the Vihara, covering basic Buddhist themes as well as introducing, in what had threatened to become a stronghold of a rather narrow kind of Theravada, the many schools of Buddhism, revealing their spiritual significance as aspects of a single Path. His talks quickly became very popular, filling the small lecture hall to overflowing. To accommodate the increased numbers, Sangharakshita arranged for a wall to be taken down, doubling the size of the hall to hold ninety or so seats—yet sometimes people would still be forced to listen to his lectures sitting on the stairs outside. The Vihara also sponsored lectures by Sangharakshita at other venues, notably the College of Psychic Science, where he again filled to overflowing a large hall.

Another regular activity initiated by Sangharakshita was the 'guided group meditation class' at which he taught the two basic meditation practices using the method he had evolved at the Summer School. Question and answer sessions at the end of one or two lecture series revealed the lively desire some people had to discuss the Dharma rather than simply listen to it being expounded, so he instituted a regular discussion group. Again he saw that Buddhism in Britain could not simply rely on bhikkhus coming from the East: everyone dedicated to Buddhism could help to propagate it. He started speakers' classes, at which those who wanted to develop their ability to give talks on Buddhism received comment and criticism on their efforts. He was thus not only teaching the Dharma but teaching others to do so. Over the Christmas and Easter holiday periods, he organised seminars during which participants would meditate and study together, avoiding the rather undignified overindulgence of the English festivities.

Sangharakshita was careful not to rekindle the old rivalries between the Vihara and the Buddhist Society. He was on excellent terms with Mr Humphreys, who clearly regarded him as a friend and ally, and he involved himself in the Society's activities as much as he could. He gave several lecture series and individual talks at the Society's imposing premises in a prestigious part of Victoria, in the heart of London. Once again, the lecture hall was not large enough to accommodate all those who wanted to hear him and several of his lectures would be given at Caxton Hall, large public rooms nearby. He would visit the Society two or three times during the course of most weeks, to give talks, participate in official functions, and lead meditation classes or speakers' classes—the speakers' classes being held at the Vihara and the Society alternately, emphasising their new-found alliance. He attended the three annual Summer Schools that took place during his first stay in England, quickly becoming their most popular and influential figure.

Although Buddhism in Britain was undergoing a phase of unprecedented growth, British Buddhists were still relatively few in number—far fewer indeed than Sangharakshita had been led to believe before he arrived. Apart from the Hampstead Buddhist Vihara and the Buddhist Society, there were two other main centres of Buddhism in London: the London Buddhist Vihara, at which there resided two or three Sinhalese bhikkhus, and the Thai Vihara, established by the Thai Government during the course of Sangharakshita's stay—both catering mainly for ethnic Buddhists from Sri Lanka, Thailand, and Burma, of whom there were quite a number resident in London. At these viharas Sangharakshita would, from time to time, give talks or participate in celebrations and the like. Besides the Hampstead Vihara, the English Sangha Trust also owned a retreat centre, Biddulph, in the Midlands, where Sangharakshita occasionally stayed to conduct retreats. Outside these main centres of British Buddhism, there were scattered over the country small Buddhist groups, sometimes with only two or three serious members and a few interested onlookers. Sangharakshita faithfully visited each one whenever he could and, in the case of groups in Brighton and Hastings, on the south coast, helped them to build their societies on a much sounder footing, drawing many new people to them with his lectures and classes.

Several universities had Buddhist societies and Sangharakshita became a popular speaker at their meetings. The Oxford and Cambridge societies were particularly lively and often attracted large numbers of students.

He was also asked by students or lecturers to speak at other, non-Buddhist, university societies. One memorable visit took him to Scotland for a weekend at the invitation of a Christian clergyman who was a lecturer in the Philosophy of Religion at Glasgow University.

Since Buddhism was beginning to become better known and to catch the public eye, Sangharakshita was asked to speak at various clubs and societies, most having either some predisposition to Buddhism, as in the case of the Theosophical Lodges he spoke at, or existing to promote understanding between people of different cultures, such as student associations or the 'Huganu Jewish Cultural Organisation'. He once spoke to a Thai Students Association on the subject of Mahayana Buddhism—which must have been revealing to them indeed, for Thailand is a stronghold of the Theravada and little is commonly known of other forms of Buddhism, which are usually considered there as mere degenerations of the Buddha's teaching. On one occasion he read poems by the great Buddhist sages Han-shan and Milarepa to a poetry club in North London.

When he arrived in England, he had intended to stay for only four months before returning to Kalimpong and his activities in India. But, as he became more and more absorbed in what was plainly very fruitful work, four months stretched to a year, and then two. Gradually, he was bringing Buddhism to life in Britain, rescuing it from the sectarianism and factionalism into which it had been falling. He was opening up to his audiences the vastness of the Buddhist tradition and, at the same time, emphasising the basic doctrines that all serious Buddhists must put into practice before they concern themselves with other teachings. He had brought order and sense into the teaching of meditation by emphasising the 'classical' practices and teaching them by means of 'guided group meditation classes'. He began to introduce people to the importance of devotion in spiritual life—as well as to the joy that giving expression to feelings of faith may bring. Previously English people had tended to approach Buddhism in a very rationalistic way, rejecting the whole colourful and mythical dimension of the tradition as a divergence from the Buddha's true message. However, when Sangharakshita introduced puja at the Vihara and at the Society, himself decorating the shrine and leading the way in the making of offerings, even the most staid supporters of the Vihara began to respond.

In his public talks, Sangharakshita was able to communicate to the Buddhists and would-be Buddhists of Britain a much fuller vision of the Dharma than they had heard before. In two years he gave well over two hundred original lectures, two or more each week, each one carefully prepared and revealing his deep personal involvement with and knowledge of his subject. Since he also taught through meditation classes, speakers' classes, question and answer sessions, and discussion groups, as well as by personal communication, he was injecting a great deal of fresh inspiration and understanding into the Buddhist community. Many of his talks were about the basic teachings of Buddhism, but he was also able to open the eyes of his listeners to the true significance of the Mahayana, to which Theravadin prejudice had frequently blinded them. He often spoke on Tibetan Buddhism, which was very little known in Britain at the time and of which he had first-hand experience, being able to show that, far from being the degenerate demon worship it was popularly supposed to be, it was one of the most vital and richest traditions in the modern Buddhist world.

He gave a few talks on Christianity and Buddhism, some at the invitation of open-minded Christians wanting to learn about other faiths and some to audiences at the Vihara, exploring the implications of new thinking within the Christian churches. In one talk on 'Buddhism and the Bishop of Woolwich' (the Bishop, whom Sangharakshita had met, was a theologian of the Church of England who, especially in his book *Honest to God*, questioned many of the traditional assumptions of the Church), he showed how the radical cleric would do much better to embrace Buddhism rather than trying to bend the Christian message into a more acceptable shape. In the few dialogues he had with Christian clergymen it became apparent that those who were prepared to talk with members of other religions were often unsure of their own. Christianity in Britain was clearly no great obstacle to the spread of Buddhism.

One of his own most popular topics for lectures was that of Buddhism in India and the conversion movement started by Dr Ambedkar. He seized whatever opportunities he could to let British Buddhists—and the wider British public—know about the struggles and triumphs of their brothers and sisters in India. His very first meeting at the Hampstead Buddhist Vihara had been dominated by questions on the new Buddhist movement in India and he had been delighted to inform the Vihara's supporters of this very important work. He wrote a lengthy two-part article on 'Buddhism in India' for the *Middle Way*, the second part of which dealt specifically with that new movement. Though he was immersed in a quite different environment, he never forgot Dr Ambedkar and his work.

Sangharakshita found himself so busy during this time that he was unable to do any major literary work—besides editing the *Buddhist*, writing a few articles, seeing a new edition of *A Survey of Buddhism* through the press, and preparing *The Three Jewels* for publication. Not only was he giving talks and classes of various kinds and travelling to various parts of the country to visit Buddhist groups, he was also looking after the running of the Vihara: answering enquiries, arranging publicity, overseeing building work, even involving himself in the financial affairs of the English Sangha Trust. Bhikkhus did not usually take such an interest in the organisational side of Buddhist work—and certainly did not display the shrewdness that he possessed in abundance. On more than one occasion he prevented the trustees from making very unwise decisions on the basis of excessive credulity in other bhikkhus. The more business-minded of the trustees were delighted.

One of the tasks that Sangharakshita found himself faced with soon after arriving at the Vihara was a very delicate one. The bhikkhu who had been living there before he came and who had been the principal cause of the rift with the Buddhist Society championed vipassana meditation. The term 'vipassana' is an important one in Buddhism, denoting primarily that insight into the true nature of life that is the goal of spiritual practice. It has however come to be used for a family of approaches to meditation common in the Theravadin world. Much that goes by the name of vipassana is no doubt beneficial, but as expounded in Britain at that time by this particular bhikkhu and a number of other people it could be quite harmful. In this case it involved very intense concentration on each movement of the body, accompanied by a kind of internal running commentary on what one was doing: 'Lifting foot, placing down,' etc. Sangharakshita quickly came to the conclusion that, far from having the effect of promoting awareness and emotional positivity, the true immediate goals of meditation, this practice, though no doubt taught with good intentions, was having a very bad effect on many of its practitioners, inducing in them a zombie-like state that Sangharakshita later came to call 'alienated awareness'. Indeed, several people who had been following the technique were suffering from severe mental disturbance, some requiring psychiatric treatment, one even committing suicide. This would clearly have to stop. However, the Chairman of the English Sangha Trust was himself a keen advocate of this form of meditation and was said to be unwilling to hear any criticism levelled at it. Indeed, Sangharakshita was warned by others that any interference with the teaching of vipassana would induce a strong reaction from him. Yet so harmful were its effects that there was no real choice. Sangharakshita waited until he was firmly established at the Vihara and then closed down classes in this particular form of vipassana practice. Although there was no unpleasantness at the time, it seems he had made enemies who later were to exact their revenge.

Naturally, Sangharakshita met a great many people. He was on good terms with all the leading figures in British Buddhism, such as Christmas Humphreys, Dr Edward Conze, Dr Saddhatissa (Head of the London Buddhist Vihara), Dr Malalasekara (Sri Lankan High Commissioner in London), and Dr I.B. Horner. As the Head of the English Sangha he found himself meeting many dignitaries, both British and foreign. He especially came to know many of the people attending his lectures and classes, whether at the Hampstead Vihara, the Buddhist Society, or elsewhere. In fact he was very popular and was greatly in demand for personal interviews—which he always endeavoured to fulfil. He ordained several shramaneras—and one 'lay-sister' observing the eight precepts—who lived for a while at the Vihara, helping him with his work. Several other bhikkhus stayed for varying lengths of time at the Vihara, including a close friend from India, the Vietnamese monk Thic Thien Chau.

For many of those attending the Vihara and the Society, a meeting with Sangharakshita was a turning point in their lives. Emile Boin, one of those for whom this was true, wrote of him at that time in the *Middle Way*: 'Like many men of his calibre, the Ven. Sangharakshita must needs be a controversial figure, a fact probably due to his almost uncanny ability to penetrate the "persona" mask of people, together with a facility of, with a minimum of words, throwing the enquirer back upon himself so that he himself discerns the nature of his problem as well as the means to its solution. Many are those who have benefited from this and found the way out of the most complex spiritual and psychological problems, whilst a handful of others, with a psychological dependence upon ideological compensations for their own inadequacies, have found his penetrating insight somewhat hard to face.'

As the months went by, Sangharakshita immersed himself more and more in the Buddhist movement in Britain. But it was not merely to British Buddhism that he had to adjust. After twenty years in the East, Sangharakshita had quite a bit of adaptation to make to the world that now surrounded him. He had to accommodate himself to the great technological and economic advances that had taken place in his absence—London was now a much wealthier and more convenient city in many ways. But, more significantly, he had to reconnect with his own cultural origins. Although he had continued to read extensively in the classics of Western literature while he was in India and had kept in touch with a few people in England, he had otherwise lived as an oriental among orientals, adapting completely to the dress, food, and customs of the people among whom he lived. He found the grace and simplicity of Indian life very congenial. He looked upon India as the land of the Buddha and saw it as bearing his own spiritual roots. Yet he had been born in the West and had found his way to Buddhism through contact with the highest and best in Western culture. A return to Britain was a return to his cultural roots. Various friends and disciples took him to see one or two serious films and to the opera—shocking some of his more rigid followers who considered that a bhikkhu should not enjoy such events.

One friend in particular, Terry Delamare, who became interested in Buddhism through Sangharakshita's talks at the London College of Psychic Science, offered to take him wherever he wanted to go. They visited Stonehenge together, the ancient megalithic monument in southern England, and in June 1966 made a six-week tour of Italy and Greece. This was a very important trip for Sangharakshita, for in Florence and Rome, Athens, Delphi, and Olympia he saw for the first time the centres of the two most important periods in Western cultural history: classical Greece and Renaissance Italy. He came face to face with many of the works of art he had first seen reproduced in the colour plates of the *Children's Encyclopaedia* when he was confined to bed at the age of eight. He was particularly impressed by the archaic sculpture at Olympia—and, for their archetypal associations, the catacombs in Rome.

By this time it had become clear to him that his future lay in Britain, although the English Buddhist movement was still far from satisfactory. There was such a legacy of prejudice, faction, and misunderstanding that at one point he had seriously contemplated abandoning the existing organisations and starting something new. It was only because his closest disciples and friends did not consider it appropriate that he did not take this course. However, despite these drawbacks, it was clear that he had made considerable progress in establishing a much healthier atmosphere amongst the Buddhists of Britain and that there were the beginnings of the possibility of a real Buddhist movement. He therefore decided that he would permanently move his base of operations to London, spending a few months each year in India to maintain contact with Dr Ambedkar's followers and to keep activities alive at the Kalimpong Vihara. He had already made provision for the future of his work in Kalimpong by founding a support group at the Hampstead Vihara, the Friends of the Triyana Vardhana Vihara, which ensured sufficient funds to meet its running expenses. It was now time to visit India for three or four months in order to tie up his affairs there. He arranged with the Trustees of the Hampstead Buddhist Vihara to return to continue the work he had so successfully begun. Many of his new English disciples were distressed to see him go and concerned that he might not return. However, he promised that he would come back early in the following year, and in September 1966 flew to Bombay, accompanied by Terry Delamare, who was to make a photographic record of the trip.

Farewell to India

Sangharakshita received a rapturous welcome from the ex-Untouchable Buddhists of Bombay, who had not seen him for two years. Over the next six days he plunged into his old routine, giving several lectures each day in various slum localities where Buddhists lived—and making a trip to the ancient Buddhist cave-monastery of Kanheri, on the outskirts of the city. Over the next two months he visited all the major centres of Dr Ambedkar's movement where he was already well-known—principally Ahmedabad, Poona, Jabalpur, and Nagpur. The new Buddhists obviously derived great encouragement from his presence among them and, as ever, he was able to inspire them to new fervour for the religion they had so recently adopted and to instruct them in its principal teachings. His tour culminated at Nagpur on the tenth anniversary of Dr Ambedkar's conversion, where he addressed a crowd of 250,000 people at the Diksha Bhumi, where the conversions had taken place.

Sangharakshita and Terry also visited Dharamsala, where they met the Dalai Lama and told him of the interest Europeans were showing in the Dharma. They also visited some friends at Dalhousie and met many of the Tibetan incarnate lamas Sangharakshita had known in Kalimpong. He took the opportunity to visit Lama Govinda and Li Gotami at Almora before spending some weeks in Kalimpong, seeing his teachers and friends and purchasing Indian and Tibetan Buddhist artefacts to sell on his return to England to raise funds for Buddhist work.

At this point, events took a dramatic turn. He received a letter from the Trustees of the English Sangha Trust telling him that he would not be welcome back at the Hampstead Buddhist Vihara. No proper reasons were given and he was offered the opportunity of 'saving face' by simply declaring that he had decided to stay in India. This astonishing piece of news came to him without any warning. Whilst he had been in England no one had expressed any dissatisfaction or raised any issues with him. He was never to be given an explanation for this extraordinary decision.

As the days went by, more letters were received, this time from his friends and disciples at the Vihara and Society. It became clear that most of those attending the Vihara were very unhappy with the Trustees' decision and were not going to accept it without question—indeed, the Trustees themselves had not been unanimous and the motion had only been passed by a majority of one, some Trustees resigning in protest. The underlying reasons for the dismissal had begun to emerge. In stopping the teaching of vipassana Sangharakshita had made enemies who were now exacting their retribution. Not only had he refused to countenance the teaching of a technique that caused many people psychological damage but he had consistently asserted his own vision of Triyana Buddhism—a Buddhism not restricted and bound by any particular school or culture. He was simply a Buddhist and drew on the entire tradition for his inspiration. Some of the Trustees had been deeply offended by this approach, since they were wedded to a narrow brand of Theravada that they considered to be the true orthodox Buddhism. Similarly, Sangharakshita recognised that many of the customary forms adopted by Buddhists were simply cultural and not intrinsic to spiritual life. Much that Eastern Buddhists took for granted needed to be re-evaluated in the West. For instance, the yellow robes and shaven head of a bhikkhu had no positive cultural significance in Britain—if anything they had a negative one and excited ridicule and contempt. Sangharakshita would sometimes wear ordinary clothes when he was travelling. The fact that he had, on a few occasions, visited the cinema and the opera offended a handful of narrow-minded people who thought that bhikkhus should not enjoy such things. Sangharakshita refused to fit into other people's expectations of what a spiritually committed individual should be—he had his own very strong dedication to the Three Jewels and his deep understanding of the Dharma to guide him and was not going to be limited by rules that had little genuine significance for spiritual life.

If the Trustees anticipated that Sangharakshita would not return to England so as to 'save face', they had badly misjudged their man. He had already come to the conclusion during his two years in London that his true place was now in the West. He had also come to the conclusion that there was a need for a 'truly vigorous and virile presentation of Buddhism' as opposed to the 'weak and tepid conventional presentation, whether Sinhalese or Thai', which could not satisfy Westerners just as it could not satisfy intelligent ex-Untouchables. He had already decided to return to London and had promised his friends and disciples that he would do so. He had no intention of breaking his word and no intention of saving the Trustees trouble by quietly saying he had changed his mind and was staying in India. The future of Buddhism in the West hung on his return to London. When he read the letter from the Trustees, dismissing him from the Hampstead Vihara, he turned to his companion and said 'This means a new Buddhist Movement.' Cut loose from the narrow and rigid confines of official British Buddhism, he was free to start again on the basis of genuine Buddhist principles.

Back in London, his friends put up a strong fight for his reinstatement. At a meeting of the English Sangha Association, the organisation of supporters of the Vihara, the English Sangha Trust's decision to terminate his incumbency was questioned and a large majority voted to have him reinstated. The Trust however held all the property and funds, and the Trustees refused to reconsider their decision. At no point would they give any reasons for their position—which of course fuelled all sorts of speculation and rumour: the Trustees were eventually constrained to issue a denial that Sangharakshita's moral character was in doubt.

Sangharakshita was able to discuss these developments with his own friends and teachers in Kalimpong. He gave both Dhardo Rimpoche and Dilgo Khyentse Rimpoche a full account of the situation and the difficulties he had had. Neither of them considered that this should make any difference to his plans, seeming to regard the troubles as a quite insignificant matter. Both strongly supported his decision to return to London and establish a new and vigorous Buddhist movement. He then stayed briefly at the Maha Bodhi Society headquarters in Calcutta where, at the urgent pleading of Valisinha, the General Secretary, he once more took over the editing of the *Maha Bodhi*. In February 1967 he left for London, stopping in Cairo on the way at the invitation of a friend and delivering two lectures on Buddhism. A new era was opening in his own life—and in British Buddhism.

Chapter Six

A New Buddhist Movement
1967–1973

Too long have I been a camel
Ship of the Desert
Too long knelt to be laden
With other men's merchandise.
Too long have I been a lion
Lord of the Jungle
Too long fought
Paper-and-tinsel dragons
Too long have I been a child
Parent of the Future
Now it is time to be
Myself.

Sangharakshita (1969)

ALTHOUGH THE CIRCUMSTANCES surrounding Sangharakshita's exclusion from the Hampstead Buddhist Vihara were unpleasant enough, it was in no pessimistic or cowed mood that he arrived back to England in March 1967. He was returning free at last of the negative and cramping atmosphere that had characterised British Buddhism till then. He was free of the petty restrictions of monastic formalism, which elevated such matters as the correct wearing of robes or not eating after a certain time above the ascetic life of genuine monasticism. He could teach the Dharma without compromise and without restricting himself to any one school.

Not only was he free to communicate the Dharma uncompromisingly, he was free to be himself. For fourteen years, Sangharakshita had functioned happily and effectively more or less within the framework of traditional Theravadin monk–lay relations. For two further years, he had experienced that traditional structure as imported into England and then interpreted in the light of English social conventions. This had been a less happy experience. The honour traditionally paid to a Theravadin bhikkhu led many Westerners to idealise him, and therefore to relate to him in a very constrained and inhibited way. It was all too easy for them to project on to him their own expectations of a spiritual teacher—and to overlook the qualities he did really have. Now he could simply be himself, communicating the Dharma in whatever way he found most effective and forming real, effective friendships with his disciples.

Even more than he had been when Kashyapji left him in Kalimpong 'to work for the good of Buddhism', he was on his own, cut loose from the models and structures that had guided him so far. Buddhism in the West was going to take a different form to those forms it had taken in the East. He was determined that it would start, at least, free from much of the formalism and rigidity that so stultifies the spiritual lives of many oriental Buddhists. He had to find a new way forward, leading his friends and followers towards a truly Buddhist way of life that could be lived by men and women in the modern West. The next few years marked a period of exceptional creativity for Sangharakshita, as he set about building a new Buddhist movement.

Since he no longer felt himself to be bound by existing models and conventions he was free to experiment and explore. He did not know what form the new Buddhist movement was to take and he simply opened himself up to what was going on around him, seeing what could and what could not be used, without preconception. His own explorations coincided with a period of exceptional ferment in the surrounding culture, with the boundaries of what could be publicly said and done being pushed back day by day. Sangharakshita dipped into some of the new and exciting currents that swirled around him. He read widely in the ideas activating many people at that time. He became involved with a circle of experimental poets, went a few times to an avant-garde arts centre, saw a number of innovative films, and even went to a rock concert or two. Finding that many of the young people he met had taken marijuana and LSD, he too tried these 'mind-altering substances' on a few occasions, having interesting but not particularly significant experiences. In these and other ways he explored what was happening around him.

Sangharakshita had now entered a no-man's-land between the old Buddhist movement and the new. He still wore the yellow robes of a bhikkhu on public occasions and still allowed himself to be referred to as

'Maha Sthavira', an honorific deriving from his fifteen years as a monk. However, although he still regarded monastic life as a very positive basis for spiritual progress, he had come to see that much traditional monastic practice was actually counter-productive since it elevated formal observance above genuine asceticism. He therefore no longer considered the traditional formalised monastic structure to be of relevance. He simply continued to use its conventions in his relations with other Buddhists in the absence of any alternative. As the new movement he created has become more established he has felt himself increasingly able to abandon the forms and styles of that old Buddhist world and to present himself exclusively in terms of the new. His has been a transitional role, between the old and the new, and it was at this point in his career, on his return from India, that he effectively stepped out of the old and began to create the new.

His break with the past was represented also in his appearance. He allowed his hair to grow down to his shoulders and sported mutton-chop side whiskers. He now wore his robes only for classes and public appearances—and even when wearing them had less the aspect of an orthodox Theravadin bhikkhu than of a shaman of some Native American tribe. Indeed, he has suggested that this period could be understood in terms of the shaman's career. The shaman usually serves an apprenticeship, during which he carefully learns the teachings of his master. But then, after a series of visions and other psychic experiences, he begins to operate independently, allowing his own vision to unfold. Sangharakshita had served his apprenticeship in the old Buddhist world and was now forced to operate independently. He had indeed a number of strange experiences around this time, which felt as though he was exploring freely and alone new frontiers of consciousness. Those who remember him at this time recall something almost raw and untamed about him, as if he existed completely beyond the reach of narrow conventions—that quality is, of course, still there in him, but perhaps less on the surface.

In many ways, Sangharakshita was very much alone at this time. But that did not seem to bother him. He has described how he would sometimes wander by himself through the streets, calling in rough working-men's pubs for a pint of Guinness, enjoying his aloneness in the midst of others. Although he was alone in so far as he had no pattern or model for what he was to do, he was not alone in that, besides his teachers and many friends in India, he had a band of devoted supporters in England. A small group of his disciples from the Vihara had worked hard to get the Trustees of the English Sangha Trust to reverse their decision to remove him. They had circularised all members of the Vihara's supporters' organisation, the English Sangha Association, rallying them to protest. At an Extraordinary General Meeting of the Association, which took place while Sangharakshita was still in India, strong, even violent feelings had been expressed on both sides. The Trustees had simply refused to reconsider their decision and still would not give any substantial reason why they did not want him to return. The overwhelming majority of members present had voted against the Trustees but to no avail. Since the Trust owned the property and funds that was the end of the matter.

The violence of the feelings stirred up by this controversy and the intransigence of the Trustees left many people completely disillusioned with organised Buddhism. Even though the great majority of the Association's members supported Sangharakshita, most of them simply dropped away from the Buddhist movement altogether—a sad but salutary lesson in the effects of disharmony within the Buddhist community. Only a dozen or so of Sangharakshita's former supporters rallied to him on his return and it was they who formed the nucleus of the new Buddhist movement he now began to build.

THE FOUNDING OF THE FRIENDS OF THE WESTERN SANGHA

As soon as he arrived back in London, he formed, with this devoted band, the Friends of the Western Sangha as the organisational basis for his work. He had much experience by now of what goes wrong in Buddhist organisations and he tried to establish the Friends of the Western Sangha on entirely new principles. It was not to be the usual society-type set-up, wherein members simply pay a subscription and do not necessarily have any effective, spiritually-based contact or communication with others in the organisation. From the start he intended it to be a community or spiritual brotherhood, founded on a common acknowledgement of and commitment to the Three Jewels of Buddha, Dharma, and Sangha. That commitment was what would determine membership, not the paying of a subscription. The emphasis within the community was to be on personal communication, as found in the vertical relationship between the teacher and his pupils and in the horizontal one between the pupils themselves. Strictly speaking one could not 'join' the Friends of the Western Sangha—one became a 'Friend' simply by participating in any of its activities. The organisational dimension of the movement was to be in the hands of those who were effectively committed to the Three Jewels.

Sangharakshita's new Buddhist movement, built on human communication and spiritual commitment rather than subscriptions and membership rules, was radical indeed for British Buddhism—perhaps even for world Buddhism. The formalism of much of the modern Theravada largely vitiates the relationship between disciple and spiritual teacher—a relationship so vital to the development of the individual. The Friends of the Western Sangha was founded on the principle of spiritual hierarchy, in full appreciation of the importance of those crucial vertical relationships being living and effective. On the other hand, in some other schools of Buddhism, notably the Tibetan, so much emphasis is placed on the vertical relationship between teacher and pupil that the spiritual significance of communication between fellow pupils is almost entirely neglected. The principle of spiritual friendship was however at the heart of the Friends of the Western Sangha.

As originally founded, Sangharakshita anticipated that there would be a hierarchy of involvement and commitment, starting with disciples and class members ('Friends'), then upasakas and upasikas who would give some assistance in the work of the movement, then maha-upasakas and maha-upasikas, followed by part-time workers and teachers who had received bodhisattva and anagarika ordination, then full-timers with bodhisattva, anagarika, or bhikkhu ordination, and finally, at the apex, the spiritual teacher.

The Friends of the Western Sangha set out for themselves the following aims and objects:

'(1) We wish to encourage the leading of a balanced spiritual life through the harmonious unfoldment of the five spiritual faculties of Faith, Wisdom, Vigour, Meditation and Mindfulness. (2) We hope to stimulate a wider knowledge and deeper appreciation of the life and spiritual significance of the Buddha as the living exemplar of the attainment of supreme enlightenment. (3) We hope to promote a more rigorous study and more ardent practice of the Dharma in all its forms, without distinction of school or sect. While remaining true to the spirit of enlightenment, we hope to present the teaching in a form suitable to Westerners. (4) We aim to encourage the study of Buddhist literature, especially the sutras, Buddhist texts, and works relating Buddhism to Western philosophy, psychology, and culture. (5) We desire to stimulate the appreciation of Buddhist arts and crafts, and to encourage the talents and interests of individuals so that these can be combined with their other practices in their pursuit of the Path. (6) We intend to help develop the Bodhisattva Ideal of aiming at the attainment of enlightenment for the benefit of all sentient beings, and to popularise the leading of a life of simplicity and non-exploitation, in accordance with the Buddhist principle of right livelihood. (7) We also hope to foster the spirit of Sangha, or spiritual brotherhood, consisting of reverence and respect for teachers (others' as well as one's own), love for fellow students, friendliness and encouragement towards newcomers and enquirers, co-operation with others, and the cultivation and maintenance of cordial relations with the Sanghas of other countries and traditions. (8) With these aims in view, therefore, we intend to celebrate the Buddhist festivals and anniversaries, to conduct retreats, seminars, lectures and meditation classes, and to help prepare persons suitable for admittance to the Order through special training courses, both practical and theoretical. (9) We also aim to maintain and support our teacher, Ven. Sthavira Sangharakshita, and his monastic disciples, as well as other members of the Sangha associated with them in their activities. (10) We intend to acquire such property as is needed, and to enter into any agreement or take lawful action, such as accepting gifts of cash or kind, towards any of these objectives.'

One of Sangharakshita's most active supporters, Emile Boin, ran a shop called Sakura, devoted to the sale of things Japanese, at 14 Monmouth Street, a side street in central London near the city's main shopping and theatre district. Transformed into a Buddhist shop with books on the Dharma, devotional objects, and artefacts from Buddhist countries, it became the information centre for the Friends of the Western Sangha. A narrow staircase led from the back of the shop down into a basement containing two rooms, one of which was now rented by the organisation and converted into a small shrine-room—later the other was also taken and used as a reception room. The shrine-room was a cavern-like space, partly tunnelled under the road, thus recalling to Sangharakshita the Roman catacombs. The shop and shrine-room became the headquarters of the new Buddhist movement and, within a fortnight of Sangharakshita's arrival from India, classes were being held there under the auspices of the Friends of the Western Sangha. On 6 April 1967 the shrine-room was formally dedicated by Sangharakshita and named the Triratna Shrine—this date now being annually commemorated as the founding day of the new Buddhist movement. From then on, one and then two classes were held each week, at first led by Sangharakshita himself.

Activities at the centre quickly began to flourish, for the times were unusually propitious to the spreading of the Dharma. Indeed, 1967 was an important year in the West—it was during that year that Eastern religious ideas were disseminated on a widespread and popular scale. Although Buddhism and other Eastern religions had been known of in Europe for some centuries, and in the last few decades a handful had even begun to consider themselves Buddhists or Hindus, the vast majority of Westerners had probably never heard of meditation or had never considered, for instance, that a religion might be non-theistic. Anyone who did turn to Buddhism tended to be older, educated and often rather neurotic. There were certainly very few young people involved in the tiny English Buddhist movement.

But a major change had been taking place during the 1960s among young people, under the influence of vast social, political, and economic changes in Western society as a whole. As the traditional Christian values that had underlain Western culture for more than a thousand years dissolved more rapidly than ever, young people began to rebel against more and more of what their parents held dear. The era has been termed the 'permissive sixties' because of the widespread relaxation of restrictions on sexual behaviour. Music was the main medium of this youth movement. There was a rapid upsurge of new and exciting rock and roll music, and the bands that made this music became very influential in forming fashion and opinion. John Lennon of the Beatles was probably correct when he declared that his band was more popular than Jesus Christ.

In 1967 several of the most popular musicians came under the influence of a movement, stemming from the west coast of America, that gave the rebellious youth culture a quite new direction. The hippie movement was a heady mixture of wild and exciting experimental music, sexual promiscuity, a complete rejection of ordinary 'straight' society, a millenarian expectation of the emergence of the New Age, and a vague mysticism derived from Buddhism, Hinduism, and Taoism. The movement had its own sacrament in the consumption of a wide range of drugs—particularly so-called psychedelic drugs such as LSD, that were supposed to give access to higher states of consciousness. In a somewhat diluted form, the hippie philosophy and style was carried all over America and Europe, influencing a great many young people who began to take drugs and to espouse something of the hippie outlook.

Self-indulgent, naïve, and destructive as this movement was in some respects, it had its very positive and creative side. Most importantly, it introduced millions of young people to Eastern culture and religion—Western popular music was, for a while, influenced by the rhythms and sounds of Indian music, several leading bands adopting sitar and tabla for some of their songs. Members of the biggest selling group of all, the Beatles, took initiation from the Hindu guru Maharishi Mahesh Yogi, and took up the practice of meditation. Many young people saw meditation as an alternative to drugs—a way to experience euphoria without the physical and mental dangers of intoxication. Some began to take a serious interest in the philosophy and religion of the East.

Sangharakshita could not have arrived in England at a more opportune time. So many young people were open to what he had to offer and they began to flock to his classes: long-haired young men, wearing brightly coloured if rather scruffy clothes, and young women in flowing, Indian-print dresses. Not only had he arrived at the crucial moment when there was a real opening for Buddhism in the West but he was the man for that moment. Whilst being entirely faithful to the essential spirit of the Dharma, he did not feel himself rigidly bound by external forms and was therefore able to communicate with young people who were determinedly rejecting the traditional patterns of behaviour they had inherited. They usually considered themselves to be radical revolutionaries—but he was in many ways more radical and revolutionary than they were, and he made a deep impression on many of the young people who came in contact with him.

The centre was very small, able to hold no more than twenty people, so larger functions were held at Centre House, a building in West London catering for the new interest in Eastern religion, hatha yoga, and alternative forms of medical therapy. Sangharakshita had first heard of Centre House during his recent visit to Kalimpong—for some reason Dhardo Rimpoche had been sent a leaflet about the place. On his return from India, he and Terry Delamare had stayed there for a few days before they found a flat elsewhere. The organisers of the centre were very sympathetic to the new movement and offered its use for lectures on Buddhism and social events promoting communication among the 'Friends'. Through some other contacts of Sangharakshita's, involved in a charity for refugee children, the FWS hired a large and beautifully situated country house, Keffolds, near Haslemere in Surrey, for a week long retreat. In this ideal setting some forty members of the circle gradually gathering around Sangharakshita were able to enjoy a deeper experience of spiritual practice.

THE WESTERN BUDDHIST ORDER

After one year, he felt ready to take the next step in the establishment of the new Buddhist movement—what he himself described as 'a historic stage in the development of Buddhism in England'. At a special day seminar at Centre House, on 7 April 1968, he ordained twelve men and women as *upasakas* and *upasikas* (male and female lay followers) in the presence of two Theravadin monks, Bhikkhus Shantibhadra and Vajirajnana, from Thailand and Sri Lanka respectively, Jack Austin, an English priest of the Japanese Jodo Shin Shu, and Taishen Deshimaru, a Japanese Zen Roshi living in France. Because many people felt uncomfortable with the word 'sangha' because it was foreign, the name of the movement had been changed to 'the Friends of the Western Buddhist Order' and these ordinations marked the creation of the Western Buddhist Order itself.

Sangharakshita, with some help from his new Order members, was for the next five years involved in a very busy schedule of activities. Besides the three or four weekly classes in meditation, discussion, and puja, he began the education of his disciples through his lectures. Each year he would give one or two major series of eight lectures at Centre House and other locations, systematically laying out his vision of Buddhism as a coherent whole and exploring connections with major currents in Western philosophy, psychology, and science. In 1967, he talked on 'Aspects of Buddhist Psychology'; in 1968, on 'The Buddha's Noble Eightfold Path' and 'An Introduction to Tibetan Buddhism'; in 1969, on 'Aspects of the Bodhisattva Ideal' and 'The Higher Evolution of Man'; in 1970, on 'Aspects of the Higher Evolution of the Individual'; in 1971, on 'Parables, Myths and Symbols in the *White Lotus Sutra*'; and in 1972, on 'Creative Symbols of the Tantric Path to Enlightenment'. In these and another fifty or more individual talks, given on retreats, at festivals, at classes, and on visits to other groups and societies, he established a clear presentation of the basic aspects of spiritual life and practice: the Three Jewels, meditation, morality, communication, even a Buddhist view of current world problems. These talks were not only of the greatest penetration and insight, replete with all the learning that Sangharakshita had acquired in his years of study and reflection, but also exceptionally lucid and approachable, delighting and inspiring his hearers. Each was tape-recorded and copies were sold widely among Sangharakshita's disciples.

Twice a year, at Easter and at the height of summer, he would conduct two-week-long retreats at Keffolds for up to a hundred people. These were remarkably happy and harmonious occasions and were, in many ways, the highlights of the FWBO calendar. Since they gave Sangharakshita the opportunity to teach his disciples what they could achieve through systematic spiritual practice in supportive conditions, these Easter and summer retreats played a very important part in the development of the movement. Given the hippie background of many participants, Sangharakshita did not always find them easy to lead since there was a constant tendency towards hedonistic indulgence, which from time to time made a retreat seem more like a 'love-in' than an opportunity for mindfulness and meditation. But he had an unfailing touch by which he deftly guided each retreat on to new heights, rather than allowing it to plunge into the threatening chaos—whilst never appearing authoritarian or moralistic. Towards the end of 1971, when the movement had definitely begun to gain momentum, he was able to introduce monthly weekend retreats, some in complete silence, held at Quartermaine, a property near Keffolds.

At the end of 1972, there was an important new development: weekend retreats began to be held for men and women separately—although Sangharakshita himself would visit the women's events to have some discussion with the participants. When he had arrived in England, he had assumed that all activities in the Buddhist movement would be open to both men and women together. The tradition found all over the world of men and women having separate spheres of activity and spending much of their time apart has largely broken down in the West, and Sangharakshita assumed that the new Buddhist movement would have no need for its reassertion. But he did find, particularly on the large Easter and summer retreats, that sexual tension and game playing did strongly influence the atmosphere and prevent many people from getting as deeply engaged in the retreat as they might have done. In fact, generally he had found that sexual relationships played far too large a part in many of his followers' lives, causing them much anxiety, distraction, and confusion. Men and women seemed to be able to get on with their Buddhist practice far better when they were apart—and most readily admitted this after experiencing a single-sex retreat. From then on, he asserted the benefit of single-sex activities in general.

Through the weekly classes at the centre, the lectures and seminars at Centre House, and the retreats at Keffolds and Quartermaine, the new Order members and other Friends gradually deepened their practice of meditation, their understanding of the Dharma, and their experience of devotion. Devotional practice had been more or less unknown in British

Buddhist circles before Sangharakshita's return, and to begin with response to this side of Buddhism had been very weak and insipid. But gradually people participated in puja with increasing energy and enjoyment and it became a popular element in retreats and classes. The major devotional ceremony used in the movement was the Sevenfold Puja, arranged by Sangharakshita from Shantideva's *Bodhicharyavatara*, and other chants were taken from Pali and Tibetan sources. Devotion was also expressed in the public celebration each year of the major Buddhist festivals: Vaishakha Purnima, Dharmachakra Day, and Kartik Purnima (now referred to as Buddha, Dharma, and Sangha Day respectively) as well as the anniversary of the Buddha's *parinirvana* or death and of the founding of the FWBO (FWBO Day) and the Order (Order Day). Usually celebration would take the form of a day of meditation and puja at Centre House, including a talk by Sangharakshita to explain its significance. Plenty of the time would be free for members of this new movement to get to know each other since Sangharakshita was careful to foster links of friendship and solidarity between the members of the Order and the movement on these and other occasions. Four times a year social events were held at which Friends would share a meal together, perhaps listen to some music or poetry—and usually conclude with a puja.

Sangharakshita's vision for the new Buddhist movement was broad and deep. He realised that, for Buddhism truly to take root in the West, a whole new culture and society must come into being. The work he was doing with his disciples was the seed of that new culture and society. He had seen in his own experience the intimate connection between Buddhism and the arts, and was keen to foster both an appreciation of the arts and artistic creativity. Several aspiring artists of various kinds attended the Centre, many of them responding very strongly to Sangharakshita's own interest in this field and to the link he made between artistic endeavour and the spiritual quest. He encouraged the formation of an arts group and himself participated in public poetry readings organised by the group at Centre House. At the end of 1969, he formed a drama group, which met at his flat to read plays—notably some by the Irish poet W.B. Yeats, strongly influenced by Japanese Noh Drama, itself underlain by Buddhist principles.

But there was much work to be done with people, even at the psychological level. When he first arrived back in England, he soon noticed the social constraint and lack of energy among English Buddhists. Even though the Friends and Order members by whom he was now surrounded were on the whole far more healthy and positive than the people he had encountered in 1964, there was still a tendency to emotional inhibition. On the first retreat held under the auspices of the Friends of the Western Sangha he had noticed this constraint, particularly in relations between his older, more staid supporters from his days at the Hampstead Vihara and those who had come since the founding of the new movement who tended to be younger and were often hippies, ex-hippies, or at least hippie-influenced. A very stiff and dull atmosphere prevailed—so he introduced some exercises he had learnt from a Western woman educationalist in Bombay, who had used them to improve communication between Indian school-teachers and their pupils. The communication exercises involve people sitting in pairs, first of all just looking at each other and, in a later exercise, one member of each pair saying certain prescribed sentences to the other, which their partner must then fully and genuinely acknowledge. In between each exercise, which lasts about five minutes, they discuss what they have experienced. In this way, participants learn really to see the person in front of them and to communicate more directly and honestly with them. The effects were almost magical: the level of energy on the retreat rose immediately and the general atmosphere became far more happy and communicative.

These exercises became a very important ingredient on all retreats. Sangharakshita realised that many people in England were dull and lacking in energy because they scarcely ever communicated fully what they felt and thought. Many people particularly found it difficult to express anger in a healthy and positive way—and so dammed up their energies behind a wall of inhibition. Much of that energy was released in the course of the exercises and was then available for spiritual practice. After a visit to the USA in 1970, he noticed that, in comparison with the Americans he met, English people were particularly dull and emotionally blocked. He therefore held four weekend 'communication seminars', during which the exercises were practised throughout the morning and afternoon. This work on communication gradually had its effect, and the level of energy and emotional positivity in the movement began to rise.

CONTACTS OUTSIDE THE FWBO

Whilst most of his work was concentrated on the FWBO itself, he did not neglect a wider range of contacts. During his time at the Hampstead Vihara he had been very popular with many of the Buddhist groups up and down the country, and most of them were keen for him to continue to visit. He was asked to give talks at a number of educational establishments, including several art colleges, where he talked on Buddhism and art. The press and news-media took some interest in him and his growing movement: the first ordinations were extensively reported and he was interviewed twice on television and several times on radio. His expulsion from the British Buddhist establishment seemed to have done him little harm and he was in as much demand as ever—outside the Hampstead Vihara and the Buddhist Society.

Sangharakshita's new work attracted interest from many bhikkhus and laymen in Britain, some of whom co-operated in the early activities of the FWBO. As has already been noted, two Theravadin bhikkhus, a Shin priest, and a Zen Roshi were present at the first ordinations, creating a kind of quorum of the Buddhist sangha and emphasising the trans-sectarian character of the order that Sangharakshita was founding. His earliest intention had been to enlist the co-operation of other ordained Buddhists in the work of the FWBO. Jack Austin, the Shin priest present at the ordinations, became Vice-President of the Friends of the Western Sangha—although he later resigned. Trungpa Rimpoche, a leading Kagyupa incarnate lama, attended some early functions of the movement, and Thic Thien Chau, a Vietnamese monk friend of Sangharakshita's, was a frequent guest on retreats and at festivals. Several Theravadin bhikkhus were in friendly contact with the fledgeling movement and its founder. Sangharakshita also had meetings with members of the Arya Maitreya Mandala, the order founded in Germany by his friend, Lama Govinda. Sangharakshita had an interesting discussion with Alan Watts, an Englishman who had spent the last few years in America and was probably one of the best-known Buddhists in the West through his popular books on Zen.

At the beginning of 1970 he visited France, at the invitation of the Vietnamese Overseas Buddhist Association, to which his friend Thic Thien Chau belonged, and La Connaissance du Bouddhisme, an organisation of French Buddhists. He gave a successful lecture for the latter and realised, from the lively and intelligent questions, that Buddhism had great potential in France. The leaders of La Connaissance du Bouddhisme were impressed by Sangharakshita and wished to continue contact and co-operation with the FWBO.

However, not all contacts with other ordained Buddhists were as straightforward and cordial. Soon after the movement was founded, several Friends had, with Sangharakshita's encouragement, contributed money towards a visit from Japan by an English Zen Roshi. She was invited to an FWBO event—but it soon became apparent that her interest was really in recruiting disciples of her own and not in co-operating with Sangharakshita. Another Zen teacher, Japanese this time, was sponsored by the FWBO, which also arranged his visa with the British authorities and accommodated him in an FWBO community. Again, he was very obviously interested only in gaining disciples for himself—and eventually declared himself to be the Buddha Maitreya during the course of a retreat on FWBO premises. From that point on, Sangharakshita has been understandably cautious about working with other Buddhist teachers—unless they have clearly shown their goodwill and willingness to co-operate.

An important opportunity for reaching new people came when Sangharakshita was invited to Berkeley College at Yale University as Visiting Lecturer in Philosophy. A student from the College had attended some of his lectures in London in 1969 and had persuaded the College authorities to invite him to give a 'Hall Seminar' in 'Buddhism for the West' for three months in the spring of 1970. Some sixty students applied for his course, although fifteen was the maximum number that could be accepted. His lecturing duties were very minimal—only two hours a week—but he also conducted a weekly meditation class at the College, which more than eighty people attended, and he was able to have a lot of personal contact with students. He quickly developed a small band of eager young friends who came to meditate with him every afternoon in his rooms. A course in the communication exercises also proved very successful. There was no doubt that there was great potential for the Dharma in America. Indeed, Sangharakshita considered transferring his activities there, but felt he could not abandon his existing disciples.

The Growth of the Movement

From its inception in April 1967 to January 1973, when he left London, the new movement was under the direct personal guidance of its founder. He took most classes, led all the retreats, gave all the instruction, and was personally involved in almost every detail of organisation—he had to erect the shrine himself and lay out the room for the first ordinations, as well as clear up afterwards. The initial level of commitment even among Order members was relatively low, on the whole, and if he did not pay attention to organisation, he could not count on anyone else to do so. He personally presided over the drawing up and registration in March 1968 of a legal structure for the organisation, chaired meetings of the governing council, and made sure that the other officers did their jobs properly.

Each week he took a class for Order members, particularly guiding them in the visualisation meditations that all members of the Western Buddhist Order can take up after ordination. He instituted speakers' classes again, helping to prepare the new Order members for giving their own public lectures. He also established a monthly class for those wanting to join the Order. Gradually the movement did develop. In 1968 several Friends decided to form a community together and rented Sarum House, a large private house in Purley, a suburb to the south of London—the community is still in existence today and called Aryatara. Sangharakshita naturally gave the members of the new community a lot of support—particularly when they began to discover that the creation of a community is not easy and often involves sorting out a lot of interpersonal issues. During the next year most of its members were ordained into the Order.

A test for the new movement came in late 1968 when a fire burnt out the shrine-room at the centre in Monmouth Street. Under Sangharakshita's personal direction, Friends and Order members rallied round to make good the damage and redecorate and re-equip the centre. But it was already clear that many of the first Order members were not going to stick with the new Buddhist movement. Some had never considered that a deeper level of involvement might be required of them and began to back away as the demands of the movement grew greater and greater. Others were disappointed that the movement was not growing as fast as they would like—but were unwilling or unable to make the extra effort needed for it to grow faster. Others again were disturbed by the influx of long-haired and ragged-clothed hippies and thought that Sangharakshita was too lax with them. Others drifted off for various personal reasons: worldly ambition, marital difficulties, or some difference of opinion with other members of the Order. Very few of those ordained in the first two years remained Order members for very long. In fact it is clear that the early Order members, with a few notable exceptions, were quite a disappointment to Sangharakshita. He was constantly exhorting them to put more effort into the work of the movement as well as into their spiritual practice.

Nonetheless, the movement gradually made progress. Another community was formed in 1969 whose members were rather more active. Two Order members took responsibility with Sangharakshita for the weekly beginners' meditation class and, when he spent three months in the USA in 1970, they successfully took over leadership of the class. In this and other ways, Order members slowly began to take on more responsibility for the new Buddhist movement.

The establishment of this new movement entailed a considerable sacrifice on Sangharakshita's part—he was unable to proceed with the literary work he had been planning for some time and that meant so much to him. When he came to the Hampstead Vihara, he had stipulated that he should have every morning free so that he could write—but this had not been possible, since he was so fully engaged in running the Vihara. The work of the FWBO demanded even more of him and, to begin with, he could not embark on any writing projects. Towards the end of 1968, he did decide to return to his memoirs and, slowly and painfully, he worked on these amidst all the other demands on his time.

One very sad and difficult burden he had to shoulder at this period was known to very few of his followers. He had to cope with the serious mental difficulties of Terry Delamare, the friend who had accompanied him to India. When they had returned to London in 1967, the two had shared a flat for a while, and, though Terry had moved out to live with his girlfriend in the summer of 1968, he had remained in daily contact with Sangharakshita, spending much of his time at his flat. Terry was a very gifted and highly intelligent man, but suffered from great emotional instability and had been receiving psychiatric treatment for several years. At times, his difficulties were so great that he considered killing himself. For the past few years his friendship with Sangharakshita had held him back from so drastic a step and Sangharakshita had spent many hours with him, talking him into a more positive mental state when he was feeling suicidal. This placed considerable strains on Sangharakshita's time and energy. Few, if any, Order members realised just how demanding and serious the situation was, and he had to cope with his friend's difficulties mainly on his own, at the same time as setting about the foundation of the FWBO. Eventually, despite all Sangharakshita's efforts, Terry committed suicide in April 1969 by jumping under a London Underground train. The two had been very close friends and this was a deep personal tragedy for Sangharakshita—but he had simply to continue with his work for the movement.

In 1970, Sangharakshita himself nearly died. In the middle of his three month stay in America, he returned briefly to England to lead the annual Easter Retreat at Keffolds. Just before he left America, he caught a severe chill and arrived on the retreat with a high fever. He conducted the evening puja and gave an introductory address, and then retired to bed. During the night, he got up and sat cross-legged in an armchair, feeling that if he continued lying down he would never get up again. He fell into a deeply meditative mood wherein he observed that 'body and mind seemed to have separated and the latter to have withdrawn to a distance of thirty or forty feet'. He realised that he could easily die but 'this consideration did not disturb me in the least. Like the two empty pans of a scale, desire for life and desire for death hung exactly balanced, without even the shadow of turning in either direction. My mood was one of profound tranquillity. Though aware of work unfinished, and friends who still depended on my guidance, I viewed the prospect of departure from it all with absolute unconcern. My usual attitude being one of wanting to finish whatever I had begun, I could not help noticing the difference, though without surprise.' Fortunately for us, Kevin Brooks, a friend who was with him at the time, realised what this mood signified and pleaded with him not to die, telling him how much he still needed him. With this, 'it was as though a hair had been placed in the pan of life, so that, by an infinitesimal fraction, desire for life outweighed desire for death. From that instant I felt energy beginning to flow into me' and he began to recover. When the doctor came next morning, he diagnosed bronchial pneumonia and said that Sangharakshita had had a lucky escape. Within a day, he was sitting up in bed, giving personal interviews to people on the retreat.

Later in 1970, he moved to a new flat in Muswell Hill in North London with two Friends, Kevin Brooks and Graham Sowter (later ordained as Siddhiratna), forming a small community. At the same time, the landlords of the centre in Monmouth Street gave notice that the building was to be pulled down for redevelopment and would have to be vacated by the middle of 1971. He now had to gear the movement up to raise funds and look for a new centre. Once again, he found himself having to exhort Order members to give more time and energy to the work of the movement. In fact, most of the help he got came from relatively new friends and he formed an 'action committee' to find and equip a new centre, consisting mainly of the most active of these, with himself as Chairman. Sangharakshita played a part in fund-raising and was to be seen behind the counter selling bric-a-brac at a jumble sale organised by some Friends—and showing surprising skill as a salesman (although he thinks he was too soft-hearted for the job). By the time the FWBO had to leave the old centre, no new one had been found and the four weekly classes had to be reduced to one composite class at Centre House—and later at a macrobiotic restaurant nearby. Fortunately, most people did stay with the FWBO through that period, which lasted for six months. (The developers' plans were never realised, and the building at 14 Monmouth Street still stands and is in commercial use.)

In January 1972, a North London borough council made available for a few years an old warehouse in Balmore Street in Highgate, pending redevelopment of the area. A Friend, Hugh Evans (soon to be ordained as Buddhadasa), and a few others pitched in to renovate and decorate the place, and classes started in these much more spacious and pleasant premises. Few of the Order members were still actively involved—most having either resigned or ceased to attend classes or help with organisational work. In fact, Sangharakshita had not performed any ordinations since August 1969. Since the level of commitment of existing Order members was, on the whole, not very high, he had decided to wait until he could raise standards. By the time the new centre opened there were signs of a new spirit among some Friends. He began preparing some of these for ordination and, in a sense, the Order had its second birth at Easter 1972 when four very active and wholehearted men were ordained.

Since the area surrounding the centre was scheduled for redevelopment, there were many empty houses awaiting demolition. Several of these houses were squatted by groups of Friends so that the centre became the focus for five or six communities, most of whose members were very involved in its activities. Order members, particularly those newly ordained, were taking more and more of a lead in the running of the movement—although Sangharakshita himself still led three classes a week, attended weekly Order meetings, and ran a class for those who had asked for ordination.

A definite breakthrough had been made and the new Buddhist movement was beginning a life of its own, independent of its founder. Members of the Sarum House community were holding classes and retreats there. One Order member, Akshobhya, who had been ordained in 1968, emigrated to New Zealand in 1971 and started an FWBO group in Auckland. Sangharakshita himself had been going to Brighton each month to take classes and now handed that responsibility over to other Order members. The Glasgow Buddhist Society's members decided that they wanted to become an FWBO group, so an Order member went to Scotland to help them. Vajrabodhi, a Finn ordained in 1972, returned to Helsinki, determined to start an FWBO centre there. The new Buddhist movement was beginning to spread and its founder and head could no longer be identified exclusively with any one centre.

For six years since the founding of the new Buddhist movement and for two years before that whilst he had been at the Hampstead Vihara,

Sangharakshita had been continuously active. He had largely to set aside his literary work and devote himself full time to teaching and organising. The time had come for him to get away. At the beginning of 1973, he left London and went with a friend, Mark Dunlop, to stay in a small chalet on the cliffs in southern Cornwall, overlooking the English Channel. He had decided to take a sabbatical for a year or more, leaving the movement in the care of the Order. He wrote a 'Personal Message to All Friends' shortly after he had gone, which was published in the *FWBO Newsletter* (published quarterly since 1968). He explained that he was *not* going away because he was tired and needed a rest—in fact he had felt more energy recently than he had ever done in his life. Nor was he going away because he was disappointed with the slow pace of development of the movement. Although he was aware that 'the movement is functioning at only a fraction of its optimum capacity' and that 'the majority of members are lukewarm in their commitment to the Three Jewels and lax in their practice of the Path', he was convinced that the FWBO was 'one of the main growing-points of the Higher Evolution in the Western hemisphere'.

Why then had he withdrawn from all programmed activities of the FWBO? 'The key to the mystery is to be found in the word "programmed"'. For so many years he had been involved in an unremitting round of scheduled activities—this had been necessary and he had been quite happy to do it since the movement needed his constant attention in its early years. 'But energy cannot be programmed indefinitely; indeed some kinds of energy cannot be programmed at all, and must either function unprogrammed or remain quiescent. *It is principally in order to release this unprogrammed and unprogrammable energy, long accumulating with me, that I have decided to take a sabbatical.* What this energy will do, once released, no one can say, least of all myself: it is a spirit, and being a spirit it is like the wind, that bloweth where it listeth; but whatever it does will undoubtedly be for the greater good of the movement in general, of myself individually, and all those who come in personal contact with me.'

There was an additional factor to be considered: Order members were now taking more and more responsibility for the running of the movement and needed to be free from Sangharakshita's close supervision in order to take on that responsibility fully for themselves. His withdrawal therefore constituted a definite stage in the training of Order members. It also had a more personal significance. Because he had been so available and so dependable for so long, many people had begun to take him rather for granted and perhaps had ceased to treat him as a human being 'but more as a piece of furniture'. 'Now that the piece of furniture has got up and walked away, it will be possible, I hope, for people to realise that it was not a piece of furniture after all but a human being. They will undoubtedly get more out of me by treating me as an individual than by treating me as a machine, even a spiritual machine. And I shall undoubtedly get more out of them. Indeed, I hope that it will now be possible for some at least of my "unprogrammed energy" to flow into an ever expanding network of spiritual friendships.'

Chapter Seven

THE FOUR GIFTS
1973–1979

I come to you with four gifts.
The first gift is a lotus-flower.
Do you understand?
My second gift is a golden net.
Can you recognize it?
My third gift is a shepherds' round-dance.
Do your feet know how to dance?
My fourth gift is a garden planted in a wilderness.
Could you work there?
I come to you with four gifts.
Dare you accept them?

Sangharakshita (1975)

IN THIS POEM, written in 1975, Sangharakshita represents what he called, in a series of lectures given the following year, 'the four things that the FWBO has to offer the modern man and woman': a method of personal development, a vision of human existence, a nucleus of a new society, and a blueprint for a new world. Whilst the lectures suggest that it is the movement that offers these things, the poem personalises the gifts—they are the poet's gifts, Sangharakshita's gifts. From the time of the creation of the FWBO to the present, he has been offering his gifts to the world with great energy, resourcefulness, mindfulness, and understanding. The movement is the manifestation of these gifts, or rather it *is* these gifts, and Sangharakshita has devoted himself entirely to guiding and inspiring its unfoldment in accordance with the principles he has expounded.

Any account of Sangharakshita's own life must therefore inevitably include something of a history of the FWBO—although there is not space here to give that history in full. During the story of the next twenty-two years we must imagine Sangharakshita at the centre of a network of men and women that grows in size and geographical extent and becomes more and more effective in the world. More and more people take up the method of personal development; the vision of human existence becomes steadily clearer; membership of the nucleus of a new society gradually increases; and the outlines of the new world built according to Sangharakshita's blueprint become ever more discernible. He is able to offer his four gifts to more and more people—and he is surrounded by more and more who help him to offer them.

A Sabbatical Year

From the beginning of 1973 he stepped aside from running the FWBO's centre in London and went to live with his companion in a small chalet on the Cornish coast. Although the area becomes a little busier in the summer season when tourists come to enjoy the beautiful scenery, it is a very quiet spot, with nothing to disturb its tranquillity but the pounding of the sea on the rocks below. One side of the main room of the tiny bungalow was taken up by a large window, looking out over the cliffs on to the sea. By this window Sangharakshita sat: reading, writing, or simply reflecting. He worked on his memoirs, wrote some poetry, and maintained regular correspondence with Order members and Friends in London.

A few people came to visit him, and he once travelled from the chalet to meet several Order members in a caravan in the New Forest, half way between London and Cornwall. He told them that far from feeling out of contact with Order members, he was constantly aware of them. In fact, at times when he was meditating he experienced the whole Order very directly, as if its members were sitting around him in a great circle. But this was no ordinary circle. The Order and the movement represented a distant echo within the world of a transcendental reality: the Order was a mundane reflection of the transcendental Bodhisattva of Compassion, Avalokiteshvara, particularly of Avalokiteshvara in his eleven-headed and thousand-armed form, representing Compassion reaching out to end suffering wherever it may be. It was as if each Order member was one of the hands of Avalokiteshvara, joined to all the other hands in the common spirit of the Bodhisattva.

On this occasion, Sangharakshita made clear the most fundamental principle upon which the Order and the movement rested: 'If anyone should ask, concerning those things which can be changed and those which cannot be changed, the answer is: anything can be changed except the Refuges.' For his new Buddhist movement there was to be no rigid formalism. All that mattered ultimately was that individuals moved forward on the path towards the ideal of human Enlightenment, a movement spoken of in Buddhism as Going for Refuge to the Three Jewels of Buddha, Dharma, and Sangha. The principle of Going for Refuge to the Buddha, Dharma, and Sangha was fundamental and all the precepts and practices could be derived from that. It was clear from these and other reflections that Sangharakshita shared with his disciples during that meeting that the unprogrammed and unprogrammable energy he wished to release by taking a sabbatical was beginning to manifest.

Meanwhile, at the centre in London, after a brief period of uncertainty, Order members had begun to take up the responsibilities left by Sangharakshita, and activities continued as before—and even began to develop further. A new step was taken with the establishment of the FWBO's own publishing wing (later Windhorse Publications), which now brought out its first book: *The Essence of Zen*, a series of four essays by Sangharakshita exploring the basic principles of Zen Buddhism, which had their origin in lectures he had given at the Hampstead Vihara in 1965.

After six months in Cornwall, Sangharakshita moved to a cottage in Norfolk. This part of England, from which his father's family originated, was well known to him from childhood visits to relatives. Situated only a hundred miles north of London, it was a sparsely populated, rural area and Sangharakshita had for some time thought that it might make a good location for a country retreat centre. A Friend, Mary Rawnsley (later Dharmacharini Sulochana), who lived with her family in a large, somewhat decayed, former rectory, had offered it for use by the FWBO. For a few years retreats and other events were regularly held there—the Old Rectory acquiring the Buddhist name Abhirati. Soon after he arrived in Norfolk, Sangharakshita conducted more ordinations during the summer retreat at Abhirati—for the first time not leading the retreat himself, but visiting only to conduct the ceremonies.

Initially, Sangharakshita had had close personal involvement with each person being ordained and had himself helped them to prepare for entry into the Order. From now on, however, he left this more and more to other Order members. He would, of course, get to know each candidate to some extent, satisfying himself that they were ready to take the important step of entering the Western Buddhist Order. But ordination classes and ordination retreats would be arranged by Order members, Sangharakshita usually taking no more part in the retreats than performing the ordinations—at the most conducting study or question and answer sessions. Over the coming years, conferring ordinations was one of Sangharakshita's constant tasks—and one that gave him much pleasure. Each year there would be two or three ordination retreats at different places throughout Britain, which he would attend for just a day or two so as to introduce new men and women into the Order. The number ordained each year has grown steadily from about ten at this period to upwards of fifty at present.

There were four upasaka/upasika ordinations and one maha-upasika ordination on this particular retreat in August 1973—the first time that Sangharakshita had conferred a 'higher' degree of ordination within the Western Buddhist Order. Maha-upasika Gotami had become a member of the Order at its foundation and had been, in many ways, the leading Order member for a number of years, dedicating herself wholeheartedly to the organisational work of the movement and giving many lectures and classes. She was now moving to Glasgow to establish the movement there, and the maha-upasika ordination represented her commitment to a far deeper level of responsibility within the movement. Although she has since resigned from the Order, she made a very important contribution at this early period.

For the rest of that year Sangharakshita remained at the cottage in Norfolk, continuing with literary work and spending time with a few people who came to visit him. He did make one journey to Rotterdam, to see Nel In't Veldt, a psychotherapist who had first come across the FWBO in London and had then attended an FWBO retreat, later ordained as Vajrayogini. Sangharakshita and his teachings had made such an impact on her that she urged him to introduce the FWBO into her own country. The visit enabled him not only to start teaching the Dharma in the Netherlands but also to have extensive discussions with Nel and her friends on the relationship of Buddhism to psychotherapy.

The topic of the relationship between Buddhism and psychotherapy was a very live one for many people involved with the FWBO, even for some Order members. Many had been interested—to varying degrees and for different reasons—in psychology and psychotherapy before becoming involved with the Dharma. Some even equated Buddhism with psychotherapy, seeing meditation, for instance, as a psychotherapeutic technique. Many coming to FWBO classes in that period wanted to explore this issue, and Sangharakshita had given a number of lectures on the subject, making a clear distinction between the Buddhist and psychotherapeutic approaches. Nonetheless, he was constantly having to reassert the difference and to prevent even some Order members from interpreting the Dharma in narrowly psychological terms.

In fact it was obvious that there were still a great many issues to be clarified within the Order—issues on which many Order members were confused. In December 1973, at Abhirati, Sangharakshita conducted the first of a series of study seminars in which he disentangled some of that confusion and shared more deeply and fully his experience of the Dharma. The texts for these seminars, of which there were to be some 150 by 1990, included canonical works from all Buddhist schools, modern presentations of the Dharma, scholarly works on Buddhism, and even texts from other religions or from English literature. He chose as the first text to be studied in this way Shantideva's *Bodhicharyavatara*. Besides being a standard text of Mahayana Buddhism, it was from an English translation of the *Bodhicharyavatara* that he had extracted the Sevenfold Puja, the principal devotional ceremony used throughout the movement.

In this and other seminars, Sangharakshita would meet with a small group of people, usually some eight or twelve in number, for periods of between a weekend and two weeks. Usually, seminars would take place within the context of a retreat, at some quiet location—although sometimes in the midst of the city they would be held in the evenings. The group would sit together in a circle for a few hours each day, and each person would read aloud a passage from the text, on which Sangharakshita would then comment, answer questions—or ask questions in order to provoke discussion. Sometimes lively interchanges would develop between Sangharakshita and other participants and thus he would be drawn to give more and more of his understanding. Discussion would often be quite wide-ranging, diverging from the text to take in subjects that Sangharakshita wanted to comment on or on which members of the group wanted to hear his views.

These seminars became a very important source of guidance for the Order, and for the next few years they were Sangharakshita's principal teaching medium. The discussions often touched on issues that were topical within the movement and so gave Sangharakshita the opportunity to clarify the principles underlying spiritual life in the light of current concerns of Friends and Order members. He was able to use the seminars to disseminate his latest thinking, and sometimes major new initiatives for the movement would emerge out of discussion. Each seminar was tape-recorded, often yielding some forty or fifty hours of valuable material. Over the years, the recordings of all his seminars have been transcribed and many of them have been published in unedited form for circulation within the Order. The seminar on the *Bodhicharyavatara* was transcribed fairly soon after it had taken place and Sangharakshita himself edited it to produce a bulky volume, published as *The Endlessly Fascinating Cry*, providing a commentary on the text as well as an insight into the concerns and preoccupations of Order members at that time. Over the next years, the editing of the transcripts of seminars and passages from seminars was one of Sangharakshita's principal literary endeavours.

He had to move again, early in 1974, this time to a cottage rented by an Order member, situated in a Suffolk pine plantation through which occasionally echoed the roar of jet engines from a nearby US Air Force base. Besides leading another seminar at Abhirati, on the *Sutra of Hui Neng*, he travelled to Aryatara for the first Convention of the Western Buddhist Order, attended by twenty-nine Order members. The event began with five more ordinations, and two days of intense discussion followed on such topics as meditation, the difficulty of finding work that supported spiritual practice, how to broaden the range of people involved with the movement, and what Order members' precise legal status was in Britain. Sangharakshita exhorted Order members to have more confidence in themselves, saying that, whereas most worldly organisations ran on 'high-powered neurotic energy' the reverse was true in the WBO where at this stage people tended to suffer from lack of self-confidence.

Several essential elements of the Order's functioning were established during this event. On the first Friday (later changed to Sunday) of each month at 7pm GMT there was to be a simultaneous world-wide Order Metta Bhavana meditation, during which each Order member would direct *metta* or 'loving-kindness' to every other. All Order members were to try to join in this practice, no matter where they were, as a means of evoking the underlying spirit of the Order. A monthly unedited newsletter, *Shabda*, to which all Order members could contribute, was to be compiled for circulation within the Order to keep them in touch with each other. Since it was no longer possible for Sangharakshita himself to have personal contact with all those who asked for ordination, each candidate was to have two *kalyana mitras* or 'spiritual friends', senior Order members who were to keep in close touch with them, help them to prepare for ordination, and advise Sangharakshita when they thought their mitra (literally 'friend') was ready to be ordained. Kalyana Mitra relationships were to be approved by Sangharakshita himself and he would perform a brief ceremony, establishing a connection between the people concerned. An Order Convenor, Master of Ceremonies, and a Librarian and Archivist were appointed as officers of the Order, in this way devolving more responsibility from Sangharakshita.

Although Sangharakshita had little to do with the day-to-day organisation of FWBO activities, he kept a close eye on what was happening. At this time he saw that all was not well at the principal FWBO centre and, soon after the Convention, he called an informal meeting of the council that ran the London centre, vigorously taking its members to task for their organisational inefficiency. He instigated a minor revolution, urging most of the older Order members to establish FWBO centres elsewhere and encouraging some young, newly ordained members to take over responsibility for the running of activities in London.

A few weeks later he was back in London again, this time to lead a retreat for Friends from the newly established Glasgow centre together with Dutch friends of Nel In't Veldt, most of whom were involved with her Gestalt psychotherapy work. Each day Sangharakshita would answer questions arising out of study of his lectures on 'The Buddha's Noble Eightfold Path'. A particular emphasis that arose during these sessions was on the need to have the confidence to act in accordance with one's spiritual vision. The combination of young and somewhat raw Scots and rather questioning Dutch people with definite views of their own produced a very lively retreat. On his return to Norfolk he led study on another series of talks during a men's retreat at Abhirati.

A Country Vihara

Sangharakshita returned to Cornwall for a further few months. This time, however, he did not keep himself as aloof as he had done previously and held a seminar on the *Udana* for a group of Order members, who camped in fields near the chalet. In August, he was finally able to settle with Mark Dunlop (later ordained as Vajrakumara) in his own small vihara in the village of Castle Acre in Norfolk, bought with a generous donation from Dharmachari Buddhadasa. Here he established a pattern that was to be continued over the coming years. He would spend periods in relative seclusion, working on various literary projects and seeing a few people who came to stay with him at the vihara, and then would make forays out into the world: to London to visit the centre there, to other groups and centres throughout Britain, and even occasionally overseas. In this way he was able to keep up some writing at the same time as continuing to guide, inspire, and stimulate the Order and movement. He strongly encouraged several Order members and Friends to move to Norfolk, seeing it as a potential stronghold of the FWBO. A community of sorts had been formed at Abhirati (although this did not last long), two Order members came to live in a neighbouring village and were able to help him in various ways and, later, several Order members moved to Norwich, the county town of Norfolk.

From the relative seclusion of his vihara, he journeyed to Abhirati for a seminar on *Outlines of Mahayana Buddhism*, by D.T. Suzuki, a noted Japanese Buddhist writer, who had been the main exponent of Zen Buddhism in the West. In the course of study, it emerged that Suzuki was guilty of great imprecision in his use of language and that often the vagueness of his terminology led him into gross error. This was a salutary lesson—for Suzuki was at that time one of the better writers on Buddhism and his work was widely known in the West. If even he, a committed Buddhist and sincere practitioner, could disseminate such confusion, what of the many other works available on Buddhism? It became clearer than ever that Sangharakshita's literary work was of exceptional importance, providing as it did a clear, accurate, and committed account of the Dharma. The seminars too were of great significance since, among other things, they gave his disciples a training in a critical approach to the reading of literature on Buddhism—indeed, to reading in general.

Another journey took him to London for a very satisfying occasion—the resolution of a long standing breach. When Sangharakshita had been excluded from the Hampstead Buddhist Vihara in 1966, Christmas Humphreys, the President of the Buddhist Society, had added his voice to the Trustees', telling Sangharakshita that he should not return to England. Since then Mr Humphreys and the Society had had no contact with Sangharakshita or the FWBO, refusing to recognise them as part of the British Buddhist scene. However, more recently, owing to the good offices of Burt Taylor, the new General Secretary of the Society, friendly relations had been opened up. Indeed, Mr Humphreys invited Sangharakshita to give a lecture at the Society, himself taking the chair—a real sign of reconciliation. This lecture, given in October 1974, on 'The Path of Regular and the Path of Irregular Steps', was attended by so many people that the Buddhist Society's lecture hall was swamped and many had to listen to it over a loudspeaker in another room. From that time until Mr Humphreys's death, Sangharakshita and he would meet once or twice a year—Sangharakshita was one of his oldest acquaintances and one of the few he could talk to about the earlier days of Buddhism in Britain. The formidable old President was clearly fascinated by the FWBO and saw it as the true successor to his own work—which in certain respects it was, since Christmas Humphreys's approach had been definitely non-sectarian and he was certainly not in favour of monastic formalism.

Later in 1974 another step was taken in the Order's relations with the wider Buddhist world. Geshe Rabten, a prominent Tibetan Gelugpa lama who had been deputed by the Dalai Lama to teach Westerners, was visiting England and an opportunity had arisen to invite him to meet Order members. After earlier experiences of other teachers at FWBO functions, there was much debate within the Order about inviting him. Sangharakshita himself had to step in to clarify the issue. He was of the opinion that the majority of Order members and Friends had, at this stage, very little to gain from contact with 'Buddhist' organisations in Britain—in fact until Order members possessed a 'high degree of spiritual vitality' such contact could do more harm than good. However, he pointed out, the Order did belong within the Buddhist tradition and was therefore connected, however indirectly, to the rest of the Buddhist world. Sooner or later, contact would have to be established with that Buddhist world so that, for one thing, what the FWBO had created would be able to act as a model for the spiritual renewal of other Buddhists—however, this could only take place once the movement really had something to offer. Nonetheless, since Geshe Rabten was, by all accounts, a genuine spiritual personality and was only in England on a visit, not to gain disciples of his own, then to give him a reception would not be a bad thing. In the event, a very cordial meeting took place, in which Sangharakshita introduced the lama to all the members of the Order present and Geshe Rabten gave a short Dharma talk.

One of Sangharakshita's major tasks over the next few years was visiting and inspiring the various FWBO centres that were beginning to spring up in Britain and overseas. There were now groups in three different areas of London, in Cornwall, Glasgow, Brighton, Norfolk, Helsinki in Finland, and Auckland and Christchurch in New Zealand. In their early stages, these fledgeling groups were often very fragile and needed a lot of support. A visit from the founder and spiritual teacher was always a very great boost. In the course of his stay Sangharakshita would get together with the local Order members individually and would have personal discussion with anyone else who wanted to see him. He was very keen to make contacts with people coming to the centre and would spend quite a bit of time with any promising Friends with whom he found himself getting on well. Besides this he would give talks, answer questions, lead discussion groups and conduct pujas at the centre. Sometimes, if the local Order members had been effective with publicity, there would be representatives of the press or radio and television wanting to interview him.

While he was visiting a centre, he would not confine his interests simply to the local FWBO: he would always want to find out about the history and culture of the place in which it was situated, visiting art galleries, museums, and famous sites—his interests were wide-ranging, indeed, encompassing the literature, history, geography, art, architecture, the people, and the flora and fauna. He would often write up an account of his more important tours for *Shabda*—some of which have been collected and published as *Travel Letters*. These open letters from various parts of the world were one of the literary forms he exploited at a time when he was too busy for more concentrated writing, and they are a fascinating record of his experience.

He visited Helsinki for a week in April 1974, giving a boost to the small Finnish sangha and attracting some media attention. At the end of the year, after a visit to the Glasgow group, he flew to the other side of the world, paying his first visit to the two FWBO groups in New Zealand. The Auckland centre had been started by Dharmachari Akshobhya, who had been ordained in England before emigrating to New Zealand, whilst the Christchurch centre was founded independently by Lim Poi Chen, a Chinese Malaysian who had discovered the FWBO in New Zealand through Sangharakshita's books. Each centre had attracted quite a number of people who were seriously interested in the Dharma. Sangharakshita spent two weeks at each, conducting study on his book, *The Three Jewels*, and meeting Friends. He led a retreat set in the beautiful New Zealand bush, attended Order gatherings, and gave a series of three well-attended public lectures. During his visit he initiated the Order in New Zealand, conducting the ordinations of eleven men and women. In addition to these basic ordinations into the Western Buddhist Order, Sangharakshita experimented with two other forms of ordination. For the last time he gave an ordination in his old capacity as a Theravadin bhikkhu: he ordained the founder of the Christchurch centre, who had earlier been ordained into the Western Buddhist Order with the name Dhammajyoti, as a *samanera* or 'novice monk'. Dhammajyoti took the *samanera* ordination because he wanted to study in a traditional context and had made arrangements to stay at a Chinese monastery in America for two years. However, Sangharakshita made it very clear that this 'monastic' ordination did not take place within the context of the Western Buddhist Order but was a special arrangement simply to enable Dhammajyoti to study Chinese Buddhism. At a final Order Day, just before his departure, Sangharakshita conferred the maha-upasaka ordination on Akshobhya and later gave him the Bodhisattva Vows.

This was, in fact, the last time that Sangharakshita conferred the maha-upasaka ordination and the first and last time he administered the Bodhisattva Vows—indeed, he had only given a 'higher' ordination on one other occasion. He later came to consider that higher ordinations were unnecessary and even a mistake, since they tended to distract from the primary commitment made on entry into the Order. Ordination is identical with the act of Going for Refuge to the Three Jewels of Buddha, Dharma, and Sangha. Although that act has to be repeated on deeper and deeper levels throughout one's spiritual life, commitment to that repetition is implicit in the one ordination and needs no further restatement. Furthermore, he has come to see that the Bodhisattva Vow is also implicit in the basic ordination. Going for Refuge itself necessarily implies altruism, and the Bodhisattva Ideal is simply that altruistic dimension of Going for Refuge. It therefore requires no separate expression.

Again, he considers that the 'monastic ordination', whether *samanera* or bhikkhu, represents the taking up of a particular life-style in pursuance of Going for Refuge, not a separate ordination. He has therefore never again conferred monastic ordination, and has introduced the anagarika *vow*—*not* ordination—for those who wish publicly to commit themselves to the celibate life. Here he has followed a well-established modern tradition of anagarikahood, which he himself had observed in 1947, and which had been taken by such Buddhist activists as Anagarika Dharmapala, who wished to work for the good of Buddhism without the restrictions that the *vinaya* rules of a bhikkhu would have imposed upon his activities. None of this was clear to Sangharakshita at this time, however. Gradually it has become more and more apparent that ordination within the WBO, although completely faithful to the Buddha's teaching, does not fit into the categories of traditional Buddhism, but constitutes something quite new and distinctive.

On his return to London in February 1975, Sangharakshita was taken directly from the airport to London's East End, to see a large, derelict former fire-station that local Order members were hoping to secure as the new London centre of the FWBO. Despite the amount of work that would obviously be needed to open it to the public, he saw the potential of the building and strongly urged that it be taken on. He then returned to his usual pattern of activities: basing himself at his vihara in Norfolk and making visits to the various centres, conducting ordinations, and leading study seminars. During one month he led three seminars—on the *Udana*, a text from the Pali Canon; *Dhyana for Beginners*, by the Chinese master, Chih-I; and *The Door of Liberation*, a compilation of Tibetan works by the Mongolian lama Geshe Wangyal. He then visited the Glasgow and Brighton centres and once more went to Helsinki, this time for four weeks. A few weeks later, he conducted a retreat in Holland—this proved a rather difficult event since most of these people had a prior involvement in Gestalt psychotherapy and were reluctant to accept the devotional side of Buddhism, expressing their reservations in no uncertain terms.

In August, he presided over the second Order Convention, at which, during eight days of meetings, forty or more Order members discussed the functioning of the Order. Once more Sangharakshita was able to clarify some areas of confusion and give the assembled Order members fresh inspiration for their individual practice and their common task. Topics considered included different ways of teaching the Dharma, the functioning of the Kalyana Mitra system, the recognition by the Order of FWBO centres, the development of devotional practices and artistic activities, and social and political involvement by Order members. The Convention concluded on Sangharakshita's fiftieth birthday.

Then there were more visits to FWBO centres and another talk under the Buddhist Society's auspices, this time held in much larger premises. All the while, Sangharakshita continued with his literary work. Even when he was not able to remain at his vihara in Norfolk, he would try to keep the mornings free from other activities so that he could keep up with his growing correspondence and carry on with whatever writing projects he had in hand. Because his time was so much broken up during this period, he could not take on any writing project that demanded uninterrupted concentration. He therefore used what media were available to him to the full, principally preparing his seminars and lectures for publication in written form. He took advantage of another medium by contributing reviews to the *FWBO Newsletter*, mainly of new books on Buddhism but including some on general topics he thought were of importance to the movement. In this way he was able to guide Order members and mitras in their reading—but he also used the reviews to make several points of his own, arising out of the material in the books under review, thus making much more than is usual of that relatively humble medium. In the Autumn 1975 issue of the *Newsletter*, for instance, there appeared a review by him (now published in a collection of reviews and articles entitled *Alternative Traditions*) of *The Heritage of the Bhikkhu*, by the famous Sinhalese bhikkhu, Walpola Rahula, mercilessly exposing the spiritual bankruptcy of his 'religio-nationalism', and showing that the widespread belief amongst Sinhalese people that Buddhism is their 'national religion', a belief that has much to do with the present civil strife in that country, is inimical to the Dharma itself.

THE NEW LONDON BUDDHIST CENTRE

Work had by now started converting the old fire station in East London into the new London centre of the FWBO. The five-storey building was eventually to contain a community of up to thirty men, a large public centre with two shrine-rooms, and the headquarters of a Right Livelihood co-operative with several businesses attached. A team of twelve men Order members, mitras, and Friends had moved into the derelict building in June 1974 and camped in the crumbling rooms. Slowly they began to bring order to the building. It had initially been projected that the new centre would be open after a year of work—in the event it took three-and-a-half years and demanded very much more money than had been anticipated. Nonetheless, although the building project did slow down FWBO activities in London for a period, it proved a very important laboratory in which were developed many of the institutions and attitudes that have now become central to the FWBO.

For a start, the conversion work had to be financed, and Order members, mitras, and Friends had to come to terms with the fact that a lot of money had to be raised. Many people in the movement, coming from a vaguely hippie background, were very uneasy about money, conceiving of it as essentially corrupt and 'unspiritual'. Sangharakshita emphasised again and again that a spiritual movement needs money if it is to have any significant impact on the world and if it is to help individuals to develop. Fortunately, the raising of funds was taken on by Dharmachari Lokamitra, who proved himself very able at mobilising the energies of the movement.

Again, many in the FWBO did not associate the spiritual life with work, particularly with hard physical labour, such as on a building site. But it was soon found that working for such a clearly beneficial enterprise has a highly positive effect. Working hard together on a common project developed a strong sense of comradeship, which provided a basis for spiritual community. Then many young people have energies that need a direct, physical outlet. Finally, in working with others against the background of the Dharma, one can learn much about oneself and can use the work itself as a means of development. Once again, Sangharakshita himself had to make all these points clear, spurring on the workers and teaching them the deeper significance of what they were doing.

It became obvious that steps had to be taken to ensure that, once the building was opened, Order members, mitras, and Friends could continue working together in some way. Starting with Friends Foods, a wholefood shop pioneered by Dharmachari Ratnaguna, businesses were established during the course of the project so as to raise funds when other sources ran dry. These laid the foundations for what came to be called Right Livelihood businesses, now so central to the FWBO. This is perhaps one of the more radical of Sangharakshita's applications of the Buddha's teaching to modern times. The Buddha himself had seen that the way in which we earn our living has to be part of our spiritual practice, and he had discussed Right Livelihood as one of the eight principal aspects of his most basic formulation of the path: the Noble Eightfold Path. The Buddha's teaching emphasised the ethical aspects of work, but Sangharakshita drew out more fully its psychological and spiritual implications, eventually showing that working with others in a Right Livelihood business could itself be a means of spiritual evolution, even of transcendental realisation. This has proved a particularly powerful tool for people living in the modern world, so dominated by economic activity. It was at this time that Sangharakshita began to work out these principles.

The twenty or so men living in the building had to organise themselves as a community in a much more thorough and systematic way than had ever happened before in the FWBO. Not without some pain at times, they learnt many lessons about community life. Originally it had been projected that there would be two communities in the building, one for men and one for women, but it soon became clear to those living there that this would not be appropriate. Life in the community was, on the whole, very positive, benefiting particularly from the fact that it was single-sex. There was a noticeable lack of sexual tension and of the polarisation and game playing so common in mixed company, especially when many are still quite young. It seemed as if men could more easily develop a softer, more receptive side of themselves in that situation, without losing their initiative and drive. That benefit would to some extent be lost by having a women's community on the next floor—as it would be to such a women's community too, for similar benefits of single-sex situations had been noticed by women. Sangharakshita recommended that there should be only one, men's, community on the premises, a women's community being sited elsewhere.

In fact, with the establishment of the community at the new centre, the whole idea of single-sex living and working took a step forward and Sangharakshita was able to draw out its benefits and lessons much more clearly. Since the idea of single-sex activities went so much against the mood of the times, there was, among some people, a certain amount of resistance and even reaction to it. Sangharakshita patiently and persistently clarified issues and imparted confidence and understanding, so that gradually the idea of separate activities for men and women became generally accepted within the movement.

What the period of building and preparation of the new London centre showed was a glimpse of a new Buddhist world that provided a complete environment in which everything supported the development of the individual. Committed Buddhists could live, work, and play together, without any need to look beyond that world—except to draw in new people. This vision was embodied in the name Sangharakshita gave to the community: Sukhavati, 'Land of Bliss' or 'Pure Land'—the ideal world of Mahayana myth, created out of the vow of the Buddha Amitabha. When he was a Bodhisattva, Amitabha vowed, it is said, that on becoming a Buddha he would form around him a world of the utmost beauty and perfection into which those who called upon him would be reborn. Here they would find all they needed to lead them to Enlightenment. Sukhavati, the Pure Land, symbolises that ideal environment whose every element aids progress on the path. It was a Pure Land that the FWBO sought to establish—what Sangharakshita came to call the 'New Society'. The creation of the London Buddhist Centre and Sukhavati community gave people in the movement a glimpse of what was possible in the future.

Sangharakshita gave a great deal of time and attention to this project, inspiring the workers, overseeing plans for the images and shrine-rooms, and clarifying issues arising for the men living and working together. Early in 1976 he came to stay for six weeks in a small flat that had been prepared for him in the community and thereafter he was a frequent visitor. During his stay in Sukhavati the third Convention of the Order was held at a nearby hall and, over four days, a variety of topics were considered by the fifty or so Order members attending—out of a total

Order of sixty. Sangharakshita emphasised that the Order transcended all boundaries, including those of class and nationality—he wanted to see the movement spread beyond the south of England, which was still its stronghold. He also explored the nature of the visualisation practices that all Order members can take up after ordination, stressing that they represent a contemplation of the goal of the spiritual life. The mitra system was now widened to include mitras who could not yet find Kalyana Mitras. Instead of being linked to two Order members, each mitra would be the general responsibility of the local Order chapter. Finally, Sangharakshita led a discussion on the place of vows in the spiritual development of an Order member.

That same year at last saw the publication by William Heinemann, a leading London publisher, of *The Thousand-Petalled Lotus*, the first volume of Sangharakshita's memoirs, dealing with his life until he settled in Kalimpong in 1950—albeit shorn, at the publisher's request, of the first nineteen years of his life (later published separately as *Learning to Walk*). The book was given a positive reception by the press. One distinguished reviewer, Christopher Wordsworth, wrote in the *Observer*, at that time one of the two 'quality' Sunday newspapers, 'His book presents an extraordinary panorama of [India] and overflows with more close quarters experiences, both seamy and serene, than most more worldly travellers could pack into several lifetimes.' Another reviewer in the *Times Literary Supplement* compared his prose to that of E.M. Forster. Since it is a straightforward work of considerable literary merit, which does not 'preach' Buddhism though it is suffused with the Buddhist perspective, the work is accessible to many who might never consider reading a book about the Dharma, perhaps opening them to Sangharakshita's teaching and the movement he has founded. It also offers an invaluable insight into Indian life—particularly throwing light on the iniquitous caste system and thereby preparing the ground for the later work of the movement in raising funds for their Indian brothers and sisters.

Sangharakshita had not only been engaged in writing; he had, as always, been reading a great deal. At this period he was very interested in the work of William Blake, the English poet, artist, and visionary, finding much in his view of life that was of relevance to Western Buddhists. Later, in 1977, he wrote an article on the subject for the *FWBO Newsletter*, entitled 'Buddhism and William Blake'. This interest was part of a pattern. Since his return to England he had been looking into various aspects of Western culture that might provide some sort of connection with Buddhism. For instance, early on he had been very interested in the

Arthurian legends of the quest for the Holy Grail. He considered that the symbolism of these legends was not merely Christian but touched on deep and universal themes, some of which had a bearing on the spiritual path. Later he researched into a widespread medieval religious movement in southern Europe of very dedicated and mystically inclined pacifists known as 'Cathars' or 'Pure Ones'. Although calling themselves Christians, the Cathars had some things in common with Buddhists. He later aired his views on these connections in a book review, later published in *Alternative Traditions*.

These and other researches were part of Sangharakshita's quest for roots for Buddhism within Western culture. He knew that his new Buddhist movement needed not only the traditional Buddhist teachings and practices but a way into the depths of the Western mind. So many Western Buddhists are Buddhists only on the surface: their deeper psychic life is not connected to Buddhism at all—often it is still essentially Christian. By seeking aspects of Western culture that have affinities with Buddhism, Sangharakshita has tried to reveal ways in which his Western disciples may transform their own inner depths, as well as appeal to the depths in others around them. And there are many currents in Western culture, usually outside Christianity, that do provide a link with Buddhism and that are clearly steps of a kind upon the Path of the Higher Evolution. Sangharakshita continues his research into these 'alternative traditions', especially into Neoplatonism, which has been a lifelong interest.

PADMALOKA

Whilst the London Buddhist Centre was being prepared, activities were developing in Norfolk. A centre had been set up in Norwich and a search had been taking place for a country retreat centre. In June 1976, Sangharakshita sold his own vihara and, together with Vajrakumara, purchased a substantial house in the Norfolk countryside with six acres of land and several outbuildings. This became Padmaloka: Sangharakshita's own headquarters, the base for the Office of the Western Buddhist Order, and the main men's retreat centre. Padmaloka also housed a community of six men who looked after the property, organised the retreats, and did some secretarial work for Sangharakshita. For the first time since he had been in India, Sangharakshita was able to collect all his books, papers, images, and thangkas in one place. In a pleasant, spacious room at the front of the building he had his study, lined with books and with a fine view of the grounds. For the next thirteen years this was his principal residence, to which he constantly returned from his many journeys. Soon he was able to conduct a series of seminars here, thereby injecting fresh clarity and inspiration into the Order and movement.

Other developments had been taking place elsewhere. Three Order members had decided to establish a centre in Manchester, in the north of England, thus for the first time taking the FWBO out of the more affluent southern part of the country. A team of women took on two adjacent derelict houses in East London and set about renovating them for use as a large women's community, known as Amaravati. Efforts were also made to establish Right Livelihood projects for the women in the community, the most successful of these being a typesetting business. The establishment of Amaravati was a very significant development since it represented women in the movement taking a much more active and independent role than previously. Until then, most of the major initiatives had come from men, women by and large playing a supporting part. To some extent, as Sangharakshita pointed out, women in the movement were tending to reproduce social convention by their collective dependency on the men. He strongly encouraged them to start breaking out of this pattern, and the establishment of Amaravati was a decisive step in this process, particularly as it involved a lot of building work, traditionally seen as 'men's work'. Sangharakshita gave a lot of encouragement to women in the movement, holding seminars for them and visiting Amaravati from time to time—the majority of his personal interviews were with women. His emphasis at this time was on women becoming more self-reliant and self-confident and this began to manifest in the growing strength of the women's wing of the movement.

Towards the end of 1976, he spent three months at Sukhavati, travelling to Brighton to give four talks on 'What the FWBO has to Offer the Modern Man and Woman'—describing his own four gifts. He then gave another major series of eight lectures in London, the first of its kind for four years, this time on 'Transformation of Life and World in the *Sutra of Golden Light*'. The lectures were held in a spacious town hall in North London, very near the Hampstead Buddhist Vihara, and some three hundred people came to hear each one, some of them travelling a long distance to be there. With the large and vigorous community at Sukhavati and more centres elsewhere in Britain, the number of those definitely committed to the movement had grown considerably and, on this occasion, Sangharakshita was addressing an audience made up substantially of that committed core. He could therefore speak in an even more direct and inspired manner than ever before, and these lectures had a special magic to them that had a profound impact on those who attended. It seemed that Sangharakshita was not simply explaining an ancient Buddhist text but was releasing the transcendental power woven into the sutra itself—allowing the Golden Light of Reality to shine forth, transforming, as he said, both life and world.

Sangharakshita began the following year, 1977, by taking a three month retreat with a friend, Andy Friends (now Dharmachari Subhadra), on the island of Arran, off the west coast of Scotland. Here he continued with his study and writing—breaking his retreat for a few days to conduct ordinations on another island, near Glasgow. Returning to Padmaloka, he continued with his round of activities: leading seminars, conducting ordinations, giving personal interviews, and making the occasional visit to one or other of the English centres. Towards the end of the year he again went to Finland, this time for ten days, his visit as usual giving fresh inspiration and clarity to Order members, mitras, and Friends in Helsinki.

In October 1977, Lokamitra, one of Sangharakshita's most senior and active disciples, began a six-month visit to India, principally to study hatha yoga, but also to make a pilgrimage to the Buddhist holy places and to see some of Sangharakshita's old haunts. For Sangharakshita this represented an opportunity for a first link between his work in the West and the work he had left uncompleted in India some ten years before. He gave Lokamitra introductions to several of his old disciples and friends in Poona, and when Lokamitra met some of them, he found that they had not forgotten Sangharakshita and the work he had done among them. They were very eager that Lokamitra should now conduct some Dharma activities for them himself. He led three meditation classes each week for a few weeks, conducted study groups, and held a week-long retreat for some of the people attending his classes. He wrote from Poona: 'I think it very likely that once the FWBO gets going in India, among the ex-Untouchables, it will be the fastest growing area of our activities.... Twenty years ago a few million people changed their religion. They therefore want to know how to live, practise, and develop as Buddhists. It is vitally important to them.... As far as I can see there is no one, besides [Sangharakshita], and no other movement [besides the FWBO], capable of working with the situation.'

By the time Lokamitra returned to England in March 1978, he had decided that he would himself take on the work of developing the FWBO in India. This decision naturally was a very significant one for

Sangharakshita, and one that gave him great pleasure. Although he had not had contact with the new Buddhists of India for more than ten years, he had not forgotten them. For some time he had been hoping that it would be possible to carry the FWBO to India and now the opportunity had come. Lokamitra had also been to Kalimpong and had visited Dhardo Rimpoche at his school, taking him a traditional Tibetan white scarf from Sangharakshita as well as a selection of FWBO publications. Dhardo Rimpoche was delighted to see disciples of Sangharakshita, making it clear that he considered that they were his disciples too. Sangharakshita had asked Lokamitra to find out what the financial situation of the school was—it was obviously very poor indeed. Lokamitra and Sangharakshita therefore decided that they would ask people in the movement to contribute towards the school's upkeep and development and an appeal was soon launched. From that time on, the school has been supported principally with funds raised by the FWBO.

During this period, Sangharakshita had been at work on what was for him a rather unusual literary project. He wrote and published a pamphlet, *Buddhism and Blasphemy*, shedding Buddhist light on a issue topical in England at that time, for blasphemy had, for a while, been very much in the public eye. In 1977, *Gay News*, a newspaper for homosexuals published in Britain, had printed a poem that appeared to suggest Jesus Christ was homosexual. It is a common law offence in England to speak or write impiously or irreverently about what Christians hold sacred, and the publishers and editor of *Gay News* had been tried for blasphemy, the first time the law against blasphemy had been invoked for many years. They were found guilty and an appeal against the conviction was dismissed.

Sangharakshita considered that the Buddhist voice must be heard on this issue since it had implications for all Buddhists in England. First of all, Buddhists could theoretically be prosecuted for openly denying the existence of God, since Buddhism is non-theistic. This meant that, in England, there was a definite limitation on freedom of religious expression. It was perhaps rather unlikely that any prosecution would be brought against Buddhists who gave a reasoned account of their non-belief—although the fact that one could even theoretically be brought gave pause enough for thought. However, Sangharakshita went further, arguing that, in order to free themselves from the psychological restrictions of their Christian conditioning, some people might *need* to openly express themselves impiously or irreverently about God—and they might not necessarily be able to do that in a reasoned and moderate way.

In forbidding blasphemous expression, the law denied an important therapeutic possibility by means of which those who felt restricted and cramped by their Christian past could free themselves of it. He argued that the law should be changed so that blasphemy was no longer a criminal offence. Some maintained that, far from blasphemy being decriminalised, the offence should be extended to include blasphemy against the sacred objects of other religions, including Buddhism. This Sangharakshita vigorously rejected. Buddhism, he said, needed no such protection.

Twice reprinted, *Buddhism and Blasphemy* was widely circulated amongst politicians, churchmen, journalists, and others. It was quoted in parliamentary debate and submitted to a Law Commission on reform of the criminal law. Sangharakshita's venture into the political arena stimulated some public interest and he made a number of useful contacts, especially as some prominent public figures were very favourably impressed by his thinking.

In 1978 fell the tenth anniversary of the founding of the Order. It was marked, in April, during the fourth Order Convention, attended by some seventy out of the total of ninety or so members of the Order, from England, Scotland, the Netherlands, Finland, and New Zealand—as well as, of course, from India, since Lokamitra was now committed to returning. With so many attending it was not possible to have the discussion sessions in which everyone participated that had been the principal feature of the three previous Conventions. This time, there were Dharma study groups, led by experienced Order members, together with lectures, group meditation, and special pujas.

Sangharakshita played a major part in the event, stressing the importance of Order members coming together in this way, so that they could get to know each other better, strengthen their common commitment, and renew their inspiration and positivity by dwelling together in the realm of the Dharma. He led all the events, chaired talks, and gave three important talks himself. The first of these, 'A System of Meditation', set out the meditation practices performed within the movement as a progression, leading to Enlightenment itself. In 'Going for Refuge' he showed that the act of Going for Refuge is dynamic and takes place on a number of different levels—indeed, Going for Refuge on ever deeper levels could be said to constitute the Path itself. Finally, in 'A Vision of History', he showed that the proper concern of history is with the struggle between the group and the spiritual community—rather than with the struggles of empires or nation-states. He briefly traced the history of various spiritual communities down the ages and then asserted that the Western Buddhist Order represented the spiritual community in a particularly pure and uncompromising form. Finally, he stressed that such a community is always in non-violent confrontation with the group. The Order should go on the offensive much more: Order members should go out into the world and draw individuals into the spiritual community since the spiritual community always needs more individuals so that it can outweigh the group—and thereby exercise a civilising influence upon it.

The Order Convention marked the beginning of the final phase of the building project at Sukhavati—all the money was now available, plans had been finalised, and a work-force of some forty Order members, mitras, and Friends was assembled. Work progressed to schedule and the centre was finally opened by Sangharakshita in a very moving ceremony—for which he had written a special poem—in November 1978. Opening celebrations were spread over a week, culminating in a talk given by Sangharakshita in a large public hall on 'Authority and the Individual in the New Society'. Widespread press, radio, and TV coverage attracted many people to the new centre and there were packed classes every night of the week from then on.

Sangharakshita brought his mother and sister to visit the new centre shortly after it was opened, and his mother was particularly impressed by the Buddha-images Chintamani had sculpted for the shrine-rooms. Sangharakshita had been to see both his mother and his father a few days after his return from India in 1964. Even though he had had no contact with them since he started his wandering in India in 1947, they had each greeted him without a hint of reproach and were very accepting of what he was doing—indeed were both very interested in his Buddhist activities. His father died not long after his return but he remained in regular contact with his mother. In fact, from this point on, he saw her more frequently than he had done previously, since she was getting quite old. As time went by, she came to consider herself a Buddhist and was very supportive of the FWBO's work in India, often giving money 'for the little children'.

The opening of the London Buddhist Centre marked a very important stage in the unfoldment of Sangharakshita's vision for there were offered all four of his gifts in one comprehensive package: the methods of personal development were taught in classes at the centre; courses and study groups examined the vision of human existence; a number of Order members were gathered together in and around the centre, forming the nucleus of a new society; and the triad of centre, community, and Right Livelihood business presented a complete new way of life, forming a rudimentary blueprint for a new world. Although all this was still only in its rudimentary form, the new centre represented a significant breakthrough, for at last it was possible for people inside and outside the movement actually to glimpse an embodiment of the vision that Sangharakshita had for so long been holding up to them. At last it was possible to see more concretely what the four gifts were that he was offering. And more and more people did dare to accept them.

Chapter Eight

HANDING ON
1979–1989

Cavern or shed, in the one-candled gloom
We know not; through the black hole of the door
The desert, where red winds howl evermore:
Within, Christ's peace; without, impending doom.
Gigantically crouched in little room,
A lion against his feet upon the floor,
St Jérome sits, the dropping sands before,
The skull beside him where the shadows loom
Blacker and blacker. In a world of sin
The empire changes hands, the Churches fight
Factious as dogs. By day the old man, stung,
Magnificently answers Augustine,
Then, dredging from the deep, night after night
Translates THE WORD into the vulgar tongue.

Sangharakshita (1968)

RETURN TO INDIA

LOKAMITRA RETURNED TO INDIA in the summer of 1978 and immediately set about establishing the FWBO in Poona—or rather the TBMSG. Since the movement in India could clearly not be considered 'Western', Sangharakshita suggested that it should be known there as the Trailokya Bauddha Mahasangha Sahayak Gana—literally, the 'Association of Helpers of the Spiritual Community of the Three Worlds'—the Order being known as the Trailokya Bauddha Mahasangha or TBM. The 'Trailokya' or 'Three Worlds' expressed the inclusive nature of the movement, the phrase encompassing both the traditional Buddhist stratification of the universe into the three worlds of sensuous experience, archetypal form, and extremely subtle archetypal form, as well as Winston Churchill's notion of the First, Second, and Third Worlds of modern geopolitics.

Lokamitra conducted the first mitra ceremonies just a few weeks after his arrival and it was not long before he had a flourishing, if embryonic, movement on his hands. The time had come for Sangharakshita himself to return to India after an absence of twelve years.

In February 1979, he flew to Bombay. He spent a day or two in the city, re-encountering friends he had not seen in all those years, and then moved on to Poona where he remained for the next two weeks. He had anticipated that his old friends and pupils in Poona would have forgotten him, but this was far from being the case—in fact, he says, not only had they not forgotten him, they had been waiting for him to come back and were overjoyed to see him. As visitors poured in to meet him, he found himself remembering the faces, even the names, of hundreds of men and women whom he had known quite well even fifteen or twenty years before—and he, of course, was delighted to see them. Invitations to give lectures flooded in from all quarters of Maharashtra, and it became obvious that Sangharakshita had left a vivid impression on the Buddhists of that state, more especially since there had been no real Dharma work done there since his departure.

He gave several talks in Buddhist localities throughout Poona, in one of which he gave a vivid description of the Windhorse mural by Padmapani at the London Buddhist Centre—this seemed particularly to please his audience. In all his talks he gave as much information as he could about the FWBO in the West, stressing that just as Dr Ambedkar's followers were 'new' Buddhists so were followers of the Dharma in the West. He led study for the mitras, and in these sessions he sensed that 'the Dharma really had been revived at last in India, and that with the starting of the FWBO in Poona something very clear and very pure had started flowing through the stagnant wastes of Maharashtrian Buddhism'. That this had happened was, he saw, in large measure due to Lokamitra, a man of considerable energy and uncompromising dedication, whose particular combination of personal qualities was exactly right for the situation.

At the end of his stay in Poona a three-day retreat was held at Sinhagad—a hill-fort with a spectacular view over the open countryside—attended by thirty-three people, including four upasakas from Britain and several Friends from Ahmedabad. The retreat culminated in the ordination by Sangharakshita of two of his oldest friends and closest helpers from his tours amongst the ex-Untouchables before his return to England. Mr Maheshkar, who had been his principal Marathi interpreter in Poona in the fifties and sixties, now became Upasaka Dharmarakshita, and Mr Vakil, who had organised his tours in Gujerat and had founded, under his guidance, the Gujerat Buddhist Society, became Upasaka Bakula. After three more days in Poona, giving talks, conducting name-giving ceremonies, and meeting many more people, Sangharakshita left for Bombay, from where, after meeting more old friends and making some new ones, he flew on to Penang in Malaysia.

The population of Malaysia is made up largely of ethnic Malays, but there are substantial minorities of Indians and Chinese. Many of the latter are Buddhists, though usually of a rather lax and degenerate kind. However, lately there had been some enthusiastic attempts at a Buddhist revival. Sangharakshita had been invited to visit the country by members of a leading organisation in this movement of renewal, the Young Buddhist Association of Malaysia, whose Secretary, Shin Yueng, had met Sangharakshita in New Zealand, during his visit in 1974, and had kept in regular correspondence with members of the Order ever since. Sangharakshita gave talks in the cities of Penang, Alor Star, and Ipoh, telling his Chinese audiences about his life and the movement he had founded in the West and in India, as well as giving them a taste of his radical understanding of the Dharma. As he spoke he became aware of the 'same kind of genuine spiritual interest that one encounters at FWBO beginners' meetings' in the West. People had come to hear him not just because they were born Buddhists but out of a deeply felt spiritual need. The FWBO could clearly prosper in Malaysia.

It obviously had prospects in Australia, too, as he found during a brief stopover in Sydney on his way to spend two-and-a-half months in New Zealand. During his first visit to New Zealand, four years previously, he had initiated the Order and now he wanted to consolidate the movement there. He travelled to each of the three centres (a third having recently been started in the capital, Wellington), meeting mainly with Order members and mitras, conducting question and answer sessions and study seminars, giving lectures, and, during a week-long retreat, receiving five more men and women into the Western Buddhist Order. Travelling extensively by car throughout the two islands, on this occasion Sangharakshita was able to see quite a bit of the New Zealand countryside, which is exceptionally beautiful, with its own very distinctive flora and fauna. Only three million people inhabit an area larger than Great Britain, and much of the countryside is unpopulated and unspoilt.

Sangharakshita pointed out to Order members there that New Zealand could really become a realm of the Dharma, a Pure Land: with such a small population it would not be impossible for Buddhists to have a significant impact on the whole nation. In fact, he said, he saw no reason why New Zealand should not become a 'Buddhist country'. Unfortunately, the very factors that gave New Zealand its potential also worked against it, for life was so easy and pleasant that there was little need to make much effort. Even within the FWBO it was hard to get people really to put themselves out for the sake of the Dharma.

From Auckland, Sangharakshita returned to Poona. At Sinhagad, during a five-day retreat, he conducted five more ordinations. Next he travelled to Ahmedabad where he was due to give two lectures—however, he developed a high fever and was unable to attend these functions. Although the fever persisted, accompanied by a piercing headache which did not leave him until he returned to England, he conducted one more ordination during a retreat held at Gandhinagar. He then returned to Bombay and flew on to London. In the course of the last three months he had initiated the Order in India and had consolidated its presence in New Zealand, as well as prospecting its future in Malaysia and Australia. It had been a very successful trip and one that gave him a great deal of satisfaction.

Consolidating the Movement

He now made a tour of centres in Britain, visiting the property in North Wales that a team of Order members and mitras was preparing for use as a meditation centre (opened in 1980 as the Vajraloka Meditation Centre). Once back at Padmaloka he had much to do. He would usually devote the mornings to more 'creative' writing. The afternoons, when he was free to do so, would be given over to correspondence—among others, he especially kept in regular contact by letter with Lokamitra in India and with other Order members overseas. In the evenings he would edit transcripts of lectures and seminars—Lokamitra had started a magazine in Marathi, *Buddhayan*, which needed a constant flow of material from Sangharakshita, and later the Western *Mitrata*, published every two months, consisted entirely of selections from his lectures and seminars.

Besides writing, one of Sangharakshita's most frequent activities, wherever he happened to be, was meeting people. Almost every afternoon, whilst he was at Padmaloka, he would have private interviews for an hour or two with each of two or three people who had come especially to see him, and he would have many personal meetings every day when he visited FWBO centres. Most members of the Order would want to spend time with him once or twice a year, particularly if they had some decision to make about their future or some difficulty or problem in their lives. Similarly, most mitras would try to meet him from time to time—and sooner or later most Friends would want some communication with him. Then there was a steady stream of old friends, Buddhists from other groups, journalists, and others interested in his life and work. As the movement expanded, the number of people wanting to meet him grew larger and larger.

Not only was he in personal contact with many people, Sangharakshita received a great many letters each day, often long and detailed accounts of his disciples' struggles and experiences, as well as minutes of the meetings of all FWBO councils world-wide and reports of activities in various places. Even though he is an exceptionally rapid reader, he would have to spend quite a bit of time every day simply reading through the mail he received. Through these letters and reports, as well as personal meetings, he had a very broad and detailed picture of the entire movement, knowing something about most people involved with it—now amounting to a few thousand—and a great deal about many. He also kept abreast of affairs in the Buddhist world in general, receiving journals from many groups in the East, as well as in Europe and America, and keeping personal contact with several individuals in other Buddhist organisations. It was clearly important that he was aware of the wider context in which his work took place, so he read a daily newspaper and followed current affairs both in Britain and internationally. He was especially concerned with events in India, since this was likely to be one of the most significant arenas for the FWBO in the coming years. He took an Indian fortnightly news magazine and followed closely the general political, economic, and social situation there. Simply keeping pace with all this information occupied a great deal of his time. He could no longer handle all this work on his own. At this time he did have some secretarial assistance at Padmaloka and could call on the community to help him with various routine matters, but it was not enough, and as time went by the volume of his work grew greater and greater.

He continued to play an active role in teaching and inspiring the movement. He held regular seminars at Padmaloka, both for men and for women, the Padmaloka community leaving for the duration of the women's events. He also presided over quarterly 'Men's Events' at Padmaloka, to which men came from FWBO centres all over Britain for a long weekend of study and talks. Sangharakshita would usually take the chair at these talks, always having something witty, thought-provoking, and inspiring to say, adding an extra dimension to the occasion. At the end of 1979 he spent another two months at Sukhavati, giving a series of eight lectures at a nearby hall. He decided that, since the emphasis of the movement in London had been so much on mundane, practical work such as building, fundraising, and organising classes at the new centre, it needed to be lifted on to an entirely different plane of inspiration. The lectures he gave, therefore, were on 'The Inconceivable Emancipation: Themes from the *Vimalakirti Nirdesha*, a Mahayana Buddhist Scripture', and they did indeed carry his audience into that realm where the Buddha met with the great Bodhisattvas and where all conceptual understanding was swept away in Vimalakirti's thunderlike silence.

Throughout 1980, Sangharakshita based himself mainly at Padmaloka. From time to time he made expeditions out to visit FWBO centres and events: he gave, for instance, a poetry reading—the first for several years—at the Croydon Centre, founded by members of Aryatara community and now flourishing with its own Right Livelihood business enterprises. In April, he attended the fifth Order Convention to which about a hundred Order members came (out of a possible hundred-and-thirty)—as usual he led all the events and chaired all the talks. More seminars took place at Padmaloka, some for men and some for women, and he gave another major public lecture in London, 'The Taste of Freedom', in which he presented Stream Entry, that first goal of the Buddhist life, in highly accessible terms. He participated in a meeting of Chairmen from all FWBO centres world-wide, answering questions and drawing points to their attention.

That year saw the opening of the Vajraloka Meditation Centre, the start of activities in Sweden, and the departure of teams to set up centres in Australia and the USA—all very much under Sangharakshita's personal guidance and inspiration. A charity called Aid For India (later renamed the Karuna Trust) was established, also at his instigation, to gather funds in the West for social projects and Dharma work among ex-Untouchables in India. Aid For India began raising money from the general public in England for the medical and educational work that Order members were beginning to undertake in Maharashtra. Teams of Order members and mitras would spend a few weeks going from door to door, soliciting covenants and donations—and usually received a very generous and sympathetic response. Not only did this make available considerable resources for FWBO work in India but it had a very positive effect on those who joined the teams. Especially it helped to generate much greater empathy among people in the FWBO in Britain for their brothers and sisters in India. Sangharakshita strongly urged Order members and mitras to participate in these fundraising teams.

Although he managed to keep up a formidable flow of work, he made sure he maintained a broad balance in his life. He never neglected his reading, which was as catholic and voracious as ever, and he continued his exploration of the arts, for instance seizing whatever opportunities presented themselves for visits to art galleries. Sometimes, of an evening, he would listen to recordings of Western classical music, and from time to time he went to a concert—at this period he was particularly delighted by Handel's operas and saw a number of them performed. Nor did he neglect close friendship. He always made sure that he had time for communication with one or two intimates, taking a walk after lunch every day with a friend, and always travelling with a companion or two—both so that they could drive for him and look after his arrangements and for the pleasure of their company.

A Retreat in Crete

At the beginning of 1981, he went with Clive Pomfret (now Dharmachari Kevala) to the Greek island of Crete for three months. He spent his time mainly reading and thinking—and doing a little sightseeing, for Crete preserves the remains of one of Europe's earliest civilisations. For the first time since he had founded the FWBO he was entirely out of contact, leaving no forwarding address, so that he could get completely away from the movement. He wanted to distance himself from his creation for a while in order to gain some fresh perspective on it—and also to see what effect his removal would have. He did not expect to come back with any major new initiatives, however, simply with a fresh overview of the entire movement. At the time, he said 'I wanted to cut myself off completely to think about the Movement, to consider whether it has been established on the right lines.' His conclusion was that, yes, it had been established on the right lines, although he saw that there was no time to waste and that Order members, mitras, and Friends needed to exert themselves for the sake of the Dharma much, much more than they generally did. He realised that he must have much more personal contact with people in the movement and returned resolved to spend more time visiting centres and meeting Order members, mitras, and Friends.

Clearly, if he was to have even more personal contact, he needed help with the ever growing volume of work. It was clear that he would have to work in a new way, with a bigger and more formal secretariat at Padmaloka. So FWBO centres raised the necessary funds and three Order members began to work full-time as his secretaries in what became the Office of the Western Buddhist Order. The Office functioned first of all as his personal secretariat, dealing with his own correspondence and arrangements, but it was also responsible for communication within the Order and movement and relations with outside organisations and individuals, Buddhist and non-Buddhist, most of which took place under Sangharakshita's personal supervision.

Whenever he was at Padmaloka, he would meet with one or other of his secretaries for an hour or so each day, discussing issues that had arisen and deciding what needed to be done. Much of his correspondence was personal and demanded some sort of reply from him individually, but there were many enquiries that the secretaries could deal with. They were also able to help him in his function as Head of the Order. Although each of the FWBO's centres is legally and financially autonomous, he himself was President of each and the spiritual teacher of all Order members, and his direct guidance was often still needed. He therefore monitored events in FWBO centres and WBO chapters very closely and, whenever intervention was necessary, he would brief a secretary who would then contact the people concerned. Again, his secretaries would act under his instructions on matters concerning relations with other Buddhist groups or in dealing with the press and news media. He was thus able to do a great deal more than he could have done unaided—but there was always more and more to do, and even keeping secretaries at work demanded more time of him.

TUSCAN RETREATS

After spending much of the rest of the year visiting centres and giving seminars, Sangharakshita initiated an entirely new development. For some time he had been concerned that those being ordained into the Order in the West were not being adequately prepared. Although Order members in centres were able to teach elementary meditation and to introduce people to Buddhism, they were not providing a sufficiently deep and comprehensive grounding in the Dharma and in the movement's basic principles. Furthermore, there were still not many Order members who were very effective Kalyana Mitras or spiritual mentors. Few had enough personal spiritual experience to spark off in others a deeper level of Going for Refuge to the Three Jewels. Another matter of concern was that, if preparation was left solely to local Order members, those newly ordained might feel a stronger allegiance to the centre from which they came than to the Order as a whole. New Order members needed, at the outset, a very definite experience of the Order's transcendence over any particular local or national grouping. Finally, since he was ordaining them, Sangharakshita needed to get to know each candidate far more closely than he had been able to do of late. All these problems had become more acute for men than for women, mainly because there were fewer women nearing readiness for ordination—and because the smaller women's wing of the Order tended to work more systematically and thoroughly.

He decided that he would have to take the matter in hand personally. He resolved that there should be a three month pre-ordination course for men at some quiet and isolated location, preferably outside Britain so that those attending, most of whom would be British, would definitely feel they had left home far behind. He himself would play a leading part in the course.

The first of these ordination courses began in September 1981, at Il Convento di Santa Croce, a former monastery of Augustinian Canons situated in southern Tuscany, near to the great cities that had been the cradle of the Renaissance. The monastery buildings had been in an advanced state of dilapidation, but the present owner had done some restoration work, using the place to stage operas. He was very glad to rent Il Convento to the FWBO for three months, having some sympathy with its objectives, as well as welcoming the money paid in rent and the building work that was to be done during the course. Sangharakshita, four Order members, and twenty-two mitras lived together at Il Convento for the next three months in an atmosphere of great harmony and inspiration, marking a new high point in the collective experience of the movement.

Sangharakshita led meditations and pujas for much of the course, spent time with each of the participants individually, and towards the end conducted seminars on Buddhist texts. Each morning during the first few weeks, study was led by Order members on edited material from Sangharakshita's lectures and seminars, making up a comprehensive basic guide to Buddhism. Questions arising out of this study were then put to him at the end of each morning. These were extraordinary events, during which Sangharakshita became more and more demanding of his hearers, insisting that they thought for themselves, often exposing layers of assumptions behind each question. At the same time he brought the spiritual realm to life, so that everyone saw and felt its reality. As the weeks progressed, he was able to develop certain ideas more and more through the answers he gave. On that first course, the principal theme was of 'Imagination' as a higher faculty by which both spiritual beauty and transcendental truth are apprehended. In the warm Italian countryside, with its rich colours and open skies, and so near to those ancient centres of art and learning, Siena and Florence and Pisa, the realm of truth and beauty really did open up for those participating in the course. In the final month twenty ordinations took place and all left with a far stronger taste of the Dharma and a far richer experience of spiritual community than they had ever had before.

These courses became an annual feature of the FWBO in the West. For the next five years Sangharakshita spent up to three months each year at Il Convento—he only attended half the third course but it became apparent that without his active presence the event could not really fulfil its function, at least for the time being, so from then on he attended each retreat for the full three months. After six courses had been held at Il Convento, Sangharakshita took part in two more courses at FWBO premises in Spain. Since 1989, although the events continue to be held in Spain, Sangharakshita himself plays no part in them, having handed the responsibility on to others.

It was not possible at that time to arrange a comparable course for women, and their preparation for ordination was spread out over a number of retreats. Sangharakshita attended women's ordination retreats each year, and supervised the process of preparation and selection, getting to know each candidate personally before accepting them.

This annual period of retreat created a very pleasant rhythm to Sangharakshita's life over the next decade. Whatever he did for the remainder of each year, he would have those three months of seclusion and quiet, with the happy routine of the retreat all around him. He was able to spend some hours each day on other work—he still kept in close touch with the movement world-wide through correspondence and he would usually also undertake some literary project. At the beginning and end of the courses, while they were being held in Italy, he would often make trips to some of the historic centres of Tuscany, particularly to Florence, with its extraordinary treasury of some of the finest in European painting and sculpture.

ANOTHER VISIT TO INDIA

On his return from the first Tuscany course, at the beginning of 1982, he visited India for the second time since the start of the FWBO/TBMSG, this time for three months. This tour is vividly chronicled by Dharmachari Nagabodhi in his book about the movement in India, *Jai Bhim! Dispatches from a Peaceful Revolution*. He toured extensively, visiting Poona, Bombay, Aurangabad, Nanded, Sholapur, and Ahmedabad, giving some forty lectures and addressing large gatherings. During three retreats, near Bhaja, at Gandhinagar, and at a People's Education Society School near Bombay, he ordained eight new upasakas. His visit concluded with an Order Convention attended by twenty-two members of the Order.

This Convention was to prove very significant in defining more clearly the place of the Order in the Buddhist world. The issue arose from a discussion Sangharakshita initiated on the nature of ordination into the WBO/TBM. Members of the Order were styled upasaka (m.) or upasika (f.), in accordance with a traditional Buddhist category, usually translated as 'lay-follower', although that is not the literal meaning of the word. However, it was quite clear that an upasaka in the Order was quite different from an upasaka as ordinarily encountered in much of the Buddhist world—being a member of the Order generally represented a far higher level of commitment. What is more, the term 'upasaka' is normally contrasted with 'bhikkhu' and suggests a layman as opposed to a monk—and usually a layman whose commitment to the Three Jewels is purely nominal, the bhikkhu being considered the real member of the sangha. The Order transcends that distinction: it is Going for Refuge to the Three Jewels that makes one a member of the sangha, not the particular way of life one follows.

To make this point clear, at Sangharakshita's suggestion, the Order members present decided to change the style of the ordination from upasaka/upasika to Dhammachari/Dhammacharini, 'Dharmafarer' or 'one who lives by the Dharma', a term found in an important early text, the *Dhammapada*, that gives far more accurate expression to what an Order member really is. Whether they lived at home with their families or followed a more monastic way of life, all were simply followers of the Dharma. Order members in the West decided to follow suit in the following year, henceforth referring to themselves as Dharmacharis and Dharmacharinis. (A complication arises here because there is a difference between the two chief canonical languages of Buddhism, Pali and Sanskrit, in the form of the word used for the Buddha's teaching: *Dhamma* or *Dharma*. The Sanskrit form, *Dharma*, is unacceptable in India because of its use in Hinduism to denote caste duty. Thus in India Order members are Dhammacharis/Dhammacharinis, whilst in the West they are Dharmacharis/Dharmacharinis.)

Since founding the FWBO Sangharakshita had functioned almost entirely through the institutions of the movement. He had, of course, met whoever from outside the FWBO, Buddhist or non-Buddhist, had wanted to see him—for instance several Christian clergymen had visited him. But, apart from his two lectures for the Buddhist Society and several television appearances, he had not accepted a public platform beyond the movement. When he was asked in 1983 to address the 'Mystics and Scientists Conference', organised by the Wrekin Trust, he decided to accept, partly so that he could see what such organisations were like. The Wrekin Trust belongs to the so-called 'New Age' movement, whose followers believe that a new era is dawning in which a new spiritual consciousness will gradually and inevitably arise within mankind. Whilst the New Age movement is usually characterised by intellectual vagueness, it is at least benign and certainly sympathetic to Buddhism. The Wrekin Trust is a rather respectable and socially conservative brand of New Age organisation, quite well established and widely known, under the leadership of its founder, Sir George Trevelyan. Their annual 'Mystics and Scientists Conference' brings together leading scientists with figures from various religious groups, attracting wide participation. Sangharakshita presented a paper that brilliantly synthesised many elements of his own presentation of Buddhism, published as *The Bodhisattva: Evolution and Self-transcendence*—although this was clearly a little heavyweight for the audience. He led a meditation class for some 150 people and, because another speaker was unable to attend, gave a further talk, this time on Dr Ambedkar and the conversion of ex-Untouchables to Buddhism. This talk was very well received indeed, perhaps particularly because of the evident strength of feeling with which Sangharakshita spoke. The Conference gave him the opportunity to meet many people, notably the eminent physicist, Professor David Bohm.

The Conference had another significance for Sangharakshita since it saw the first appearance of my own book, *Buddhism for Today: A Portrait of a New Buddhist Movement*, which is an introduction to the institutions and ideas making up the FWBO. Sangharakshita considered this to be a particularly important event for him personally since it was the first full-length book brought out by an Order member other than himself. 'In addition to possessing its own intrinsic value, the book therefore represented the devolution of yet another of my functions and responsibilities on to the "senior and responsible" Order members. Something more had been *handed on.*' He says that he felt 'rather like a man who, in his old age, holds his first grandson in his arms and knows that his line will continue'—although the real sign that his line would continue, the handing on of responsibility for ordinations, had yet to come.

After the conference, Sangharakshita journeyed on to Wales, where he stayed for the next three months with Dharmachari Prasannasiddhi in a cottage near Vajraloka Meditation Centre. For some time, he had been finding that he no longer had at Padmaloka the undisturbed tranquillity he needed for his writing. The Office of the Western Buddhist Order had grown more and more busy, for there were now some two hundred Order members active all over the world, all generating work for the Office, and more retreats than ever were being held on the premises. Even though community members tried to keep him free from interruption, nonetheless, with the busy hum of Padmaloka all around him and always accessible to interruption, it was difficult to get on with his writing. He had recently decided to establish a small vihara for himself, keeping Padmaloka as his main residence but retiring from time to time to a smaller and more secluded situation where he could get on with writing undisturbed. A suitable house had been found in the south of France, but when it came to the point Sangharakshita realised that he still needed to be closer at hand to guide the movement in Britain. Plans to buy a house in Britain had fallen through for lack of funds. This three-month retreat in Wales was the best he could do, for the time being, to bring about the conditions he needed for his writing.

He began his retreat by writing a long letter to *Shabda*, describing his recent activities, and then started preparing for publication a work he had written some years previously when he was in Kalimpong. This was a detailed account of the canonical literature of all Buddhist schools and traditions, and it needed updating since much new material had more recently come to light. The importance of this work in the total scheme of Sangharakshita's teaching is very great for it shows, for the first time ever in Buddhist history, how all the canonical works of all the Buddhist schools are parts of one spiritual whole. His vision of the unity of Buddhism was here applied in yet another field. The book had originally been entitled *The Word of the Buddha*, but since that title had now been used by another author it was published in 1985 as *The Eternal Legacy*.

CONFLICTING DUTIES

The tension between Sangharakshita's more public work for the movement and his writing was becoming stronger and stronger. His direct guidance was clearly still needed to keep the FWBO moving on to fresh heights—even to prevent it from falling back into confusion and impotence. He still needed to have a lot of personal contact with people throughout the movement. He still needed to keep a close eye on what went on in all the various centres, communities, and co-operatives. He was still the only one able, for instance, to unravel the complexities of relationships with other Buddhist organisations. Even if he had handed on something with the publication of *Buddhism for Today* there was still much more that had not been handed on. All of this required of him a very active participation in the life of the movement.

At the same time, he felt a strong impulse to write. There was so much that he had to say that could only really be said in writing, especially as he was addressing not only his present disciples but also generations yet to come. He had started the movement, and had established it on a firm basis, but he was looking now into the distant future. He knew that the movement needed far more clarity and inspiration if it was to survive through the centuries. Through his writing he could provide something of that inspiration and clarity. The immediate needs of the movement and the demands of his writing were more or less incompatible—a tension he has had to live with ever since the movement was founded. More and more he has felt that his writing is his greatest priority and has tried to arrange everything else around it—but this has been far from easy to achieve.

He returned from Wales to Padmaloka to take up the many duties that had accumulated there for him. By this time there were nineteen FWBO centres throughout the world in nine different countries and the demands on him were growing greater and greater all the time. But he did not allow himself to become bogged down in merely overseeing the organisation of the movement. He also ensured that there was always fresh inspiration to lead it on to new spiritual heights. During this period he began a series of talks to Order members on themes from the life of the Buddha. In one, 'A Case of Dysentery', he stressed that Order members must really care for each other, seeing each other not from the point of view of usefulness but as human beings with a common spiritual aspiration.

In fact, this theme began to emerge more and more at this time, as Sangharakshita stressed the importance of spiritual friendship at every opportunity. So many of the difficulties that people experienced in their spiritual lives could be attributed to lack of real friendship. So many disputes and disagreements could be resolved if people got to know each other more deeply. Without a far stronger appreciation and experience of spiritual friendship, the Order could not long survive. Not only that, true friendship was one of the greatest delights of human life, as he knew from his own experience. To bring this theme more to life within the Order he led a seminar for senior Dharmacharis on *The Duties of Brotherhood in Islam* by Al Ghazali, a leading medieval Islamic thinker. This proved exceptionally interesting, partly for what it revealed of the Islamic outlook, but especially for the very lofty, yet practical, vision of friendship it upheld, giving Sangharakshita the opportunity to reveal his own, yet loftier, vision. For him spiritual friendship was itself a path by which the self-transcendence of Enlightenment could be achieved. Sangharakshita pursued this theme further in a seminar on the poem 'Ode to Friendship' by the great English writer, Dr Samuel Johnson, long a favourite author of his.

As we have seen, he tried to give himself more time for other work by attending only half the third Tuscany Ordination Course in 1983—but this was an experiment he was not able to repeat for another six years. Immediately after he returned from Italy, he left for a third trip to India, this time for only three weeks and principally to perform ordinations. He gave a talk to a crowd of 5,000 people at Dapodi in Poona, dedicating the site of the Bahujan Hitay medical centre. He formally opened the new retreat centre at Bhaja, cutting the ribbon and giving the vihara the name Saddhamma Pradipa. The first activity of the new vihara was a three-day ordination retreat at which eight new Dharmacharis were created. The two-day Order Convention that followed was attended by every Order member in India—by now totalling thirty-six, including Western Order members working there permanently. At Worli in Bombay, Sangharakshita gave a final talk on the theme of Buddhism and Marx to a large audience, speaking for nearly two-and-a-half hours—his longest talk yet, although the audience listened with complete attention throughout.

A Stream of Creativity

When he returned to England, Sangharakshita set to work preparing a paper to be read at the sixteenth anniversary celebrations of the founding of the Western Buddhist Order in April 1984. He had long contemplated clarifying the relationship between ethics and Going for Refuge and, in particular, the reasons for the adoption of the ten precepts taken by Order members at ordination. Although the ten precepts form an important set of ethical principles found in all Buddhist traditions, they have never before been formally adopted by any Buddhist order. Sangharakshita wrote a very careful and systematic appraisal of the precepts, showing them to be *The Ten Pillars of Buddhism*, the most all-inclusive and fundamental of all ethical principles—another very important issue had been illuminated for the sake of both present and future generations.

A little later he took up another theme of significance to both the present and the future—indeed on the outcome of this issue depended whether or not there would be future generations. He prepared a paper on *Buddhism, World Peace, and Nuclear War*, which he read to five hundred people at a hall in central London and again at the Croydon Buddhist Centre. This stream of creativity was continued during the fourth Tuscany Course, during which he read two papers, *The Journey to Il Convento* and *St Jerome Revisited*, exploring the Buddhist Path in terms of Western art, myth, and symbol. The following year, once more settled at Padmaloka, Sangharakshita completed work on *The Eternal Legacy*—launched by his reading of another paper, *The Glory of the Literary World*, at a large public gathering in London. He then began work on the second volume of his memoirs, describing his establishment of the YMBA in Kalimpong and his first meeting with Dr Ambedkar.

His Sixtieth Birthday Year

During 1985, he visited several FWBO centres in Britain and participated in the women's ordination process retreats, conducting some ordinations. He attended the Order Convention, chairing talks, answering questions, and reading from work in progress. For two weeks he led study for FWBO chairmen from all over the world on *The Forest Monks of Sri Lanka*, an ethnographic study by Michael Carrithers, an English academic. This investigated the attempt by modern monks in Sri Lanka to get back to the original spirit of Buddhism and it proved very instructive for Order members trying to live the Buddhist life in the West. Through the text Sangharakshita was able to explore with his senior disciples some of the deeper principles behind the movement.

He was constantly aware of the need for greater understanding of spiritual life among his disciples. He still did not consider that Order members were sufficiently knowledgeable about the Dharma or able to communicate it to others. Again he felt he must take the matter in hand himself. A new study course had been instituted for mitras in the West, using nine of his lecture series as a basis. He decided that study leaders needed to be more thoroughly prepared before they could lead groups on this material and undertook to train them himself. Over the next three years, groups of Dharmacharis and Dharmacharinis listened to each lecture, discussed it among themselves, and then asked Sangharakshita questions on points that were not clear or that provoked further reflection. In this way, he built up a commentary on his own lectures that would be invaluable to those leading study in the future.

1985 was, from several points of view, an important year for the movement and therefore for Sangharakshita. A retreat centre, Aryaloka, was established near Boston, in America—although the FWBO had been present in the USA for some years, this marked its effective implantation. Even more significantly, a property was purchased near the northern Welsh border that became Taraloka, the women's retreat centre. Sangharakshita had been keen on this project for some time, emphasising that the women's wing of the movement would not really be established on a sound spiritual footing until it had some such base. This was the fruition of his policy of encouraging the women in the movement to be independent of the men—under Sanghadevi's able leadership, the necessary funds had been raised, the property purchased, designed, and converted entirely by Dharmacharinis and other women. There was a noticeable increase in confidence amongst Dharmacharinis and women mitras from this moment on, and the women's wing began to develop much more strongly than ever before.

However, the most important development of that year took place in December 1985 when, for the first time, Sangharakshita handed on the conferring of ordinations. He had been planning to go to India that year to ordain some twenty new Dharmacharis, but his mother's health had been very poor and she was uneasy about him being out of the country for so long. He therefore seized the opportunity to devolve a major responsibility: he asked three senior Dharmacharis—Kamalashila, Suvajra, and me—to go to India to conduct the ordinations on his behalf.

This was a development he had been considering for some time. Two years previously he had asked all Order members in the West for their views on who should conduct ordinations in the future—most had expressed reservations about anyone else doing so whilst Sangharakshita himself was still alive. It was clear that it would be difficult to begin the process in the West. He knew that Order members and mitras in India generally had much greater faith in their spiritual teacher than did his

Western disciples. They would much more readily accept his appointment of others to carry out the ordinations. It was therefore clearly best to begin in India. The ceremonies were conducted with complete success and no one doubted the validity of the ordinations—in fact, everyone rejoiced that the spiritual vitality of the Order had been expressed in this way. The following year, three Western Dharmacharinis, Shrimala, Ratnashuri, and Padmashuri, completed the process by performing the ordinations of Indian women. Something else had been handed on.

Although he had been unable to go to India himself, Sangharakshita resolved to make a substantial contribution to the work there by writing a book about Dr Ambedkar. There is still no biography of Dr Ambedkar published in the West, and there is no book-length study of the movement of mass conversion to Buddhism that he initiated. In fact, hardly anything is known of that movement outside India, and there is very little understanding even of the terrible blight of Untouchability, perhaps one of the greatest social evils of the modern world, especially with the demise of apartheid. From his very first public appearance in London in 1964, Sangharakshita has striven to spread some knowledge and appreciation of that great modern hero, Dr Ambedkar, and to awaken sympathy for the ex-Untouchables, both in the hearts of Western Buddhists and the public at large. He had certainly ensured that those involved with the FWBO in the West had a close and practical involvement with their brothers and sisters in India—to date the Karuna Trust has raised some five million pounds for development projects amongst them. But he wanted to make sure that as many people as possible could learn about Dr Ambedkar and what he had done for his people. He particularly wanted everyone involved with the FWBO to understand his true significance, because Dr Ambedkar had vitally important lessons to teach Order members, mitras, and Friends. Sangharakshita wanted the FWBO's future generations to be heirs to Dr Ambedkar's message that social, economic, and political changes were essential, but that they had ultimately to be underlain by a spiritual commitment.

He started to write a booklet on this theme but quickly found that he had enough material for a small but substantial book. For six months during 1986 he worked on this when he could, finally launching *Ambedkar and Buddhism* at a special celebration in a public hall in London in December 1986 to mark the thirtieth anniversary of Dr Ambedkar's death.

However, he had no uninterrupted period of writing. He had the usual visits to FWBO centres to make, the women's ordination course retreats to attend and ordinations to give, study courses to take for mitra study group leaders, and many people to see. He gave two public talks in London, on FWBO Day and Buddha Day, a poetry reading at the Norwich Centre (a collection of his poems, *Conquering New Worlds*, was also published in 1986), and seven short talks for television. He had the singular distinction, in this year, of being the first Buddhist to give a lecture in one of the most important centres of English Christianity: the chapel of King's College, Cambridge, a masterpiece of English Gothic Perpendicular architecture, built in the fifteenth century. King's College itself is one of the most prestigious places of learning in the country, noted particularly for its training of Church of England priests. It was a very strange experience for English people to hear a Buddhist speaking about the great Mahayana text, the *Saddharma Pundarika Sutra*, at this one-time stronghold of the English Christian establishment. Later that year he received another distinction from the Establishment, Buddhist this time, when *The Eternal Legacy* was awarded the Christmas Humphreys Annual Book Award as the best new book on Buddhism, which had 'made an outstanding contribution to the literature of basic Buddhism'.

GUHYALOKA: THE SECRET REALM IN SPAIN

The previous year had seen Sangharakshita's sixtieth birthday, and Order members, mitras, and Friends all over the world contributed some £150,000 as a birthday present for him. Some of this money was spent on renovating his quarters at Padmaloka, the rest was set aside to buy him what he really needed: a secluded vihara. A search had been carried out in various parts of Europe for a suitable property, and now a small bungalow had been discovered, high up in the mountains of eastern Spain. Two hundred acres of land were for sale, consisting of a mountain valley, enclosed on all sides by high limestone cliffs. Terraces had been cut into the valley slopes on which olive and almond trees grew, although these had not been cultivated for some time and pines and small oak trees were beginning to replace them. A delightful rustic spring poured out into a ancient stone-carved basin at the bottom of the valley. Hardly a sound could be heard but the singing of the birds. It was a very rare spot indeed. Sangharakshita immediately named it Guhyaloka, 'Secret Realm', and agreed to its purchase. He would stay in the small bungalow, in the midst of the valley, and a semi-derelict farmhouse at the bottom would house a community of men who would look after the valley. Here the men's ordination courses would be held so that Sangharakshita could participate in them fully, whilst having his own separate quarters. A team of Dharmacharis and mitras immediately set to work to prepare the place for the next year's ordination course.

Towards the end of 1986, after he had attended the men's ordination course, the last to be held in Tuscany, and done some sightseeing in Rome and Naples with Prasannasiddhi, Sangharakshita visited Guhyaloka to see how the building work was getting on and to do a little Dharma work in Spain. Arrangements had been made for him to give three talks in the cities of Valencia, Alicante, and Benidorm, all close to the mountains in which Guhyaloka is situated. From the success of these, and the publicity in press and radio they attracted, it became clear that there was plenty of scope for the FWBO in Spain—in fact it was becoming obvious that, wherever Sangharakshita's message could be put across clearly, there were people who would respond. Unfortunately, Sangharakshita's time in Spain was cut short on Christmas Day by a sudden and painful illness. A swollen prostate kept him in agony for some hours till medical help could be brought from the nearest village, six miles away down a very poor road.

Sangharakshita cut short his visit and returned to England for further medical treatment. He was advised to have an immediate operation and, after careful consideration, decided to do so. The operation, which turned out to be a quite major one, took place successfully at the beginning of 1987, and he was well on the way to full recovery when infection set in. This left him very weak and able to do very little, and necessitated a second operation in April of that year.

Being often unable to write through weakness, he did quite a bit of reading during this period, but as soon as he could he continued with his second volume of memoirs—on which he had done no work for two years because of other commitments. There were, of course, plenty of other commitments now as well: he gave a major talk at the Buddha Day festival celebrated jointly by all British FWBO centres, conducted women's ordinations, led study on more lecture series for mitra study group leaders, participated in the eighth Order Convention, and gave many private interviews: more than a hundred in one six-week period. In August 1987 he went to Guhyaloka for three months to participate in the first men's ordination course there, also spending a few days giving talks in the nearby cities, and launching *El Sendero del Buda*, a Spanish translation of his lectures on the Eightfold Path.

Over the years, the act of Going for Refuge to the Buddha, Dharma, and Sangha had emerged more and more clearly in Sangharakshita's teaching as the central and definitive act of the Buddhist life. The whole Order and movement ultimately rested on that act. It was by virtue of 'taking' the Three Refuges from Sangharakshita (or one of the preceptors appointed by him, themselves having once 'taken' them from him) that one became a member of the Order. There was a coincidence of his Going for Refuge with that of all Order members, expressed in the ordination ceremony. The whole Order thus sprang out of Sangharakshita's own Going for Refuge and therefore, in a sense, rested upon it. It was clearly vitally important that he shared more fully with the Order his understanding of this definitive Buddhist act and how he had arrived at it. Returning to Padmaloka from Spain at the end of 1987, he settled down to write a systematic account of his slowly deepening realisation of the full significance of Going for Refuge to the Three Jewels. He read his paper, published as a small book, *The History of My Going for Refuge*, to the assembled Order members at the twentieth anniversary celebrations of the Order in London in April 1988. Many Dharmacharis and Dharmacharinis had been unaware of all the steps and stages whereby he had come to his present view of the matter. All or most were reasonably clear on what he now thought, but they did not realise that he had had to piece together a living appreciation of this essential spiritual principle from the shattered fragments of tradition inherited by present-day Buddhism. Once again, here was a crucial aspect of his experience that could only be expressed through the careful medium of the written word. Another vital piece of his vision had been handed on to his present and future disciples.

IN THE FOOTSTEPS OF AMBEDKAR

After visiting various FWBO centres in Britain, Sangharakshita left for Guhyaloka where he planned to spend five months or so, participating in the ordination course and doing some writing. However, these plans were soon to be modified. He was approached by a television producer who, after reading *The Thousand-Petalled Lotus*, wanted to make a film about him. More research revealed that here was a very good story indeed: an Englishman who had lived in India, brought Buddhism to the West, and was now very actively involved in the revival of Buddhism in the Buddha's motherland. Western people had become accustomed to gurus coming from the East and building large followings amongst Westerners. Here was something quite new: a Westerner taking an Eastern religion back to India. It was an excellent story, and it seemed that there was material for not one but two films: one about Sangharakshita's work in general and one about him in India. In fact the television company was willing to fly him to India and would film him making a tour. This was too good an opportunity to miss and, during a hasty visit by the producer to Guhyaloka, arrangements were made for Sangharakshita to return to England for a week to do some filming there for the first programme and then to fly out to India at the end of the year for the second.

The three-week Indian tour in October 1988 began with a large event at Worli, a suburb of Bombay, where 10,000 people came to hear him speak. As he moved around Maharashtra—giving talks, laying foundation stones, leading retreats, conducting ordinations—the cameras turned. Everywhere he went he was greeted with great jubilation and thousands of people came to see him—for so many people in Maharashtra he represented the greatest hope they had had since Dr Ambedkar died. All this was captured by *In the Footsteps of Ambedkar*, a television documentary about Sangharakshita in India, later shown throughout Britain. Another film, rather unfortunately entitled *The Enlightened Englishman*, gave a more general view of his life and work.

Although so much important work was being done at this time, it was not an easy period for Sangharakshita. He had still not entirely recovered his health after the operations of the previous year. What is more, there were some serious difficulties in the movement in Britain. An Order member who had been close to Sangharakshita in the early days of the FWBO had suddenly become deeply embittered, starting what appeared to be a sustained campaign directed towards Sangharakshita and the movement. His actions, which were inevitably sensed as something of a betrayal by a one-time friend, naturally saddened Sangharakshita, but he dealt with it calmly and patiently. Again, the Chairman of one FWBO centre had begun to act in a way that seemed insensitive and dictatorial, and was even, it was felt, mistreating some of the mitras. Sangharakshita had to intervene personally, insisting that the new movement he had founded must never permit such high-handed behaviour. The centre was reorganised on a new and more positive basis, but the Chairman, a long-standing member, resigned from the Order. This again was saddening for Sangharakshita, although he was determined that such conduct would not be tolerated.

Towards the end of 1988, he learnt that his blood pressure had become dangerously high and that, unless he immediately took medication and had a complete rest, he might soon be dead. He had to drop all his responsibilities forthwith and withdraw from Padmaloka, staying once more in a small cottage in Wales with Paramartha, a Dharmachari from New Zealand who is now his constant companion, simply reading and resting. Although he had been forced to change his way of life under such dramatic circumstances, it was clear that a change had to be made anyway. He could not go on carrying responsibilities spread over such a wide area—trying to fulfil several major literary projects as well as overseeing a rapidly expanding spiritual movement. He had to take a step back and leave more of the running of the movement to others. He resolved that, medical reasons apart, it was time for him to function in a completely new way.

After briefly visiting FWBO centres in the south of England, he based himself at his flat in Sukhavati, leaving his secretariat at Padmaloka where it would not be constantly demanding attention from him. He would live very quietly in London, free from organisational responsibilities, writing, and meeting a few friends. He was not, however, retiring from the movement. Far from it: he simply wanted to operate in a more effective way. Even though he was no longer in such regular contact, his guidance and inspiration were still very much felt throughout the movement.

Perhaps the most important effect of this resolution was that he would no longer be giving ordinations to men in the West. He would not attend the ordination course at Guhyaloka. He would not even make the final decision as to whether individual men should be ordained or not. When Kamalashila, Suvajra, and I had visited India to conduct ordinations in 1985, it was very explicitly as his emissaries, acting on his behalf. He had said whom we should ordain. He had thought up the names. But now he was going to leave the whole matter entirely to the ordination team at Padmaloka. Suvajra and I performed some ordinations at Padmaloka under his guidance in January 1989, but then, in July of that year, we conducted seven ordinations at Guhyaloka without reference to him. Sangharakshita was now free to devote himself more fully to his literary work since that major responsibility was now completely handed over.

Chapter Nine

URGYEN
1989–1995…

I am the Windhorse!
I am thought at its clearest,
Emotion at its noblest,
Energy at its most abundant.
I am Reverence. I am Friendliness. I am Joy.
I only among beasts
Am pure enough, strong enough, swift enough,
To bear on my back the Three Flaming Jewels.
The pride of the lion is not enough.
The strength of the bull is not enough.
The splendour of the peacock is not enough.
With what joy I sweep through the air,
Bearing age after age
My thrice-precious burden!
With what joy, with what ecstasy, I fulfil
The greatest of all destinies!
Plunging or soaring, I leave behind me
A rainbow track.

Sangharakshita (1975)

IN AUGUST 1985 Sangharakshita had celebrated his sixtieth birthday. Some twenty of his close friends and senior disciples gave him a surprise birthday dinner at Padmaloka, with appropriate entertainment. After we had enjoyed a sumptuous feast, we listened to music in his honour, and rejoiced in our teacher and friend. Among the speeches, Prasannasiddhi read out a letter he had received from Sangharakshita that he felt expressed vividly his own experience of the man. In that letter, Sangharakshita recalled that forty years ago he had experienced a tension between 'Sangharakshita I', who wanted 'to enjoy the beauty of nature, to read and write poetry, to listen to music, to look at paintings and sculpture, to experience emotion, to lie in bed and dream, to see places, to meet people' and 'Sangharakshita II', who wanted 'to realise the truth, to read and write philosophy, to observe the precepts, to get up early and meditate, to mortify the flesh, to fast and pray'. Indeed it was some years before he was able to bring the two together so that they became something like 'Sangharakshita III'. He now felt a new Sangharakshita emerging—but actually it was not a Sangharakshita at all: it was Urgyen. This name, the Tibetan for the land of which Guru Padmasambhava had been king, had been given to him by Khachu Rimpoche in 1962, in the course of the Padmasambhava initiation. He had never really used it since. Now he felt it to represent this new spirit emerging within him. Urgyen, we were warned, would be far more uncompromising than Sangharakshita had ever been. Urgyen was, in fact, not willing to compromise his ideals at all.

Some of us were a little surprised to find that Sangharakshita considered himself to have ever been willing to compromise his ideals. Our own experience was that he was a man who never let go of what he knew to be right. Nonetheless, he himself felt that he had been too obliging—perhaps even that he had not been 'angry' enough, in the sense of speaking unpalatable truths, clearly and unequivocally, calling a spade a spade and a fool a fool. Whether or not he had been too obliging before, there is no doubt that it is as Urgyen that he has stood out more and more, especially during these last few years. In some of his published writings he has pitilessly exposed the confusion and even dishonesty in the arguments he is dissecting, or has very directly expressed some forthright ideas. In personal communication and in public utterance he has been even more bracingly challenging—many an audience has realised that one must think very carefully before posing him a question. At the same time he remains as cheerful, friendly, kindly, and amusing as ever—perhaps even more so than ever before. Age has certainly not blunted his idealism nor has it reduced his spiritual vigour. Urgyen is even more spiritually vital than any of the previous Sangharakshitas.

Urgyen—or Sangharakshita as we will continue to call him in this public tale—since his return from Wales, spends much of his time at his flat in the London Buddhist Centre complex. The four-room apartment adjoins Sukhavati community and is relatively secluded from the busy centre and its even busier surroundings. As Sangharakshita has said, it is, curiously enough, easier for him to find tranquillity in this crowded setting than in the peaceful Norfolk countryside. He lives with Paramartha, and the two of them have settled into a very full and satisfying routine together. Sangharakshita usually gets up at 4.30 or 5 a.m. and does some reading: he often uses this time to check through manuscripts by Order members or others, or proofs of his own writing, or else he does some more weighty study—at present it is the works of Plotinus, the great Neoplatonic philosopher, that he is likely to take up. At 6.30 a.m. he and Paramartha sit for meditation. After breakfast, he gets down to writing whatever his major literary project of the moment might be. He continues with this work undisturbed, apart from a brief break for coffee, until lunch is brought to him from the Cherry Orchard, a vegetarian restaurant next door to the London Buddhist Centre run by Dharmacharinis and women mitras.

After lunch, he and Paramartha go for a walk in a neighbouring park, partly for enjoyment and partly for exercise to help keep his blood-pressure down. He then rests for half an hour or so, going through his mail or sometimes reading a newspaper. Reading then occupies him till four o'clock. As he has done since he was a child, he reads a great deal, getting through five or six books each week—always serious works or literary classics: he keeps abreast of most new scholarly works published on Buddhism and reads widely in many other fields. After tea at four o'clock, he either carries on with whatever he had been writing in the morning or else attends to correspondence. At six the cook from Sukhavati community brings supper, after which he often sees one or two people for half an hour or so each. He then continues with correspondence or his writing project or reads a bit more. The day finishes with he and Paramartha meeting together over a hot drink, reporting-in to each other about their day and discussing whatever has struck them as of importance. He retires to bed at ten o'clock and reads for a while before going to sleep.

This routine is occasionally varied, for instance, by an outing to the centre of London for the afternoon, visiting bookshops, or an art exhibition or the like. Every two or three months he spends a few days at Padmaloka, consulting with his secretaries and clearing up any business he may have there. These visits usually coincide with an Order weekend or other event, and he takes advantage of the opportunity by chairing a talk and seeing many people. Most years he spends a month or so at his vihara in the beautiful valley of Guhyaloka, where he and Paramartha keep up their usual routine—differing only in that there are few if any people to see.

Even though the handing on of responsibility for ordinations has marked a major step in Sangharakshita's withdrawal from detailed responsibility within the movement, nonetheless a number of weighty duties still remain to him. He is still the fountainhead of authority: appointments to the leading responsibilities emanate from him. Further, he is still the principal unifying factor for the FWBO world-wide. Most Order members still consult him before making any major changes or taking any new initiatives. He still keeps in touch with developments in the movement all over the world and intervenes when he sees the need for correction. Particularly, he still is the chief guardian of clarity of ideas and doctrine. Finally, he has ordained some four hundred Order members who are therefore his personal disciples, requiring his guidance and advice. All of this makes his present 'withdrawal' a very relative one—in many ways he has been more active and involved than ever.

Throughout the last six years, in fulfilment of his unifying function, he has paid visits to FWBO centres world-wide. From time to time he makes short tours to one or more of the British centres, having visited them all at least once during this period, notably reading poems on the theme of 'Friendship' on several occasions and launching his new publications. Indeed, the reading of his own and others' poetry has been one of the media he has used on a number of occasions—at one point he threatened to do nothing else. He has not confined himself to Britain, however. Early in 1992 he again returned to India, making a historic visit to Nagpur, the city in eastern Maharashtra where the first mass-conversions to Buddhism had taken place in 1956 and where he himself had not been seen since 1966, twenty-five years earlier. In many ways this was the crowning glory of his work in India, returning to the centre from which it all began. He has also taken something of a personal interest in the establishment of Buddhist activities in Germany and has twice visited the FWBO centre in Essen. As the movement has begun to blossom in the USA, he has taken a close personal interest in its development there too. He visited the country in 1990, for the first time since he lectured at Yale in 1970, spending three weeks at Aryaloka Retreat Center and meeting most people involved with the movement there. In 1993 he returned, receiving into the Order the first two Americans to be ordained on American soil. He then spent some weeks touring FWBO centres on the west coast and meeting a number of leading American Buddhists. In October 1994 he went to Tucson, Arizona, to lecture at a conference on Buddhism and then visited the FWBO's San Francisco centre.

Looking at reports of Sangharakshita's travels, it is impressive that, whilst he clearly works very hard during his tours, he always finds time for cultural activities. If there are noted museums or art galleries in the neighbourhood he will visit them and he is occasionally taken to the theatre or a concert or opera. An inspection of the local bookshops is mandatory. These activities are, for Sangharakshita, not entertainment, but a source of spiritual nourishment and understanding, and he always undertakes them in a very thorough manner, often preparing fully in advance. A cultural trip with him can be very illuminating, his casual observations bringing meaning and beauty to flower in quite unexpected ways, and his further reflections casting new light on spiritual life and experience.

Since he is still the movement's principal unifying factor it is clearly important that people in the FWBO all over the world should have the opportunity to see him from time to time—and, apart from his travels to various centres, he has made a point of appearing at the FWBO's big public occasions. From time to time he has launched books, given poetry readings, chaired talks, and conducted pujas at large public gatherings in various places. In both 1990 and 1991 he attended celebrations of the founding of the Order and the FWBO, held in the impressive Victorian Town Hall in Manchester, as well as the succeeding ones held in London. At the 1991 celebrations he gave a public talk on 'The Five Pillars of the FWBO', these pillars being ideas, practices, institutions, experimentation, and imagination. In March 1991 he personally supervised a large public programme to commemorate the first anniversary of the death of his teacher and friend, Dhardo Rimpoche, and in 1994 he ceremonially placed a portion of Rimpoche's ashes in a stupa at Padmaloka.

He has been especially concerned to continue guiding the Order he has founded. He attended the European Order Conventions in 1989, 1991, and 1993, playing an important part in each. At the annual celebrations of the founding of the Order in 1990 he read a paper entitled *My Relation to the Order*. His position is complex, even ambiguous, and it is vital that Order members understand his place in the Order, since that is part of understanding what the Order itself is. His role emerged in his paper as a transitional one, neither still a part of the old Buddhist world nor fully part of the new, as represented by the Western Buddhist Order. In this way he clarified another issue, guiding Order members of the future in the meaning of their own spiritual community. At the WBO Day celebrations in 1991 he read 'The Cave', a moving short story he had written about a meeting between a young monk and the Buddha. He used the 1993 WBO Day celebrations to outline fifteen points he wished Order members to consider. In 1994 he addressed a gathering of Order members and mitras who had children, giving them 'Fifteen Points for Buddhist Parents'. This was felt to be something of a turning point, since Sangharakshita had till then given little systematic attention to the raising of children from a Buddhist point of view. It represented no 'change of policy', however, merely the natural unfoldment of his thinking in accordance with the developing needs of the movement.

He has also taken advantage of other means of contact with Order members. Until the mid-eighties one of his main teaching media was the seminar, in which he would comment systematically on a text. Since then one of his principal media has been the answering of questions, usually submitted to him in advance in writing—in that way ensuring that both the questions and the answers are carefully considered. From time to time he has conducted such sessions for groups of Order members. For instance, in 1990 he spent one evening a week for six weeks in this way with the Order members in the East London region, thereby clarifying quite a number of contentious issues. He led an important session in 1994 for those involved in Windhorse Trading, the movement's most successful Right Livelihood business, which wholesales and retails giftware, especially through its chain of ten shops called 'Evolution', and which has achieved the distinction of being listed for three years running as one of the hundred fastest growing private companies in Britain. During the sessions with Windhorse Trading's leading Order members, Sangharakshita showed clearly that work in such a context is itself a spiritual practice that can lead to Insight.

Sangharakshita's interests have always been predominantly literary, but he has been increasingly aware of the possibilities of new media of communication. He has greatly encouraged the use of video in the movement and has appeared in a number of films made by Clear Vision and Lights In The Sky, the two British FWBO video units. In 1993 a film, *In the Realm of the Lotus*, was made by the Finnish art critic, J.O. Mallander, about Sangharakshita's views on art and spiritual life, which has been shown on Finnish television and later published as a book. Indeed, it seems that public interest in his life and ideas is growing since he has appeared frequently on radio and television in Britain, as well as being interviewed a number of times for the press, both in Britain and internationally.

Over these last years, Sangharakshita has become an increasingly respected figure in the Buddhist world. This gives him much satisfaction, since for many years he had been seen, at least by some in the British Buddhist scene, as something of an outsider. But Buddhism, both in Britain and the USA, has now developed far beyond the narrow sectarianism of the sixties and there are today many sincere Buddhists outside FWBO circles. Some of the leading figures among them have been very happy to have contact with Sangharakshita, and in the last years he has had quite a number of cordial and fruitful meetings with other Buddhist teachers. It seems that he is now considered one of the elders of Western Buddhism and that many are realising that he has already thought about and resolved some of the most pressing problems facing Buddhism in the modern world. Tangible recognition of his leading role came when he was invited, as a distinguished Buddhist teacher, to speak at the European Buddhist Union's 1992 Congress in Berlin, where he spoke on 'Buddhism and the West: The Integration of Buddhism into Western Society'.

This growing respect towards him has not diminished Sangharakshita's frankness on what he considers to be the faults of many Buddhist groups today. In the May–July 1994 issue of *Golden Drum*, the movement's magazine, Sangharakshita wrote of the 'Idols of the Marketplace', three modern views that, especially in the USA, are being increasingly confused with Buddhism: 'democratisation', 'feminisation', and 'integration'—democratisation, however appropriate in society at large, undermines the notion of spiritual hierarchy; feminisation, in the sense that Sangharakshita uses the term, negates those masculine qualities so essential to spiritual life; and the integration of spiritual life into ordinary worldly life overlooks the necessity for renunciation. Sangharakshita is determined that if he is to be respected it is for what he actually believes and teaches.

Despite all these activities and the six or seven hundred people he meets each year in personal interviews, Sangharakshita has continued with his literary work. By dint of making sure he writes a few hundred words most days, he has managed to maintain a considerable output. Besides a number of articles and open letters, in this period he has completed and published a 500-page volume of memoirs, *Facing Mount Kanchenjunga*, covering the period 1950–1954, and is well into another. In *The FWBO and 'Protestant Buddhism': an Affirmation and a Protest*, published in 1992, he carefully dissected an article about the FWBO written by an English academic. In the course of this exercise in dissection he exposed many common misunderstandings about spiritual life and Buddhism in general and the FWBO in particular. In 1993 he clarified another important issue, both for the FWBO and for the entire Buddhist world, in his *Forty-Three Years Ago*, in which he presented his reflections on his own bhikkhu ordination. He showed in this work that the monastic formalism so common in the Buddhist East rests on the shakiest foundations—and that it must therefore simply be dispensed with. He is not, however, against monasticism itself, and in this paper makes clear what he means by monasticism, celibacy, and the anagarika vow. Far from rejecting genuine 'Sutra-style monasticism', Sangharakshita says that one of the things that has most pleased him in these last years is that a growing number of Order members have taken the anagarika vow by which they dedicate themselves to a life of celibacy. A rejoinder to *Forty-Three Years Ago* by an Australian bhikkhu prompted more reflections from Sangharakshita on this subject, published in 1994 as *Was the Buddha a Bhikkhu?*

Besides these works, a number of other books and pamphlets by him have been published over the last three years. Some of these have been reprints of works written by him many years ago, a few being published for the first time. Others have been the fruit of a new venture by Windhorse Publications, the 'Spoken Word Project', dedicated to publishing in written form his numerous oral teachings, found in his lectures and seminars. Another aspect of Sangharakshita's literary work is encouraging others in their endeavours. As more of his disciples have written books, he has read through their manuscripts, often more than once, and made careful comments on their work. He has the great skill of being both critical and encouraging at the same time.

THE FINAL TASK

Perhaps his most important task of all, at which he has been steadily working for a number of years, is the final handing over of his responsibilities within the Order and movement. He has studied closely the difficulties many Western Buddhist groups have experienced on the death of their founders, leading often to permanent divisions and loss of spiritual momentum. Learning the lessons of their experience, he is trying to avoid for his own movement the internal dissension, schism, and degeneration that have racked so many others. He wants personally to oversee the handing on of the leadership of the Order and the movement, rather than leave it to the fates after he has gone. Not, of course, that he can ever 'retire' as founder of the Order—he realises that, as long as he is alive, he will always carry the founder's responsibility. However, he wants to see that whatever responsibilities can be handed over are passed on well before his own death—indeed, he says that he would like to be alive when his successors hand them on to their successors, so that he can oversee that process too.

Having handed on the ordination of men to a small team of preceptors in 1989 and commenced the handing on of women's ordinations, in 1990 he took another important step. Since the foundation of the FWBO, he had been President of each of the autonomous charitable organisations that governed FWBO centres world-wide. At this point he resigned all his presidencies and invited centres each to choose a replacement from among ten or so senior Order members designated by him. These would fulfil the responsibility he had formerly carried for ensuring that each centre functioned in accordance with the basic principles of the movement and in harmony with the Order and movement as a whole.

He took a further decisive step during the Order Convention in 1993. He gathered together most of those then acting as Presidents and Preceptors, telling them that it was to them that he would be handing over his remaining duties. They were to form a college, gathering around the Public Preceptors—the Public Preceptors being the men and women who perform the part of the ordination ceremony that marks the formal accession of a new Order member to the Order. It is the Public Preceptors who have the future of the Order in their hands and therefore carry the final responsibility for ensuring its spiritual integrity. They would form the core of the Preceptors' College that would, with the addition of other senior Order members, provide the collective leadership of the Order and movement. He asked them to find a large house where most of them could live together and where they could establish their secretariat. Once that was done he would begin to pass on his last responsibilities. He stressed that this was not a matter of simply 'handing over the files'. His responsibilities ultimately are not administrative but spiritual. What he has to share with his successors are his concerns for his disciples, for the movement, even for the world. He has to pass on to them his understanding of the Dharma, his vision of the Order and the movement, and his links of spiritual friendship. He has to finally hand on responsibility for the process that he initiated in April 1967—that had its roots in his own experience of the transcendent truth of the *Diamond Sutra* at the age of sixteen.

In 1994 a large house was purchased in southern Birmingham and a few of the Presidents and Preceptors have moved in. Over the next year or so, more will be arriving either to live at the house or nearby. Gradually the members of the Preceptors' College are beginning to gather, and Sangharakshita is giving quite a bit of his time to contact with its members, individually and collectively. His present plan is to continue living in London until the end of 1996, when he will leave England for a year or two. He wants to be away from the movement in Europe so as to give time for the College members to function independently in their new responsibilities. He himself will probably spend some time in New Zealand and in the USA.

Precisely what Sangharakshita will do in the future it is hard to say. He has never been a man whose plans can be easily guessed at. He could, at any time, plunge into some new work. He says that he wants to make writing and personal contact his priorities. He wants to complete the second part of his memoirs, which is to consist of reminiscences from the period 1957–1964, covering his contacts with his Tibetan teachers and with the ex-Untouchable Buddhists. He has plans to write a personal account of the period 1964–1969, during which he was at the Hampstead Buddhist Vihara and then founded the FWBO and WBO. He would like to write a 'History of My Encounters with Christianity', a substantial paper on Buddhism and Neoplatonism, a supplement to *A Survey of Buddhism*, a commentary on the Bodhisattva precepts, and a study of reason and emotion in English literature. He is also considering a work that will place all his thinking in a clear philosophical context. He says that he would like to do some more purely creative writing as well, for instance he has projected a long poem on the myth of Orpheus.

Whatever his future productions, there is a facet of his life which will continue to unfold and which is far harder to define and quantify. Perhaps we can only speak of it as his spiritual experience. A visit to Sangharakshita is not simply intellectually stimulating and clarifying or emotionally bracing and encouraging. If one chooses to look, one senses within him or behind him something very subtle and refined, yet very powerful indeed, the almost tangible presence of a consciousness greater than one normally knows. It is as if the larger part of him sits in some other dimension, far more real and ample than this one. He has said that he has had a continuous experience recently of the complete meaninglessness of time, and it is indeed as if he looks at the world from a timeless realm. He finds himself less and less interested in the personal difficulties and organisational problems that still occupy so much of his time. His own attention is more and more focused on the great and fundamental issues of existence. Whatever the frontiers of consciousness he is now exploring, there is little doubt that he will continue to do so as long as he is alive—and no doubt beyond death, if we are to accept the traditional Buddhist perspective.

Naturally, any talk of the future in connection with a man of seventy must acknowledge the approach of death. Although his health is basically good and he still has plenty of energy, he knows that death is more and more imminent—indeed, that it could come at any time. This is something that he makes a point of acknowledging, and has done for some years. In 1985, during his sixtieth year, he published a paper, *St Jerome Revisited,* in which he explored the inner meaning of the image of St Jerome in his cave, bent at his desk as he translates the Bible into Latin—an image commonly depicted by Italian Renaissance artists. Before St Jerome on his desk stand an hourglass and a skull, embodying his awareness of the march of time and of time's inevitable outcome in death. Sangharakshita clearly identified himself with the Christian translator, for, as he says, he too has been a translator—a translator not from one language to another but from one culture to another, even from one dimension to another. It seemed, from that time onwards, as if he too had an hourglass and skull on his desk, and that he too was more and more conscious that he could not count on having much more time to finish his own work of translation. He says that he does not at all mind the thought of dying and is quite happy to do so whenever death comes. He simply wants to make as sure as he can in the meantime that the work he began in founding the FWBO and WBO will continue without him.

There is little doubt now that his work will survive him, and not merely survive but continue for many years to express more and more vividly his founding vision. He is by nature a careful and thorough man and he has thoroughly and carefully established and consolidated his new Buddhist movement. In founding it he distilled the experiences and reflections gathered over many years of active Buddhist life, first in India and then in Britain. Since then, he has laid out its basic principles with great clarity and he has thoroughly trained his leading disciples in them. He has written and spoken on a very broad range of topics, leaving future generations abundant inspiration and guidance. He has very conscientiously and prudently prepared the movement for a new leadership to take over from him. It is of course possible that he will have many years left to him and that he will contribute much more before he dies, but even if he were to go now he would leave a real and lasting mark upon the world.

It is in his care for the continuance of his work that Sangharakshita's true quality is finally revealed. It is, in a sense, not hard to achieve something in life, but it is rare indeed to ensure that what one has achieved is passed on successfully to others. Sangharakshita has done—and continues to do—his best to make sure that his own work will enrich the lives of many generations yet to come.

Perhaps we should conclude by recognising what it is that Sangharakshita himself considers his work to be. The vision that he has embodied in his new Buddhist movement is one of individual development towards the goal of highest perfection, known to Buddhists as Buddhahood. What he has attempted is to create, or at least to initiate the creation of, a culture that encourages and supports the development of individual men and women. That culture, that movement, as Sangharakshita sees it, must be comprehensive if it is to be effective, including the economic, social, and political aspects of human life, as much as the intellectual, artistic, and spiritual.

But his new Buddhist movement is not simply offered to those who happen to become involved with it. He sees it as a contribution to the world Buddhist tradition, which finds itself in crisis as it confronts the modern age. He hopes that the FWBO will act as a challenge and a model for the spiritual renewal of that tradition. He hopes that other Buddhists will be inspired and instructed by his work, so that they too will create vital spiritual cultures in which high human endeavour thrives.

His purpose is wider yet. He regards these present times as largely ones of degeneracy and increasing barbarism, as the civilising ideals that have formed the best in our culture are progressively lost. He hopes that his work, inspired by the Buddha's supreme vision, will help to keep alive the guttering flame of civilisation that alone marks out human life from that of the animals.

Bibliography

As will be gathered from the pages of this outline of Sangharakshita's life, he has written a great deal himself. Those who wish to know him more fully therefore cannot do better than to read systematically through his writings. Below are a selection of works which will act as an introduction to him. For a more exhaustive bibliography, see Windhorse Publications' list.

Autobiographical

Learning to Walk, Windhorse, Glasgow 1990.
The Thousand-Petalled Lotus: The Indian Journey of an English Buddhist, Allan Sutton, Gloucester 1988.
The History of My Going for Refuge, Windhorse, Glasgow, 1988.
Travel Letters, Windhorse, Glasgow, 1985.
Ambedkar and Buddhism, Windhorse, Glasgow, 1986.

Background Material

Sangharakshita: A New Voice in the Buddhist Tradition, by Dharmachari Subhuti, Windhorse, Birmingham 1994.
Buddhism for Today: A Portrait of a New Buddhist Movement, by Dharmachari Subhuti, Windhorse, Glasgow 1988.
Jai Bhim! Dispatches from a Peaceful Revolution, by Terry Pilchick, Windhorse, Glasgow 1988.
The Wheel and the Diamond: The Life of Dhardo Tulku, by Suvajra, Windhorse, Glasgow 1991.

Selected Writings

A Survey of Buddhism, Windhorse, 1993.
The Three Jewels: An Introduction to Buddhism, Windhorse, Glasgow 1991.
The Eternal Legacy: An Introduction to the Canonical Literature of Buddhism, Tharpa, London 1985.
The Ten Pillars of Buddhism, Windhorse, Glasgow 1984.
Conquering New Worlds: Selected Poems, Windhorse, Glasgow 1986.
Hercules and the Birds and Other Poems, Windhorse, Glasgow 1990.
A Guide to the Buddhist Path, Windhorse, Glasgow 1990.
New Currents in Western Buddhism: The Inner Meaning of the Friends of the Western Buddhist Order, Windhorse, Glasgow 1990.

INDEX

The Windhorse symbolizes the energy of the enlightened mind carrying the Three Jewels —the Buddha, the Dharma, and the Sangha—to all sentient beings.

Buddhism is one of the fastest growing spiritual traditions in the Western world. Throughout its 2,500-year history, it has always succeeded in adapting its mode of expression to suit whatever culture it has encountered.

Windhorse Publications aims to continue this tradition as Buddhism comes to the West. Today's Westerners are heirs to the entire Buddhist tradition, free to draw instruction and inspiration from all the many schools and branches. Windhorse publishes works by authors who not only understand the Buddhist tradition but are also familiar with Western culture and the Western mind.

For orders and catalogues contact

WINDHORSE PUBLICATIONS
UNIT 1-316 THE CUSTARD FACTORY
GIBB STREET
BIRMINGHAM
B9 4AA
UK

ARYALOKA
HEARTWOOD CIRCLE
NEWMARKET
NEW HAMPSHIRE
NH 03857
USA

Windhorse Publications is an arm of the Friends of the Western Buddhist Order, which has more than forty centres on four continents. Through these centres, members of the Western Buddhist Order offer regular programmes of events for the general public and for more experienced students. These include meditation classes, public talks, study on Buddhist themes and texts, and 'bodywork' classes such as t'ai chi, yoga, and massage. The FWBO also runs several retreat centres and the Karuna Trust, a fundraising charity that supports social welfare projects in the slums and villages of India.

Many FWBO centres have residential spiritual communities and ethical businesses associated with them. Arts activities are encouraged too, as is the development of strong bonds of friendship between people who share the same ideals. In this way the FWBO is developing a unique approach to Buddhism, not simply as a set of techniques, less still as an exotic cultural interest, but as a creatively directed way of life for people living in the modern world.

If you would like more information about the FWBO please write to the

LONDON BUDDHIST CENTRE
51 ROMAN ROAD
LONDON
E2 OHU
UK

ARYALOKA
HEARTWOOD CIRCLE
NEWMARKET
NEW HAMPSHIRA
NH 03857
USA

Also From Windhorse

SUBHUTI

Sangharakshita: A New Voice in the Buddhist Tradition

Today Buddhism is a growing force in Western life, sowing the seeds of a spiritual, cultural, philosophical, artistic, and even economic revolution. Among the personalities at the heart of this development is a remarkable Englishman: Sangharakshita.

Sangharakshita was one of the first Westerners to make the journey to the East and to don the monk's yellow robe. In India he gained unique experience in the main traditions of Buddhist teaching and practice. His involvement with the 'mass conversion' of ex-Untouchable Hindus to Buddhism exposed him to a revolutionary new experiment in social transformation. More recently he founded one of the most successful Buddhist movements in the modern world—pioneering a 'living Buddhism' that seems ideally suited to our times.

Highly respected as an outspoken writer and commentator, he has never been afraid to communicate his insights and views, even if they challenge venerated elements of Buddhist tradition.

But what are those insights and views? How have they arisen and developed? Here one of Sangharakshita's leading disciples offers an account of his evolution as a thinker and teacher.

328 pages, Index

ISBN 0 904766 68 3

£9.99, $19.95

SANGHARAKSHITA
A SURVEY OF BUDDHISM

Now in its seventh edition, *A Survey of Buddhism* continues to provide an indispensable study of the entire field of Buddhist thought and practice. Covering all the major doctrines and traditions, both in relation to Buddhism as a whole and to the spiritual life of the individual Buddhist, Sangharakshita places their development in historical context. This is an objective but sympathetic appraisal of Buddhism's many forms that clearly demonstrates the underlying unity of all its schools.

'It would be difficult to find a single book in which the history and development of Buddhist thought has been described as vividly and clearly as in this survey.... For all those who wish to "know the heart, the essence of Buddhism as an integrated whole", there can be no better guide than this book.' *Lama Anagarika Govinda*

'I recommend Sangharakshita's book as the best survey of Buddhism.' *Dr Edward Conze*

544 pages, Bibliography, Index
ISBN 0 904766 65 9
Paperback £12.99, $24.95

SUBHUTI
BUDDHISM FOR TODAY

To be a Buddhist does not mean wearing strange robes or adopting Eastern customs. *Buddhism for Today* explains how a Buddhist life can be lived here and now in the Western world without rejecting our cultural background.

Ranging from meditation through devotional practice to the problems of practising 'right livelihood' in a consumer society, this book is also a survey of the Friends of the Western Buddhist Order, a movement which is allowing thousands of Westerners to live wholeheartedly as Buddhists in the modern world.

Since its first appearance this popular work has excited much interest—and even controversy.

212 pages, Index
ISBN 0 904766 34 9
£7.50, $12.95